The Problem-solving Process in Modern Organizations: Learning from Psychosocial Theories

THE PROBLEM-SOLVING PROCESS IN MODERN ORGANIZATIONS: LEARNING FROM PSYCHOSOCIAL THEORIES

Seyed Ali Fallahchay

SOCIETY Publishing

www.societypublishing.com

The Problem-solving Process in Modern Organizations: Learning from Psychosocial Theories

Seyed Ali Fallahchay

Society Publishing
224 Shoreacres Road
Burlington, ON L7L 2H2
Canada
www.societypublishing.com
Email: orders@arclereducation.com

ISBN: 978-1-77469-419-0 (Hardcover)

ABOUT THE AUTHOR

Seyed Ali Fallahchay PhD., is a Professor at the University of Mansford. He, also, teaches at Raffles Design Institute in Indonesia. Dr. Fallahchay earned his Doctorate from De La Salle Araneta University in the Philippines. He earned his Bachelor in Engineering of Industrial Forestry from the University of Azad Islamic, Iran. In 2011, he became a licensed engineer. While pursuing his post-secondary education, he managed his own distribution company in Iran. He also managed a manufacturing business in the Philippines. Dr. Fallahchay has a passion for teaching. In 2015, he started teaching at several colleges and universities in the Philippines. Later, he became the Director of Research and Development at one of the University in Philippines. Dr. Fallahchay has authored five (5) books — Modern Scientific Communication, The Economic of Innovation, Data Science and Decision Making: An Introductory Text for Students and Practitioners, Business and Administrative Communication, Communication in Everyday Life, and Handbook of Group Decision

TABLE OF CONTENTS

LIST OF FIGURES

PREFACE

Organizations face many problems today. It, therefore, makes sense that these organizations seek efficient ways of solving those problems. Psychosocial theories have tried to explain, predict, and describe organizational problems. This has been done to make it easier to solve any challenges that organizations face over time. It is from that background that the problem-solving process was born. This is a systematic model that can be applied to different organizations regardless of context and the nature of the problem they may be facing.

There is always a danger of becoming reductive when describing solutions to problems. This is because problems are complex and diverse. Similarly, the solutions to them must be more sophisticated than merely crudely applying a set of predetermined solutions. Nevertheless, the problem-solving process is a useful guide for organizations and increases the possibilities of growth or even development following a problem. More importantly, the problem-solving process allows for lessons to be gleaned from the experience so that they can be applied to future problems.

Of course, the book itself will touch on the merits and dangers of over-relying on heuristics to solve problems. The past may not always be a good indicator of the present or the future. Hence, the organization must cultivate the foresight and patience to be able to evaluate a problem solution in an objective manner. This involves seeing the wood from the trees and accepting reality as it is. Indeed, there may be situations in which problems are intractable and cannot be resolved completely or satisfactorily.

This is where pragmatism enters the problem-solving process. Hence, an organization must do its best to deal with its present reality and future without losing sight of its own limitations. This is particularly true when dealing with a market and a business ecology that is predetermined by many factors that may not necessarily be within the immediate control of the organization. The best businesses are the ones that make the right compromises at the right time, and yet do not lose their identity in the process. These are the businesses that can apply theory to practice.

Problems are a necessary and unavailable part of life. There is hardly any entity that has not dealt with problems. They are challenges that need to be overcome. A systematic approach based on theory and practice is therefore useful to people from all walks of life. If humans had perfected the art and science of solving problems, it would make life so much simpler. Alas, this is a work in progress.

This book offers a unique opportunity to explore the classic problem-solving process from a theoretical and practical point of view. It will be a useful text for undergraduates in a range of disciplines that include business management, administration, entrepreneurship, psychology, social work, and leadership studies. The book has wide applicability because of its practical approach that reconstitutes and represents complex theories in ways that are useful to those that are running or engaged in organizations. The problem-solving process is not confined by disciplinary boundaries and is, therefore, a peripatetic concern.

CHAPTER 1

OVERVIEW OF THE PROBLEM-SOLVING PROCESS

CONTENTS

It is appropriate to commence this book with a chapter that provides an overview of the problem-solving process. Hence, we explore ways of defining a problem in an organization. This leads to a differentiation of facts and opinions. This chapter emphasizes the role and benefits of consultation throughout the problem-solving process. It also implicitly addresses the challenges of organizational factionalism. Ultimately, the chapter guides readers towards a more precise and concise statement of organizational problems before setting certain expectations and standards for a possible resolution. This overview of the problem-solving process begins with definitional challenges.

1.1. HOW TO DEFINE A PROBLEM IN AN -ORGANIZATION?

Defining a problem in an organization becomes a problem itself (Dutse, 2013; DyReyes, 2008; Egan, 2009; Egloff and Bhalla, 2014; Evans, 2005; Farndale et al., 2008; Fetscherin and Heinrich, 2014). It is important to distinguish general problems from the problems that occur in institutions, companies, businesses, enterprises, or an organization. For a problem to be classified as an organizational problem, it must span several units of production or departments. Hence, such a problem will affect the organization in its entirety rather than impacting only one unit or individual. For example, having a dispute with your manager maybe a personal or team problem, however, it will not rise to the seriousness of an organizational problem until it starts impacting on several departments.

Perhaps one analogy is to consider the ways in which social scientists distinguish problem from social problem. In this instance, a social problem has a significant negative problem on a significant portion of a population for a significant period to the extent that it harms the relations between and among people. An individual problem may be severe, but it is not given the same priority as would be the case if it was a social problem. Organizations follow the same pattern by prioritizing organizational problems (Amos et al., 2008; Anckar et al., 2002; Anwar and Sun, 2013; Anyim et al., 2011; Arbulú et al., 2015; Argenti, 1996). The rationale is that it is imperative to limit the damage that might arise from any organizational problem. Of course, the fact that a problem impacts on many departments means that it is more difficult to resolve than if it were an issue for an individual within the organization. The occasional sickness of an employee is nowhere as problematic as four departments recording very high sickness absence levels.

Because organizational problems impact on several departments, solutions to them necessarily also have a peripatetic aspect (Turyakira, 2018a, b; Visser, 2012; WHO, 2018; Wilkinson, 1997; Williamson, 2008). That means, organizational problems are solved collectively and have several stakeholders who must be consulted during the resolution process. It is the reason why it is said that organizational problems call for a team effort when trying to resolve them. This presents problems as well as challenges. For example, many hands may increase the impact of individual effort. At the same time, the involvement of many people can create new bureaucracies that make it challenging to quickly resolve the problem. In any case, Figure 1.1 summarizes some of the key considerations when defining a problem. Whereas organizations may experience several problems, existing literature has identified some of the most common issues that organizations will encounter in their existence.

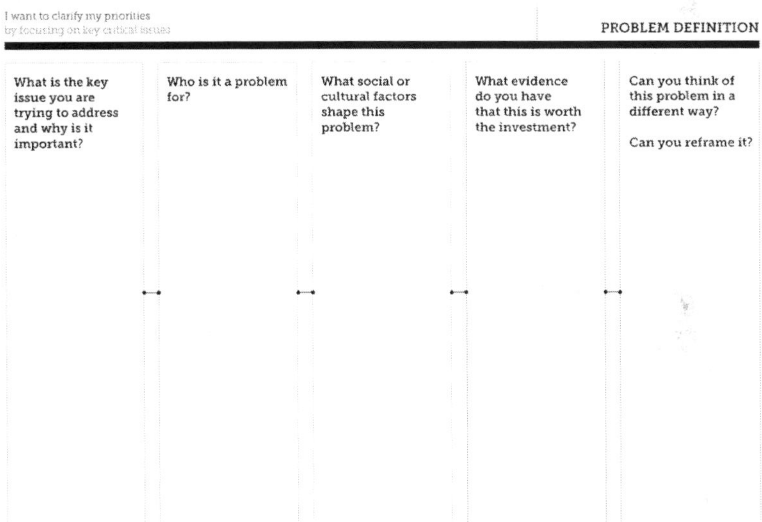

Figure 1.1. Problem definition in development.

Source: DIY toolkit.

One of the problems that organizations may face over time is a lack of clear direction (Lee and Park, 2009; Leggett, 2007; Lengnick-Hall et al., 2009; Leuenberger, 2006; Leung et al., 2015; Li, 2009). This means that there is no leader or manager of principal stakeholder who can provide direction to the staff. Two causes have been identified in existing literature as leading (potentially at least) to a lack of direction in an organization. The first problem emanates from leaders who are insular and refuse to engage with the rest of the team to discuss their strategies or ideas for that in the direction of the organization. The ability to persuade others to follow a given direction is one of the critical competencies of a leader within an organization.

The lack of clear direction means that there is no overall strategy that employees can follow (BIS, 2015; Baker and Esherick, 2013; Bannò and Sgobbi, 2016; Barry et al., 2000; Bekker, 2014; Bell et al., 2011). Hence, team leaders will try to fill the gaps by setting targets that may not necessarily fit in with strategic goals that a leader has conceptualized. It is important to be clear at this point that not having a clear direction does not mean that there are no discernible goals or even a strategic goal in the organization. Some leaders and executives may have a very clear vision of what they want but are then unable to communicate that vision to their colleagues and subordinates in a way that is persuasive. This comprises the inability to be persuasive to the rest of that stakeholder body in an organization. It is a fatal failure in most executive positions.

Another potential source of problems are organizations that focus too much on execution and do not look for realignment and consultation (Saji and Ellingstad, 2004; Sakuramoto, 2005; Samah et al., 2013; Schlögl, 2005; Schmid and Adams, 2008). Such organizations may find difficulties in the future because they will not have a reference point for all the activities that are taking place. That means that many people will be engaged in a lot of hard work but with no tangible benefits that reflect on the goals that were conceived by the leadership team. It is therefore the responsibility of the leadership team to ensure there is a clear and reasonable balance between the execution of strategy and the conceptualization of communication of that strategy. So, the first step is to have a clear vision and the second step is to ensure that vision is shared with all people that operate within an organization.

Organizations may face difficulties in blending different personalities into a coherent team (Pavlatos and Paggios, 2009a, b; Peng and Huiling Chen, 2011; Phillips and Gully, 2014; Pitts, 2009). This is of course a natural consequence of the move towards diversity and inclusiveness. If you cast the net wide, it is likely that you will find differing personalities that may not be consistent with each other. The leadership team must pay attention to the overriding interest in ensuring that the teams operate in a cohesive and logical manner. Very big personalities, particularly in the creative industry, can become harmful to an organization if they cannot blend with each other. A simple disagreement can become an existential threat for the organization if the leadership and management teams cannot reconcile the different personalities that have been recruited into the organization.

That is why the human resource management team may engage in significant and extensive psychometric testing to ensure that the workforce acquired through recruitment and selection is cohesive (Tarafdar et al., 2014; Thursfield and Grayley, 2016; Toner, 2015; Too and Weaver, 2014; Torre Edoardo and Luca, 2013). Hence, the people that enter the organization must be consistent with the ethos of that organization. In addition, they must be adhering to the values of the organization. That is how you construct and embed a coherent organizational culture. Hence, the recruitment and retention practices must be cognizant of the need to blend personalities within the organization. The problem becomes more intense when the people involved are very high up in the hierarchy of the organization.

It can be rather challenging to reconcile personalities that a diametrically opposed to each other (Bernini and Cracolici, 2015; Berthon et al., 2009; Bilson et al., 2013; Bjerregaard, 2011; Black, 2005; Brandsen and Pestoff, 2006). Hence, the organization must acknowledge the reality that at some point they may have to let go of certain employees that do not fit into the organizational culture. That does not mean that the organization only employs "yes people." Instead, it means that there is an overall blend and coherence to the personalities that operate within the teams of the organization. As Figure 1.2 shows, actors in a system or situation can be part of a problem. Hence, they must be included in the solution to that problem. Excluding actors in a problem situation is one of the reasons why organizations are unable to find lasting solutions to their problems.

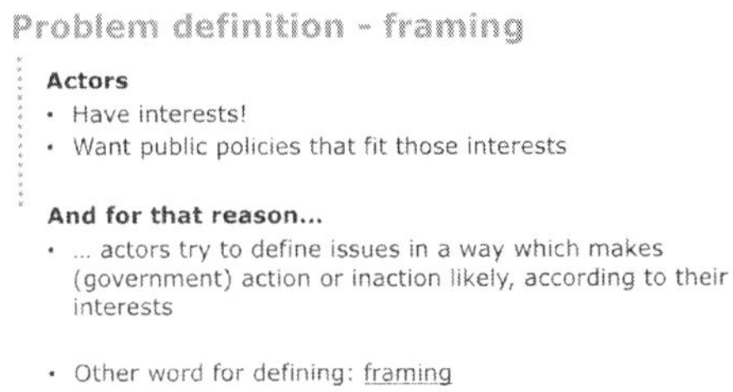

Figure 1.2. Framing a problem.

Source: Chris Jan Geugies via YouTube.

Organizations sometimes face problems because they are unable to come up with system and structures that allow them to develop desirable behavior and competencies (Hansen and Olsson, 2011; Harney and Dundon, 2006; Harris and Brown, 1998; Harrison and Lock, 2004; Hartmann, 2014). That goes back to the issue of recruitment and selection. You need a certain spectrum of incompetence to accomplish the objectives and goals that are important to an organization. For example, you may have people who have good intentions but do not have the competency and behavior that is required to achieve the goals that have been sent by the leadership team. That can become a problem for organizations that do not have the will to sack employees who are simply incompetent. This is a problem that has been a challenge for the public sector because the jobs in that sector are effectively jobs for life. Hence, it is very difficult to get rid of someone that is incompetent if they can follow certain basic rules and do not engage in behavior that is serious enough to be classified as gross misconduct.

In any case, the human resource management team must be very clear in the development of a job description and person specification so that applicants are aware of the key competencies and behavior patterns that are required for the job role that they are applying for (Hansen and Wernerfelt, 1989; Hansen and Olsson, 2011; Harney and Dundon, 2006; Harris and Brown, 1998; Harrison and Lock, 2004). An effective organization must grow with its employees and not leave them behind. For instance, some organizations have accumulated significant experience and subject matter expertise in their respective fields or niches. Yet, those same organizations have not paid enough attention to issues of technical talent and competency within their employee teams. That means that whereas the organization is rated very highly in terms of its overall image of competencies, the people that contribute to their overall competency are lacking in some respects.

Once again, the role of the human resource management team cannot be underestimated.

Communication is the glue that holds an organization together (Fetscherin and Heinrich, 2014; Finkelstein et al., 2007; Gil-Pareja et al., 2007; Gruman and Saks, 2011; Guest et al., 2003). Organizations that have failed to develop an effective communication system are going to collapse because people working in them will not know what other people are doing. Two extremes have imagined existing literature. One extreme is where there is excessive communication to the extent that business secrets cannot be secured. For each member of the team, such excessive communication can overwhelm them to the extent that they are unable to undertake the key priorities within the organization. Another extreme that has developed within certain organizations are situations where people so afraid of confrontation or blame that they are no longer engaging with each other. Poor communication breeds contempt and confusion.

Another danger of poor communication is that the necessary messages are not sent to the right people in turn or in the right format (Schmid and Adams, 2008; Schuler, 1989; Sedmak and Longhurst, 2010; Sendawula et al., 2018; Supply chain Management and Logistics: Zara, 2013). If such an inept communication modality is not satisfactorily resolved, then there is a very high chance that certain dissatisfied and confused employees will work in ways that are contradictory and even harmful to the objectives or goals of the organization. Some individuals may avoid confrontation at all costs and therefore do not communicate bad news. That is the negative aspect because it means that problems cannot be resolved in time. Other people use communication to belittle others and engage in bullying or harassment which is unhelpful to an organization.

The modalities of communication and the manner of communication must be consistent with the values and priorities of the organization (Songa et al., 2012; Sparrow and Makram, 2015; Speer and Potter, 2000; Steers et al., 2004; Stevens, 2002). This must be part of an overall communication strategy that is shared with all members of the team. It should be possible to recognize the culture and values of an organization by examining its communication channels and the messages that have been sent. If necessary, a communication specialist might be hired to improve the nature and modalities of communication within an organization. This is a wise investment given the negative issues that might arise out of poor communication. Certainly, it can prevent an interpersonal conflict from becoming an organizational problem.

Some organizations face the problem or a deficient in terms of a lack of awareness (Papasolomou and Melanthiou, 2012; Parker et al., 2013; Parry et al., 2008; Patiar and Mia, 2009; Pavlatos and Paggios, 2009a). This means that the organization is not clear about its internal and external environment. The modern business ecology can be very complex and challenging for organizations that do not invest in strategies that allow them to scan their internal and external environments. Examples include situations where the organization is facing unauthorized and damaging information leaks to the media, briefing wars, whispering campaigns, and backbiting among staff members. It is important for an organization to keep abreast of the developments within the industry because the market remains competitive on both the demand and supply side.

Improved awareness increases the likelihood of producing output that is attractive to the supply and demand markets (Gruman and Saks, 2011; Guest et al., 2003; Hansen and Wernerfelt, 1989; Hansen and Olsson, 2011; Harney and Dundon, 2006). If the products that have been produced are not appropriate for the market because they are outdated, the organization producing them will soon fall out of business. Similarly, if an organization is not investing in the latest techniques for developing staff and recruiting the best people, there is a risk that the same organization will fail to find the right workforce for achieving its goals. Typically, the organizations that are not paying enough attention to the internal and external environment will be out of step with the markets. However, organizations that are agile and dynamic should be able to deal with complexity and velocity within their selected markets. To fully understand organizational problems and their solutions, it is important to distinguish fact from opinion.

1.2. HOW TO DIFFERENTIATE FACTS FROM OPINIONS WHEN SOLVING PROBLEMS?

One of the key challenges facing a decision-maker is the ability to distinguish facts from opinions (Williamson, 2008; Willmott, 1993; Wysocki, 2013; Yang and Chen, 2006; Zhang and Wen, 2008; Zheng, 2017). A fact comprises any statement that is made but can be proven to be false or true. In contrast, an opinion comprises an expression of feeling or perspective that cannot be proven to be either true or false. It is important to note that opinions can be based on facts. Opinions can also be based on emotions. Furthermore, opinions may be constructed deliberately to mislead others in a manipulative construct. The decision maker must glean some insight into the motivations and behavioral patterns of a person expressing opinions. For example, a latently malignant influencer within the organization may express an opinion that has the potential to mislead. The dangers posed by such rogue elements are worsened by the fact that the person expressing a misleading opinion may successfully mask their own true intentions.

Negative forces may utilize carefully constructed opinions to sway an organization along a pathway that is going to threaten its existence (Li et al., 2006; Lock, 2007; Loorbach, 2010; Lorenzo-Romero et al., 2013; Loundes, 2001; Lycett et al., 2004; Maneesh et al., 2009). This is a tactic that can be used by competitors who wish to get rid of strong players in a segment or niche. However, there are times when people may express facts that are uncomfortable for the organization. Yet, this may be the types of facts that are necessary for the organization to engage in self-reflection and self-criticism. It takes a certain level of maturity to acknowledge and even act upon facts that are inconvenient. Such maturity distinguishes the great leaders from those that are merely keeping an organization afloat. Great leadership is then tasked with distinguishing fact from opinion, as demonstrated in Figure 1.3.

Distinguishing between Fact and Opinion

The ability to distinguish between fact and opinion helps people think for themselves and resist being manipulated by others. Knowing the difference also helps you developing paragraph-writing skills.

FACTS	OPINIONS
• Can be proved true or false. • Can be checked. • Are specific. • Look like details. • Include statistics and dates (often contain numbers) • Includes examples. • Cite evidence or proof.	• Are subjective (e.g. I believe...) • Contain value judgments (i.e. they make something sound good or bad) • Uses adjectives. • Look like explanations. • Make personal comments (e.g. I think you should...) • Are often phrased as compliments or put-downs

Examine the following statements. Next to each, write the letter "F" if it is a FACT or an "O" if it is an OPINION.

_____ It is 85 degrees Celsius outside.
_____ It is hot outside.
_____ It is a horrible steam bath outside.

Sometimes statements include both Facts and Opinions. The following is an example. Read the statement. Then underline the parts that express Facts and circle the parts that express Opinions.

Mr. Ocampo said, "I can't stand this horrible humidity. The weatherman reported that it is 37°. This climate is terrible."

You have just applied the skill between fact and opinion.

Figure 1.3. Distinguishing facts from opinions.

Source: StudyLib.

When reading literature and guidance points, facts may speak for themselves (Kay et al., 1994; Kerzner, 2003; Khan et al., 2011; King et al., 2000; Klikauer, 2014; Kluike, 2015; De Kok et al., 2006). In this case, the decision-maker must consider the facts and their relevance to the situation that they are dealing with. That situation could be an organizational problem that requires decisive action to alleviate a further deterioration in the operational capacity of the team. When making decisions, it is important to acquire information from reliable sources. Such sources may include academic literature, employees, and publications that emanate from industry professionals or otherwise qualified trend analysts. In evaluating the factual basis of literature, it is important to understand that language can be manipulated to present opinions as fact. Hence, the decision-maker must ensure that they are not inappropriately swayed by flowery language or persuasive rhetoric that hides the key points that they must deal with in the decisions they are making.

All of these are part of the tactical positioning that communicators may use to persuade others toward their point of view or even change the course of direction (Abramovsky et al., 2004; Abu-Saifan, 2012; Ahimbisibwe and Nkundabanyanga, 2016; Ahmad and Schroeder, 2003). Another tactic that managers must be wary of is cases where questions that are leading in nature (and therefore elicit a response that the questioner wishes to present in the first place). These may be loaded questions that divert attention away from the priority areas on to distractions that do not really impact on the operational capacity of the organization. Hence, managerial resources are spent on issues that do not matter whilst simultaneously ignoring those that ought to matter most. A decision-maker or problem-solver should not allow themselves to be distracted from the key issues that need their attention. They must also be on the lookout for those that cleverly lose language to obscure organizational goals, objectives, values, and priorities.

That does not mean that emotional rap language is necessarily a negative thing (Egloff and Bhalla, 2014; Evans, 2005; Farndale et al., 2008; Fetscherin and Heinrich, 2014; Finkelstein et al., 2007; Gil-Pareja et al., 2007). For example, advertising relies on emotional language. The problems only arise if that emotional language is manipulative or misleading in some way. Generally, the decision-makers in an organization are presented with a range of information that includes facts and opinions. Distinguishing the opinions from the fact is a key requirement. The next stage involves making a decision that is appropriate for the situation. Indeed, opinions could be accurate because they may highlight an issue that can later be supported by facts. The decision-maker must exercise indiscretion to explore opinions and look for evidence to either give them credence or discredit them. The people giving opinions may feel slighted if their contribution is minimized or written-off as being prejudiced right from the beginning. One of the tasks of communication is to bring everybody on board whilst making the right decisions at the right time.

That approach calls for highly sophisticated monitoring and evaluation frameworks that can evaluate the range of sources and their quality when making decisions (Lengnick-Hall et al., 2009; Leuenberger, 2006; Leung et al., 2015; Li, 2009; Li et al., 2006, 2013). This is what is known as judging facts and opinions before coming to a conclusion. An appropriate mixture of opinions and facts that are carefully considered elicits a much higher quality decision than situations when a decision is based on opinions or facts alone. This is particularly true when considering externalities and nuances of the situation may have heightened the quality of the eventual decision. Manage and supervisors need to ascertain whether facts are as reliable as presented instead of being clouded by manipulative rhetoric or malignant intention. Figure 1.4 reiterates some of the key distinctions that the decision-maker will consider.

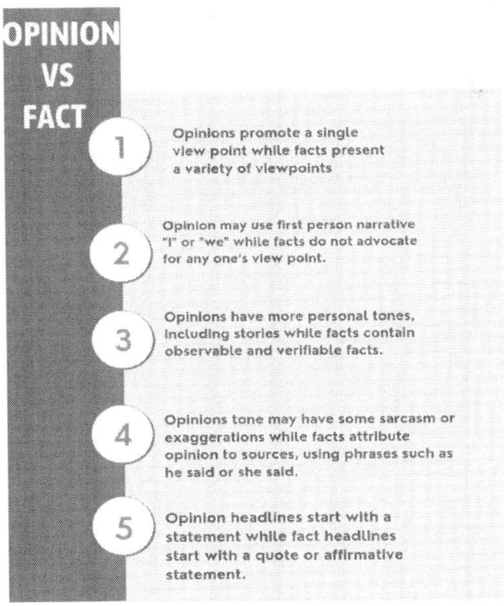

Figure 1.4. The big difference between facts and opinions.

Source: Dubawa.

Managers should not ignore opinions because they reflect the nuances of perspectives within the organization (D'Ippolito and Timpano, 2016; Dartey-Baah and Amoako, 2011; Day and Schoenrade, 2000; Deery and Nath, 2013). Unintentionally or intentionally, the expression of an opinion provides important insights into a personality. This can be very important when constructing a team and ensuring that there is unity within the team. Indeed, the presentation or expression of contrarian opinions may help the organization to avoid future sabotage by individuals who have expressed negative opinions about a change program. That does not mean stigmatizing and victimizing employees that may have an unconventional opinions and unconventional methods of work. Communication is an important tool for eliciting opinions, even from those members of staff that may be unconventional in their perspective.

It is important to interrogate and even challenge opinions so that they better reflect reality (Schlögl, 2005; Schmid and Adams, 2008; Schuler, 1989; Sedmak and Longhurst, 2010; Sendawula et al., 2018). There is the famous adage that people can be entitled to their opinion, but not to their facts. This is an important protection for decision-makers so that they can query and interrogate opinions without having to accept them at face value. In recent times, the issue of political correctness has meant that certain victimized groups may engage in the furtherance of opinions that cannot be realistically challenged despite their paucity. No manager can risk criticizing established victim categories without facing additional social approbation. Of course, there are managers that engage in discriminatory behavior that must be challenged. That does not mean that all opinions must be taken for face value.

The true measure of a leader is the ability to engage in difficult situations and to challenge bad practice so that they can guide the organization towards success (Wilkinson, 1997; Williamson, 2008; Willmott, 1993; Wysocki, 2013; Yang and Chen, 2006; Zhang and Wen, 2008). Unfortunately, that can become a hard and thankless task in an era of sensitivity. For example, when an accusation of harassment or discrimination is made there is a tendency for managers to avoid any performance management issues that relates to the alleged victim. This is because they may feel that any such action could be construed as a form of victimization. A good decision-maker should be able to critique opinions in an objective and coherent way. If they are disputing a certain opinion, they should provide very clear reasons as to why we have come to that conclusion. Indeed, the process of evaluating facts and opinions before announcing a final decision can produce much better outcomes than if things were presented as a fait accompli.

Strong opinions can be problematic, but they can also be important for improving organizational performance in the long run (Obeidat, 2012; Odrakiewicz, 2012; Okotoni and Erero, 2005; Onyx and Maclean, 1996; Ozturk and Rumens, 2014; Papasolomou and Melanthiou, 2012). An effective leader or manager should be able to acknowledge and act upon facts and opinions regardless their personal animosity towards the source of those facts and opinions. Leaders are not required to act upon any fact or any opinion that is presented to them, even if it is irrelevant to the problem-solving process. Instead, they should be able to evaluate the facts and opinions on their merits. When this type of evaluation is undertaken throughout the operations of an organization, it becomes easier to defend the decisions that are subsequently made. This can have practical implications on processes such as Recruitment and training. Facts and opinions about an issue or personality of framework of project should be curated for future reference. Then the rationale for making a certain decision should be explained in case the decision has to be reviewed in the future. In making these decisions, it is imperative to consult wisely and widely.

1.3. THE VALUE OF CONSULTING WITH ALL FACTIONS WHEN SOLVING PROBLEMS

The ability to consult extensively is a key competency for managers, regardless of the size of the organization that they are working in (Sakuramoto, 2005; Samah et al., 2013; Schlögl, 2005; Schmid and Adams, 2008; Schuler, 1989; Sedmak and Longhurst, 2010). This is particularly important when solving organizational problems because by their very nature, these types of problems affect different departments within the organization. That means that there will be many factions that have an interest in the resolution of that problem. Through consultation, it is possible to understand the perspectives of all the interest groups and ensure the decisions are made in a comprehensive and holistic way. Certain professions such as medicine have made consultation an integral aspect of work. Figure 1.5 describes the consultation process before engaging in high-risk surgical procedures. This is a demonstration of the widespread acknowledgment of the importance of consultation in organizations.

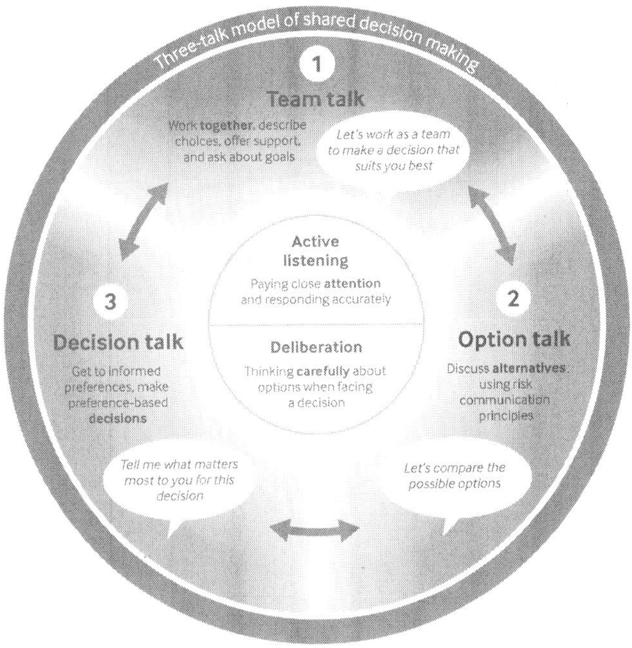

Figure 1.5. Shared decision-making for high-risk surgery.

Source: BJA Education.

Existing literature highlights the importance of keeping one's ears to the ground when managing a diverse team because many of the insights that might support a management decision will emanate from different stakeholders of factions within the group (Subhas Chandra et al., 2010; Tarafdar et al., 2014; Thursfield and Grayley, 2016; Toner, 2015; Too and Weaver, 2014). A consultation is a form of education for managers. It helps leaders understand the attitudes, beliefs, and behaviors of different stakeholders in the entity that they are entrusted to run. This form of consultation can take different directions depending on whether the organization is in the public sector or the private sector. For example, some of the organizations that have flatter hierarchical structures will be able to engage in feedback loops that rely on word-of-mouth. Others have more formal approaches to consultation in which communication must be clearly documented and categorized according to certain standards that prevail within the organization.

Nevertheless, it must be noted that recently some organizations have downgraded word-of-mouth feedback in terms of preparing strategy

(Lashley and Burgess, 2007; Le, 2017; Leary, 2001; Lee and Park, 2009; Leggett, 2007; Lengnick-Hall et al., 2009; Leuenberger, 2006). One of the reasons for this downgrade is the justifiable suspicion that word-of-mouth is not reliable in terms of communicating the right information at the right time. It can veer dangerously into management by rumors. Instead, some organizations prefer formal communication that is linked to specific problems within the organization. The consultation net can be as wide as desirable depending on the priorities of the organization. However, there are certain groups of stakeholders that must necessarily be consulted.

For instance, it is important to engage with the people that own the company and the leadership team (Peng and Huiling Chen, 2011; Phillips and Gully, 2014; Pitts, 2009; Podoshen et al., 2015; Priola et al., 2014; Rasim, 2008). At the same time, you must also consult with partners or members of a supply chain who impact on your business and who are impacted on by the activities of your organization. Indeed, public sector organizations have a duty of care and a duty to consult with members of the public who support them directly or indirectly through taxation. Research has shown that consultation increases the likelihood that development initiatives will be accepted in a community. By contrast, projects that are implemented without adequate consultation are likely to face resistance from the local community.

It is a cost-effective decision to consult before implementing project as opposed to merely ramming them through via the executive power route (Min et al., 2008; Mitchell et al., 1997; Moore and Birtwistle, 2004; Moore and Doyle, 2010; Morrison and Milliken, 2003). This is because the costs of dealing with resistance are demonstrably much higher than the cost of consulting extensively. That is why some organizations have come to the conclusion that it is in their best interest to engage in consultation as part of the development process. Moreover, it is thought that consultation allows for better ownership of public-sector initiatives. The public sector is statutorily and morally expected to engage in extensive consultation. However, the private sector is also increasingly adopting this stance, not least because its main stakeholders are the owners and the customers who purchase products and services from them.

Consultation in the public sector can offer salutary lesson to private-sector organizations (Sharma and Upneja, 2005; Shatte et al., 2014; Sinclaire and Vogus, 2011; Singh and Masuku, 2014; Singh et al., 2016). For example, extensive, and meaningful consultation helps to shape the nature and quality of the products that are delivered to the client or customer. The organization will get an insight into the tastes and preferences of their target market. This is very important in the private sector where competitive markets require that businesses can quickly and flexibly respond appropriately to the needs of service users or customers. Those that respond late or inappropriately will eventually be pushed out on the market. Similarly, consultation motives and modalities already exist in the public or third sector. A case in point is the adoption of participatory practice in healthcare (see Figure 1.6).

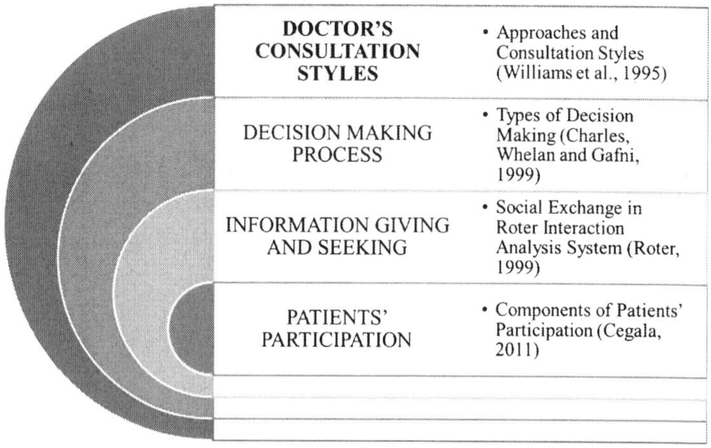

Figure 1.6. Participatory decision-making in medicine.

Source: Nurul Nadia Haron (2014).

In the public sector, there exists a series of service level agreements that are reviewed on a regular basis (Pitts, 2009; Podoshen et al., 2015; Priola et al., 2014; Rasim, 2008; Rose Ragins, 2004; Rosenthal, 2013; Rosser and Eccleston, 2011). Indeed, some social care authorities have recently instituted and empowered important interest groups from the community to direct and instruct the health authority to prioritize certain aspects. In effect, development, and care is subject to the norms and values of a community rather than being imposed in a top-down approach. This can be an improvement from the old approach in which the public was expected to accept the decisions that were taken by senior managers within the public sector. This dictatorial approach was seen as the norm and led to a democratic deficit in which bureaucracies were prioritized over the needs of service users.

As scrutiny over the expenditure of public taxes has increased, the need for consultation has also increased (Leung et al., 2015; Li, 2009; Li et al., 2006, 2013; Lock, 2007; Loorbach, 2010; Lorenzo-Romero et al., 2013). The formulation of policy through strategic consultation increases the likelihood of success. However, that does not mean that consultation should become a barrier to progress. For example, the consultation process should not be so long or so onerous that it prevents high-priority projects from taking place. One danger that public-sector organization must be aware of is that of consulting retrospectively. This is a mistake because it means that members of the public have been taken for granted. Indeed, such retrospective consultation may be deployed to avoid scrutiny or to prevent significant sanctions being imposed by the funder or controller for failing to consult as required.

The private sector must continuously scan its internal and external environment so that it keeps abreast of key developments that might impact on its operations (Kluike, 2015; De Kok et al., 2006; Korczynski, 2002; Kotas, 2014; Köllen, 2013; Lashley and Burgess, 2007). For example, businesses must be aware of the changes in attitudes and perceptions of their client base so that they can produce items and services that respond to those needs. Consultation has often had a positive effect in terms of reputation of management. This is particularly the case in the private sector because consultation allows for explanations of the reasoning or rationale behind certain decisions to be shared with customers. Hence, previously negatively perceived decisions may have better reception following extensive consultation.

Therefore, consultation offers the opportunity to win hearts and minds (Mia and Patiar, 2001; Milosevic et al., 2010; Min et al., 2008; Mitchell et al., 1997; Moore and Birtwistle, 2004). Planning through consultation helps to direct the growth and trajectory of the organization. This ensures that growth and development within the business is in tandem with the expectations of the market. In that way, the organization or business does not become obsolete. When engaging in consultation, it is very important to have an understanding of the key drivers of opinions and decision. In the public sector these are known as opinion leaders. They are a key resource for quickly reaching the rest of the community. However, consultation should not be an exclusive activity that does not pay attention to other players within the organization. For example, you can consult with partners, experts, local authorities, funding organizations, clients, customers, and even your own employees. Indeed, there is evidence in existing literature that consultation has led to the development or imagines of creative ideas.

When undertaking consultation, it is important to understand who is and who is not a stakeholder (Rose Ragins, 2004; Rosenthal, 2013; Rosser and Eccleston, 2011; Saenz and Pérez-Bouvier, 2014; Saji and Ellingstad, 2004). Existing literature suggests that a stakeholder is anyone or any entity that affects the actions of an organization. Stakeholders also include anyone or any entity that is affected by the actions of the organization. The Stanford Research Institute started the norm of using the word "stakeholder" in 1963. According to the institute's definition, stakeholders comprised all groups without whose support the organization would stop existing. Edward Freeman continued developing the concept of a stakeholder in the 1980s.

The terminology of stakeholders and consultation has ever since been widely used in the business sector and in construction projects (Hopkin et al., 1979; Hunter and Katz, 2012; Huselid, 1995; Ibrahim and Zailani, 2010; Ichniowski et al., 1997; Ifinedo, 2016). The term has become so popular that certain projects require consultation and evidence to support it as a prerequisite to funding. This is particularly true of those products that are supported by the public or third sector. Certainly, non-government organizations (NGOs) have engaged in extensive consultation to understand their client base and to understand the ways in which their target community is organized. This was a response to evidence that there have been far too many examples of projects that have failed because the local community was disengaged. Indeed, critics have argued but ignoring the prospective of local communities is a form of neo-colonialism. Hence, the stakeholder has been extended to include virtually anyone that has an interest in a project. Nevertheless, this broad definition of a stakeholder must not be allowed to stymie the delivery of key and priority projects. Consultation is always a balancing act between engaging with stakeholders and ensuring the delivery of scheduled projects. That calls for a clear statement of a problem in ways that are understandable to stakeholders.

1.4. HOW TO SPECIFICALLY STATE A PROBLEM IN AN ORGANIZATION?

The problem statement is an integral aspect of the problem-solving process in an organization (Stone et al., 2015; Stoorvogel et al., 2017; Storey et al., 2006; Subhas Chandra et al., 2010; Tarafdar et al., 2014; Thursfield and Grayley, 2016). It is an art and a science to state an organizational problem in a succinct manner whilst elaborating on the key issues that need to be addressed. The problem statement describes an area in the structures of the organization that needs to be addressed through interventions. The problematic aspect or area is given priority because it is impacting on the operations and effectiveness of the organization. Figure 1.7 shows examples of effective problem statements.

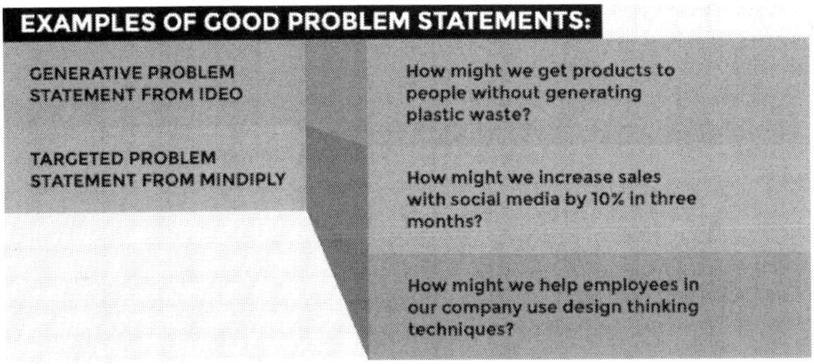

Figure 1.7. Problem statement examples.

Source: NEXEA.

It is not enough to simply state that there is an organizational problem because there are always contextual issues that must be addressed (Kotas, 2014; Köllen, 2013; Lashley and Burgess, 2007; Le, 2017; Leary, 2001; Lee and Park, 2009; Leggett, 2007). For example, the statement must explain the nature of the problem and its impact. The problem that is referenced in the statement may be an area of concern or condition that must be improved to ensure that the organization can achieve its goals. Hence, the reader of that statement is quickly apprised of problems related to difficulties that need to be neutralized or eliminated. There are organizations that create problem statements that reference a key question about the market operations which must be systematically addressed through the transformation of the various departments that are affected. Then there are problem statements that focus on practice points that need to be improved. You should develop a problem statement after a deliberate and structured investigation that provides you with an understanding of the nature of the problem.

Managers have reported significant problems when preparing a problem statement because there are too many potential distractions that must be ignored (Newell and Simon, 1972; Nica, 2015; Obeidat, 2012; Odrakiewicz, 2012; Okotoni and Erero, 2005; Onyx and Maclean, 1996). For example, the symptoms that are associated with the problem may add to the confusion of understanding the problem. That means that the decision-maker or analyst is trying to describe the symptoms of the problem rather than describing the problem. Hence, there is some form of diagnosis when preparing a problem statement. Another issue that may arise is where the analyst or decision-maker is trying to prematurely find solutions. Hence, they may write a problem statement that includes half-baked solutions that are not appropriate for the situation. Early and inappropriate solutions might distract the intervening team from properly investigating the problem that they are faced with.

Furthermore, the urgency to deal with a problem means that the statements may be rushed through without considering all the nuances of the challenges that the organization is facing (Chang et al., 2006; Chen et al., 2011; Chevalier and Mazzalovo, 2008; Chung, 2015; Clegg and Palmer, 1996). It is natural to seek easy and quick solutions to alleviate the pain of frustration that is associated with an organizational problem. However, reflexive actions are not necessarily the most appropriate approach to dealing with short-term problems. One of the reasons for this reluctance is the fact that the symptoms of a problem may be masking a deeper issue that requires significant investment and investigation. Therefore, the analysts try to save time by insisting on identifying quick solutions before they have understood the background and nuance of the problem. Ideally, the problem statement should trigger interest and curiosity for further investigation the manifest and latent issues.

When writing a problem statement, it is important to avoid incorporating solutions because they are not needed at this point (Finkelstein et al., 2007; Gil-Pareja et al., 2007; Gruman and Saks, 2011; Guest et al., 2003; Hansen and Wernerfelt, 1989). At the same time, you should not be including causes within the statement because they are not necessarily part of the brief which must be precise and concise. It is important not to engage in the blame game when writing a problem statement. This is a problem that public-sector organizations are facing where every member of the team is looking to ensure that they are not blamed for failures within the organization. Moreover a problem statement that is tinged with the blame game likely to provide self-serving narratives that does not reflect a full and accurate picture of the situation. That means that the decision eventually arrived at, and associated conclusions will not be fully supported by empirical evidence. Although not specifically referenced in the characteristics of a good problem statement (Figure 1.8), objectivity, and the lack of blame games are implicit requirements.

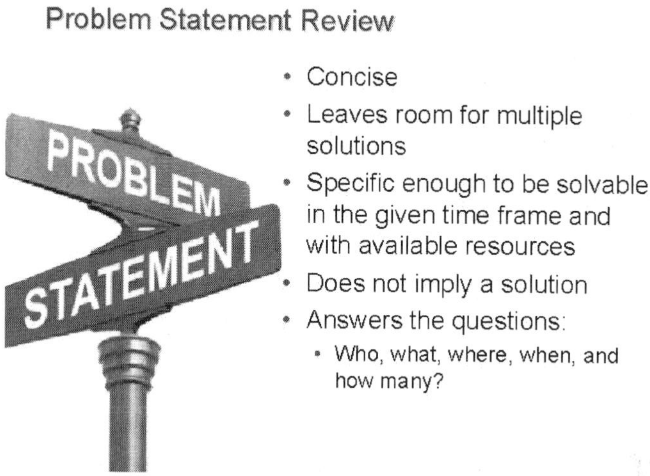

Figure 1.8. Characteristics of a good problem statement.

Source: SlideToDoc.

In many cases, a problem statement describes a gap between what is and what ought to be (Ismail et al., 2005; Jansen et al., 2008; Jian Wang et al., 2010; John et al., 2014; Johnson and Clark, 2008; Jurevicius, 2016). This is a modality that is used in social sciences when describing social problems. Performance and success must be necessarily and desirable in an organization. Hence, deficits between goals and reality are problematic whilst surpluses are almost always welcome. There is no point in investing organizational resources on to gobs that is desirable or neutral. For example, the organization may be reporting a level of performance which is far below the expectations and that is a problem. However, performance that far exceeds expectations is celebration and may be used for brand promotion. Ideally, the problem statement should focus on the future status of operations which are being hampered by a current problem or bottleneck. It is advisable to include relative and absolute measures that can help the reader to identify and quantify the gaps that have been referenced.

There is a systematic approach to a problem statement which may be used depending on the protocols that are prevalent within the organization (Cunniff and Mostert, 2012; Cunningham, 2011; D'Ippolito and Timpano, 2016; Dartey-Baah and Amoako, 2011; Day and Schoenrade, 2000). The first step is to identify the gap or the pain that exists today. The second aspect is to describe a location and timeframe within which the problem occurs. Hence, it is important to describe when and where the problem was first observed. A good problem statement also highlights the context of the problem, bearing in mind existing trends. Another aspect is to describe the impact of the problem. In this case, you are trying to identify a gap in terms of the personal, environmental, quality, time, and cost implications of the problem. Then you should describe the importance of the problem to the organization. For example, some problems are limited to a few teams whereas other problems affect an entire department or the entire organization. The highest priority problems with deep or extensive impact should be addressed first before the lowest priority problems with shallow or limited impact. This calls for an understanding of the standards and expectations within the organization that is trying to analyze its problems.

1.5. UNDERSTANDING STANDARDS AND EXPECTATIONS IN ORGANIZATIONS

It is important to understand the expectations and standards of an organization when resolving problems (Deery and Nath, 2013; Dumay et al., 2010; Dutse, 2013; DyReyes, 2008; Egan, 2009; Egloff and Bhalla, 2014; Evans, 2005). Resolving problems is an organizational goal and therefore the procedures that are used for setting goals act as a reference point when solving problems. Standards and expectations provide the decision-maker (or the person given the responsibility for intervening in an organizational problem) insights into the minimum acceptable level of performance (or resolution) that they are supposed to achieve. Figure 1.9 shows the intersection of standards and expectations in organizations.

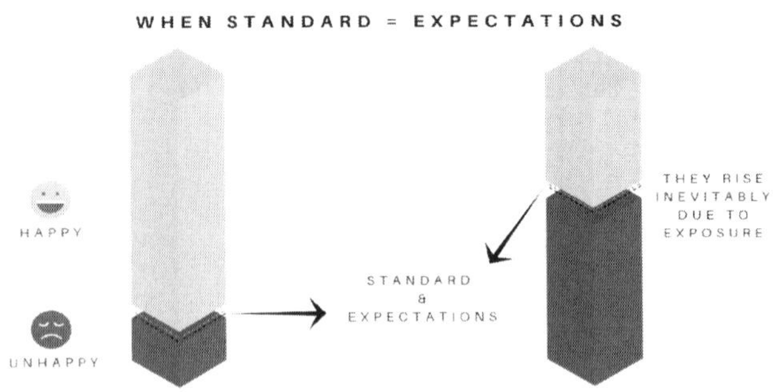

Figure 1.9. Intersection of standards and expectations.

Source: Medium.

A combination of standards, and expectations helps to orientate employees within an organization (Capko, 2003; Carraher, 2013; Chang et al., 2006; Chen et al., 2011; Chevalier and Mazzalovo, 2008; Chung, 2015). Without these three elements, it becomes difficult to influence and shape the activities of employees as they execute their roles and responsibilities within the structures of the organization. Furthermore, the lack of goals of Standards means that it is not possible to identify and fully appreciate outcomes after a problem has been resolved. Standards are an elementary unit of success. Indeed, some organizations may brand themselves based on their standards. These can be included in the mission and vision statements. The training manual as well as the job recruitment paperwork will reference certain standards. If there has been successful integration, all members of all teams will have a good idea of the standards and expectations for all their activities. The gaps start to emerge when there is confusion about the nature of expectations and standards as well as the best ways of meeting them.

Existing literature has highlighted the so-called "Pygmalion Effect" when setting standards and expectations in an organization (Onyx and Maclean, 1996; Ozturk and Rumens, 2014; Papasolomou and Melanthiou, 2012; Parker et al., 2013). This means that expectations of employees will orientate them towards performing to achieve those expectations. If there is an expectation of high performance, there is a likelihood that the level of performance will increase as well. Similarly, if there are little or no expectations of performance, it is likely that employees will not be motivated or orientated. Hence, the affected employees will not modify their activities and efforts to achieve the goals or objectives of that organization. In the resulting vacuum, some diligent employees may set goals and expectations for their own work depending on their personal values. However, there is no guarantee that those standards and expectations will be universal or consistent with the strategic goals of the organization. Besides, the piecemeal approach to standards and expectations might lead to significant inconsistency and variability in performance as you explore different parts of the organization. Clearly, this is not acceptable.

That development of standards is a collaborative effort that includes various stakeholders within the organization (Ichniowski et al., 1997; Ifinedo, 2016; Ismail et al., 2005; Jansen et al., 2008; Jian Wang et al., 2010; John et al., 2014). Hence, the resultant standards are a reflection of the norm, values, and principles of the organization. That is why standards are used as a unit of measure to explain the levels of performance or achievement when resolving organizational problem. This is particularly important when undertaking comparative analysis. The standard or expectation will quickly inform the assessor about the level of performance. From that, they will be able to compare it with the expected level and then decide whether it is a case of underperformance or overperformance. Indeed, many companies give feedback in terms of the extent to which employees or teams have achieved the expectations of the organizations. The resultant interventions in terms of training and other aspects of performance management are also benchmarked against the expected standards. In fact, adopting such an approach will reduce the risk of being accused of unfairness or favoritism during performance evaluations.

Organizations have used standards and expectations as an adaptive strategy for fulfilling certain goal and objectives (Phillips and Gully, 2014; Pitts, 2009; Podoshen et al., 2015; Priola et al., 2014; Rasim, 2008; Rose Ragins, 2004). In other words, setting the standard is an implicit indicator a goal or objective. It clearly communicates the goals and expectations of the organization to all the members of staff who are responsible for achieving them. That is why sophisticated communication channels are an indicator of organizational competency. Additionally, there should be mechanisms for informing workers of the various ways in which they can achieve the goals or objectives that are set for them. Moreover, there must be a sufficient level of appropriate resources to achieve these goals. This is when performance management is logical and acceptable. The alternative is a performance management framework that is unnecessarily arbitrary and therefore inherently unfair. Nevertheless, it is also important to remember that customers are part of the stakeholder group and also have certain expectations or standards (see Figure 1.10) which must be met.

Figure 1.10. Managing customer expectations.

Source: One-Stop Information Shop.

Once the goals, standards, and expectations of the organization have been communicated to the entire workforce, it is imperative that there is ownership and acceptance (Le, 2017; Leary, 2001; Lee and Park, 2009; Leggett, 2007; Lengnick-Hall et al., 2009; Leuenberger, 2006; Leung et al., 2015). That ownership and acceptance will motivate and orient workers so that they can engage in specific activities that are known to achieve the targets that have been set for them. The organizational goals, standards, and expectations should be part of the work plan for teams and individuals within the organization. The leadership team has the responsibility to monitor and evaluate the work plans and their achievement to ensure that the problems that have been identified and are being worked on. The failure to deal with issues of acceptance and ownership can lead to resistance from the teams which are in turn a waste of time for the organization. In setting standards, monitoring, and evaluating them, the use of modern technology might be recruited to facilitate the process.

The use of technology and advanced Techniques can be critical when resolving intractable organizational problems (Turyakira, 2018a, b; Visser, 2012; WHO, 2018; Wilkinson, 1997; Williamson, 2008; Willmott, 1993). That is why modern organizations have attempted to automate virtually all their activities including those that relate to human resource management, accountability, monitoring, and evaluation. Of course, the use of technology has its limitations which managers should be aware of. A machine can never really replicate the human touch and there will be gaps that have to be filled using the available human resources. The idea is to use human resources in the most efficient and effective manner rather than wasting them on things that could be achieved using technology. In most cases, there is some level of complementarity between the work that is achieved by technology and the work that is achieved by human effort. When a proper balance is struck to achieve this complementarity, organization can succeed in virtually all contexts. In all this, the technical support provided by the human resource management team should not be ignored.

Human resource management teams can be a critical resource in terms of overseeing the modalities for resolving problems (Nagalakhmi and Trivedi, 2015; Nagasawa and Fukunaga, 2015; Najam, 2000; Nath, 2011; Newell and Simon, 1972; Nica, 2015). However, that is only one part of the overall structures and infrastructure that is responsible for understanding and resolving problems. It is important that organizations do not overload the human resource management team with tasks that should be dealt with by individual workers, supervisors, managers, or leaders. The team is there to provide technical support based on its superior knowledge of employment law and practice. It is not a replacement for good operational management. Standards can help to homogenize performance across teams and individuals that may be very diverse in their competency or even experience. Hence, the use of standards has been closely associated with the factory model. That does not mean that there are no standards for higher-level professions that give employees some laxity. The key is to understand the market, workforce, and organizational priorities before amalgamating them into a coherent business or organizational strategy.

Chapter 1 Summary

This initial chapter has provided an overview of the problem-solving process. Some of the key areas that have been tackled include definitions, facts, opinions, factions, interest groups, and the modalities for starting problems. Above all, the chapter has shown that standards, goals, and expectations must be referenced when solving organizational problems. Chapter 2 will focus more on the processes of solving organizational problems.

CHAPTER 2

THE PROCESSES OF SOLVING PROBLEMS IN ORGANIZATIONS

CONTENTS

This chapter considers the processes through which organizations go through when resolving their problems. The elements of these procedures include the identification of the problematic aspects of the operational process before accessing the right data and information to resolve them. Moreover, the chapter emphasizes the importance of considering alternative solutions before settling on the final ideal option. Besides, the chapter explores the ways in which alternative solutions are assessed, evaluated, and implemented depending on the choices that have been made by the organization through its designated decision-makers. During this process, there is an acknowledgment of the need to align solutions to the strategic goals of the organization. Hence, this chapter provides management professionals and other employees with a framework for resolving problems. Organizations, regardless of whether they are public, private, or third sector should pay attention to these processes. We start off the chapter by considering the processes that allow the organization to identify problems related to its processes and content.

2.1. IDENTIFYING SPECIFIC PROCESSES IN AN ORGANIZATION THAT HAVE PROBLEMS

Decision-making in the organization can be improved if there are clear processes for identifying problems within the organization (Bercu, 2012; Bernini and Cracolici, 2015; Berthon et al., 2009; Bilson et al., 2013; Bjerregaard, 2011; Black, 2005). Identifying the real problem (as opposed to merely focusing on its symptoms and causes) improves decision-making. There are a series of leadership tools and techniques that can be referenced by the management team win trying to resolve problems within the organization. Choosing a specific technique or tool will be a decision for the leadership team. However, that decision must bear in mind the costs implications so that they can be balanced against the known benefits of using that option. That is why organizational problems are often solved at different levels. Indeed, this is recognition of the peripatetic nature of organizational problems.

The ability or inability to resolve organizational problems can have dire consequences for the leadership team as well as other operational activities (Crawford, 2016; Cunniff and Mostert, 2012; Cunningham, 2011; D'Ippolito and Timpano, 2016; Dartey-Baah and Amoako, 2011). Leaders should try to engage with the procedures and processes of the organization so that they can identify any loophole or obstacle to resolving problems.

That way, the leaders can ensure that the productivity of the organization is not hindered by the inability to identify the right problems at the right time. Many institutions and businesses have collapsed because entirely preventable problems were ignored until they turned into intractable crises. The diligent managers are always on the lookout for any issues that may impact on the operational efficiency of the team that they are leading. This calls for a proactive approach that does not wait for problems to happen before responding or taking any preventative or corrective action.

Optimal decision-making is not an automatic process (Day and Schoenrade, 2000; Deery and Nath, 2013; Dumay et al., 2010; Dutse, 2013; DyReyes, 2008; Egan, 2009; Egloff and Bhalla, 2014). It requires investment in terms of resources and expertise. Moreover, the organization should ensure that its leadership team has been trained extensively in the art and science of dealing with organizational problems. These training programs should not only look at the outcomes of the problem resolution process, but also the ways in which the organization has reached this point. During that process the organization will try to distinguish the real problem from its symptoms. Figure 2.1 represents an example of how problems can be identifying by considering the trajectory of a project life cycle. This then becomes a tool for picking out those situations that are likely to become problematic in the future.

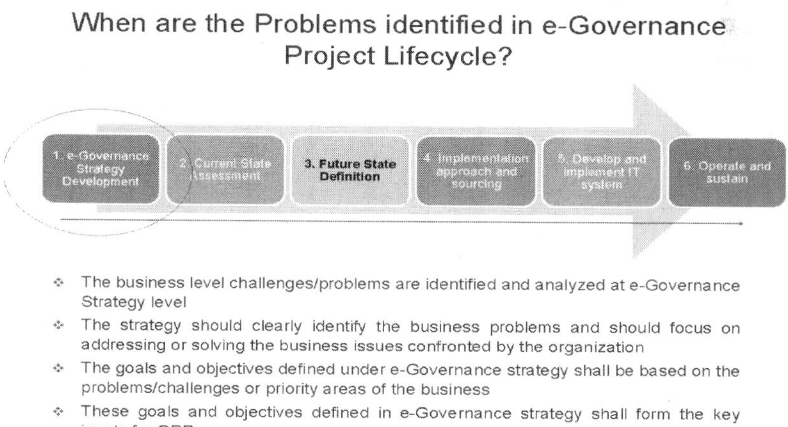

Figure 2.1. Identification of problem in the process and vision.

Source: SlideToDoc.

One of the most frustrating things for managers is coming in too late to resolve a problem that could have been dealt with effectively in its earliest stages (Speer and Potter, 2000; Steers et al., 2004; Stevens, 2002; Stewart and Walsh, 1992; Stone et al., 2015). For example, there is a lot of design and execution that are embedded within the process before you can get the outcome of a resolution to an organizational problem. These are investments that cannot be replaced or re-allocated since they have already been deployed towards a solution that has not worked. It is far better to take a lot of time during the planning phases so that you are clear about the problem before proceeding with any interventions. The costs of these undesirable and inappropriate interventions soon mount up and make it difficult for the organization to deal with the real priorities that deserve attention.

One of the problems that managers have faced is designing and executing solutions to a range of problems in the organization only to find that they are not relevant to the real problem (Podoshen et al., 2015; Priola et al., 2014; Rasim, 2008; Rose Ragins, 2004; Rosenthal, 2013; Rosser and Eccleston, 2011). This retrospective reflection on the appropriateness of solutions to organizational problems has been a waste of resources. If it is entirely unpreventable, at least the failure to find the right solutions should be used as a learning curve for the leadership team so that we can do better next time. The use of scenarios and other demonstrations of the problem situation can be important in reducing the error rate for the decision-making process. Making mistakes in the pilot scheme or in the early stages of the resolution process is not as expensive as rolling out the entire change program and later discovering but it is not appropriate for the problem that has been identified in the organization.

The solutions themselves must be carefully evaluated to ensure that they are not causing more problems (Meyer-Sahling et al., 2018; Mia and Patiar, 2001; Milosevic et al., 2010; Min et al., 2008; Mitchell et al., 1997). Quite often, the selection of an option to resolve a problem takes resources away from certain parts of the organization. Hence the leadership team must ensure that the selection of resources to allocate to the resolution to a problem is thorough. All options should be subjected to a monitoring and evaluation process to ensure that they are fit for purpose. Indeed, we might borrow from the economics of cost-benefit analyzes. If possible, an opportunity cost evaluation should be undertaken to identify whether there are other better ways of dealing with the problem than the ones that are currently presented. The wider the net is, the more likely it is that the organization will develop an extensive knowledge of the problem. However, expanding the information base too much can also be harmful in as far as it masks the real issues that pertain to the organizational problem.

Managers have sometimes complained that the lack of appropriate data when making decisions about organizational problems (Anckar et al., 2002; Anwar and Sun, 2013; Anyim et al., 2011; Arbulú et al., 2015; Argenti, 1996; Arthur and Dworkin, 1991). That means that their hands are tied when trying to resolve organizational problems. Therefore, it is critical to engage in a research process that's elicits key information about all the nuances of a problem in an organization. It is important to remember that resolving organizational problems does not necessarily require lots of data. There are situations where a brief outlook with clear and succinct information will be sufficient to resolve the problem. Indeed, excessive data collection might mean that the manager misses the woods from the trees. The manager should cultivate the capacity to pick up the critical aspects of any presentation. This is particularly important when the manager has a wide remit that requires them to explore different organizational plans at different times during their working schedules.

If we take the example of the collapse of large corporations such as the Lehman Brothers, it becomes clear that data alone cannot resolve problems (Rosenthal, 2013; Rosser and Eccleston, 2011; Saenz and Pérez-Bouvier, 2014; Saji and Ellingstad, 2004; Sakuramoto, 2005). One of the issues is the fact that these problems are deeply embedded within the structure, procedures, and values of an organization. It is advisable to explore the events and symptoms that underpin the problem. This is a precursor to any corrective action, and it is a critical stage in the research process. Objective data has the advantage of not being tainted by the subjectivity of the human gaze. However, objective data is necessarily reductive in nature and may therefore not highlight the complex dynamics that underlie the major problems which the organization is facing. An appreciation of the nuances of organizational problems is of the essence when trying to resolve them. Figure 2.2 demonstrates a knowledge management initiative framework that might be useful in structured organizations which have specific rules and procedures for dealing with problems.

Knowledge Management Initiative Framework

	Plan	Deploy	Maintain
Strategy	Identify the business requirements and benefits of knowledge management and ensure these are addressed by the initiative	Gain buy in and alignment from stakeholders on the execution of the knowledge management campaign – demonstrate clearly the value proposition	Foster a culture of knowledge sharing and collaboration by growing communities of knowledge organically
People	1) Identify key contributors and guardians of knowledge. 2) Identify key consumers of knowledge. 3) Identify a knowledge management evangelist to manage content and lead knowledge communities as facilitators and guides.	1) Encourage contributors to create and share knowledge through corporate wide recognition. 2) Train users on adopting a collaborative approach to locating, updating, and using shared knowledge. 3) Train knowledge management leaders on the technologies and then let them lead training for the rest of their functional communities.	1) Ensure knowledge management leads continue to review, approve, and organize submitted content. 2) Collect feedback from users of knowledge management process and technology for future improvements. 3) Reward key contributors and consumers of knowledge.
Process	1) Review all sources of knowledge within the organization and create a process for migrating to the identified locations. 2) Identify gaps and develop plan to create missing knowledge. 3) Design and develop taxonomy to organize knowledge	1) Design a process architecture to guide creating, capturing and managing knowledge. 2) Validate process design with KKHs and other key knowledge management SMEs 3) Identify communities of knowledge specific processes	1) Conduct regular reviews of the repository to maintain relevancy and quality – alternatively use a rating system 2) Use a card catalog system to track in-process documents 3) Track key metrics around knowledge management objectives to track ongoing performance
Technology	1) Identify where knowledge is currently stored and accessed including shared drives, web applications platforms, and cloud products. 2) Evaluate existing solutions used as well as other hosted and on premise solutions (RFI/RFP) 3) Align requested features and functions with the business requirements.	1) Plan and migrate knowledge and content to the new platform 2) Implement the taxonomy structure and metadata properties to allow for improved navigation and relevant search results 3) Implement various tools and mediums for knowledge sharing such as Blogs, Forums, Document Libraries, Wikis, and Intranet Portals	1) Customize the platform as new features such as wikis and blogs become available – community needs 2) Refine taxonomy and tags as needed to reflect company vocabulary and industry terminology updates 3) Continue to improve and optimize the user experience through surveys and rapid platform releases

Figure 2.2. Addressing the challenges of knowledge management.

Source: Kenny and Company.

Existing research has shown that those leaders who hold a single point of view or perspective may not fully understand the problem in the organization and will therefore not be able to effectively deal with it (Parry et al., 2008; Patiar and Mia, 2009; Pavlatos and Paggios, 2009a, b; Peng and Huiling Chen, 2011). Rather, it is advisable that managers expand their viewpoints and consider the subjective aspects of the problems within the organization. The accumulation and analysis of extensive data may not satisfactorily answer these critical questions. That is why the age of big data has not effectively resolved all the problems that organizations face today. Experts call for a more holistic approach to problem-solving because it delivers results that are long-lasting as well as dealing with the underlying issues. Of course, holistic conceptualizations of organizational problems take time and resources. This is something that the organization must consider and invest accordingly to ensure it gets the best results. Skimping on the problem-solving process is never a particularly productive strategy. If anything, it may render the resultant solutions unsustainable in the long run.

Big data was supposed to open a new era of quick solutions as supported by advanced technology (Sendawula et al., 2018; Supply chain Management and Logistics: Zara, 2013; Sharma and Upneja, 2005; Shatte et al., 2014). However, those expectations have not always been fulfilled as organizations struggle with the data deluge. If anything, the problems faced by all sizes of organizations are becoming even worse. Managers should invest in investigating the root causes of problems rather than only looking at the comforting Halo of big data. In this way, the leadership teams can prevent problems from occurring again in the future. This is the proactive approach which is preferred in modern organizational management. There is no single formula that will work for every organization. Instead, the leadership team should explore and experiment with different options to find the ones that are optimal for their environment on the priorities of the organization.

Existing literature has suggested several stages, formulas, models, and theories that might be considered appropriate for selecting problematic areas of the organization that require specific interventions (Phillips and Gully, 2014; Pitts, 2009; Podoshen et al., 2015; Priola et al., 2014; Rasim, 2008; Rose Ragins, 2004). Nevertheless, a systematic approach has its advantages which should not be ignored. Through the adoption of systematic approaches to problem solving, organizations can reduce their costs and improve the chances of eventual success. Moreover, a systematic procedure will allow the organization to take calculated risks that are backed by science and appropriate data sets. This is where decision-making is led by science and information. However, that does not mean that managers should suppress or ignore their gut instinct. Sometimes, good old-fashioned management can save the day.

Modern managerial science is not meant to stifle the creativity of leaders, managers, and supervisors (King et al., 2000; Klikauer, 2014; Kluike, 2015; De Kok et al., 2006; Korczynski, 2002; Kotas, 2014; Köllen, 2013). Rather, the science of management is meant to ensure a more authentic approach to problem-solving. At the same time modern management techniques are meant to ensure that managers do not get into trouble with employees concerning performance management issues. Hence, the problem-solving process becomes a systematic endeavor that is underpinned by principles and values. If an organization has well-settled and well-embedded values, they will be reflected in the problem-solving process that is adopted by employees. Moreover, those values and principles will ensure that there is no dissonance between the strategic goals of the organization and the resolution of any organizational problem.

Organizations are structured in such a way that they are systems in effect (Najam, 2000; Nath, 2011; Newell and Simon, 1972; Nica, 2015; Obeidat, 2012; Odrakiewicz, 2012; Okotoni and Erero, 2005). Hence, there is input, throughput, and output in an organizational context. The system of an organization is so complex that it includes sub-systems and ecological dynamics which contribute to the creation or even the resolution of problems within that organization. Managers should be particularly wary of contributing factors that are latent in their presentation. It is very easy to miss these critical aspects while prioritizing the manifest aspects of the problems. The manifest aspects are all the symptoms that clearly present themselves when the manager or leader first encounters the problem. It is for this reason that it is never advisable to try and solve problems without having the benefit of sufficient data about them.

2.2. THE DANGERS OF TRYING TO SOLVE PROBLEMS WITHOUT DATA

As already hinted in the previous sections of the book, data is a key ingredient in the resolution of organizational problems (Stewart and Walsh, 1992; Stone et al., 2015; Stoorvogel et al., 2017; Storey et al., 2006; Subhas Chandra et al., 2010; Tarafdar et al., 2014). There will be many big data problems that the organization must overcome before it can successfully resolve all the problems within its docket. For example, the organization may have to select a data analysis method that is valid and reliable. It is estimated the last three years account full nearly 90% of all the world data. That means that in the last 36 months, nearly 2.5 quintillion bytes of data were generated daily. Social media is responsible for a significant portion of this data. We are looking forward to a future that is dominated by big data. However, that also means that there are likely to be increasing data problems. Figure 2.3 summarizes the data science process which many organizations are increasingly referencing.

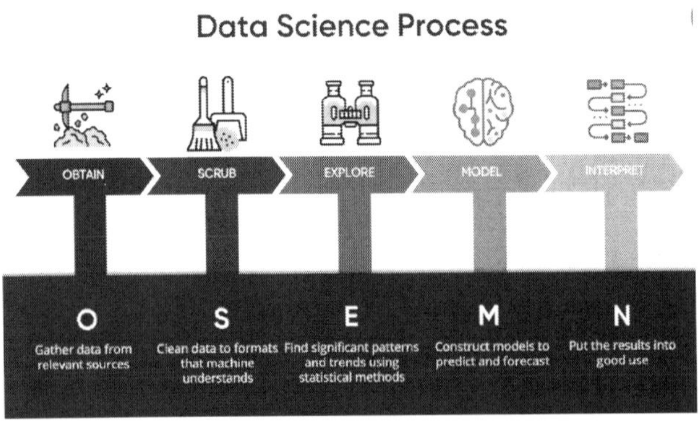

Figure 2.3. Five steps of a data science project lifecycle.

Source: Towards Data Science.

To that end, organizations relay on big data (Abu-Saifan, 2012; Ahimbisibwe and Nkundabanyanga, 2016; Ahmad and Schroeder, 2003; Alshallah, 2004). This is regardless of whether they are in the private sector or the public sector. There can be extraordinary benefits from big data if it is used wisely and strategically. The increase in big data has meant that leadership teams across a spectrum of organizations are using data as a key decision-making tool. Big data offers the possibilities of using information to solve organizational problems that have existed in the business world for a long time. A series of laws have been enacted by various parliaments to ensure that the use of data is consistent with the respect for human privacy and dignity. A case in point is where explicit consent is required to access certain types of data. This is particularly true of data if it is of a personal nature or information that has the capabilities of harming those who are vulnerable in society. Some critics have argued that the restrictions on access to Big Data could lead to bureaucracy and red tape that prevent free enterprise. However, the protection of the vulnerable in society takes precedence in these matters.

If data is to be used in the decision-making process, there must be cleared guidelines on how is stored and accessed (Anyim et al., 2011; Arbulú et al., 2015; Argenti, 1996; Arthur and Dworkin, 1991; Ashton et al., 2010; Assink, 2006). Therefore, many enterprises have developed clear protocols on access to information that is used in the problem-solving process. Some of the key issues that will be addressed include the storage of data, the protocols for collecting data, informed consent, best storage of data, and key decisions as to who has a right to access to the data. Critically, there are specific restrictions on the use of data. For example, it is unacceptable for anyone accessing data to use it for purposes that are different from that which was stated at the access point or during the informed consent process. This is particularly true of data that is used for marketing purposes without the explicit consent of the clients who may have inadvertently provided it to the data collection agency.

Organizations may identify one department that is responsible for the collection and coordination of various databases that are used in the operations of that organization (Tarafdar et al., 2014; Thursfield and Grayley, 2016; Toner, 2015; Too and Weaver, 2014; Torre Edoardo and Luca, 2013). Moreover, certain specialist departments such as human resource management may be called upon to provide their expertise in this respect. The use of data for making decisions can make managers complacent because they may perceive the day that contains all the answers that they need for the questions that I raised in the organization. Nevertheless, it is imperative to understand that big data is just one aspect of the Arsenal of tools that may be available to a manager when they are trying to resolve a problem. Besides, the data must be arranged in such a way that it can provide meaningful insights to those who access it for purposes of making decisions.

There is no escaping the data-driven economy. The businesses that refuse to adjust to this new reality are likely to be driven out of their core markets (Hansen and Olsson, 2011; Harney and Dundon, 2006; Harris and Brown, 1998; Harrison and Lock, 2004; Hartmann, 2014). Hence, it is advisable to look for pragmatic solutions that are consistent with the strategic plan of the organization and provides employees with optimum opportunities to achieve those goals without compromising their personal values or the law. One of the problems that any organization will face is the lack of understanding when data is accessed and interpreted. Typically, managers feel that those who gather data then proceed to present it in highly technical terms that are opaque and virtually inaccessible to other employers. Such complexities do not make it easier to rely on such data to resolve organizational problems. Hence, it is advisable that the professionals who are collecting data for purposes of decision-making present in formats that are accessible and understandable to managers. The data science approach (as summarized in Figure 2.4) can be useful when seeking ways of making information more accessible to end-users.

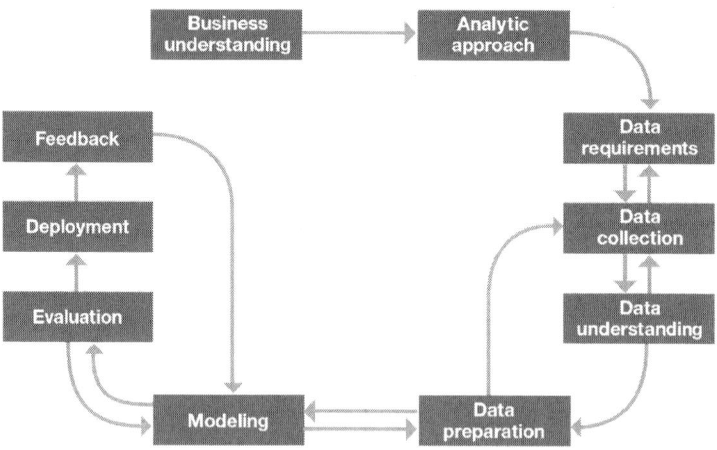

Figure 2.4. Data science approach for problem-solving and business strategy.

Source: Medium.

Additionally, the organization can arrange for training and development for senior managers and supervisors so that they can fully understand the various databases that are utilized within the organization (Moore and Birtwistle, 2004; Moore and Doyle, 2010; Morrison and Milliken, 2003; Mosher, 2013; Mujeeb and Ahmad, 2011). Alternatively, data must be presented after meticulous review to ensure that it is appropriate for the audience for which it has been presented. It should be a performance management issue if data is consistently being presented in opaque and inaccessible formats. Another issue that might arise when facing big data is the high cost of purchasing that data or even accessing it. The informational needs of organizations will continue to expand as the complexities of the markets where they primarily operate becomes apparent.

Other organizations have complained that they are faced with too many choices when accessing data (Sakuramoto, 2005; Samah et al., 2013; Schlögl, 2005; Schmid and Adams, 2008; Schuler, 1989; Sedmak and Longhurst, 2010). That means that the deluge of information does not allow them time to process it and converted into workable decisions. The industry has produced very complex systems for managing data and this may not be suitable for professionals who have expertise in other areas. For example, a social worker, lawyer, or doctor may find difficult to engage in complex accounting and the associated processing systems that do not directly refer to their professional role. It is therefore important to break down data into sets and formats that are readily accessible for those that need them. In some cases, it could involve summarizing the data or picking out key issues that are relevant to the organizational problem. Research has shown that excessive and irrelevant information prevents the processing of priorities.

Data security is becoming a major issue for organizations (Matías-Reche et al., 2009; McGill and Wooten, 1975; Memili and Welsh, 2012; Menke et al., 2007; Meyer-Sahling et al., 2018). This is because there has been a parallel development of hackers and other nefarious groups who access and abuse data that is held on the databases of various organizations. The design of these databases must therefore address security issues and ensure that access is restricted to those who are authorized. Indeed, the failure to bridge security gaps can lead to legal consequences for the offending organization. Part of data protection legislation is designed to punish those businesses that fail to adhere to the tenets of the policy. One of the important infringements is granting access to those who should not have access.

Despite the growth in data, there has been very limited attempt to increase the quality of the data that is provided to the public (Hartmann, 2014; Haworth and Hughes, 2015; Hennigs et al., 2013; Hermansson, 2020; Hopkin et al., 1979). A case in point is where marketing agencies are given access to databases that have been collected for alternative purposes. This may lead to unsuccessful cold calls seeking to sell merchandise and a negative response from the potential customers. The negative responses from customers who deal with unsolicited telephone calls highlights the importance of ensuring that the quality of data that is used for solving problems in an organization is very high. Access to inaccurate data is as bad as not having any data at all. Therefore, it is the responsibility of all actors within the organization to ensure that any mistakes and mishaps in the data are corrected at the earliest opportunity.

Moreover, organizations must overcome several compliance hurdles when maintain sets of public data (Egan, 2009; Egloff and Bhalla, 2014; Evans, 2005; Farndale et al., 2008; Fetscherin and Heinrich, 2014; Finkelstein et al., 2007). Failure to comply with these regulations may mean that the organization no longer has access to the data. Technology has provided some solace in terms of quickly processing vast amounts of data. However, modern technology can increase the complexity of data and make it difficult to make decisions based on the information that is being produced. In some ways, technology has sometimes outpaced the technological skills of enterprises. That is why some organizations have complained that they lack the skilled workers that can engage with the various big data access point. Hence, these organizations are not using all the big data that is available to them simply because they do not have a member of staff who can access and process data. In any case, the datasets available to organizations are continuously growing and changing so that the complexity becomes very difficult to manage. The challenges of relying on big data highlight the importance of looking for alternative solutions before settling on one.

2.3. THE IMPORTANCE OF GENERATING ALTERNATIVE SOLUTIONS TO PROBLEMS

It does not follow that the first solution that is identified when analyzing an organizational problem will be the most suitable option (Calabrese, 1997; Capko, 2003; Carraher, 2013; Chang et al., 2006; Chen et al., 2011; Chevalier and Mazzalovo, 2008). That is why it is very important to acknowledge and seek alternative solutions to a problem before investing in a single option.

There are solutions that are viable and those that are not viable. Based on the skill and experience of a manager or decision-maker, the consideration of options will play an important role in deciding which option a suitable for the circumstances. By implication, solutions which are not suitable will be discarded or modified accordingly. For example, a suitable option is one which is within the facility, power, and authority of the decision-maker. The problem-solving process can borrow from the strategies and tactics of integrative negotiation as demonstrated in Figure 2.5.

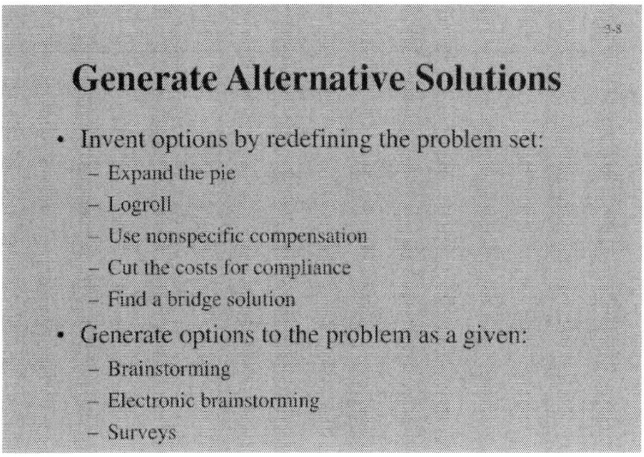

Figure 2.5. Strategy and tactics of integrative negotiation.

Source: Slide Player.

One of the most common errors that managers make is to assume that they can control the behavior of other members of the team in much the same way as they are able to control their own behavior (Hennigs et al., 2013; Hermansson, 2020; Hopkin et al., 1979; Hunter and Katz, 2012; Huselid, 1995; Ibrahim and Zailani, 2010). The complexity and diversity of an organizational team means that there is always the risk that's one of the elements within the structural will not be easily compliant. A case in point is where there are personalities that are resistant or otherwise impossible to manage using standard protocols. A skilled manager will look for options that can circumvent the challenges that are presented. This is the implication of resolving problems in a creative way. It is a very different proposition from situations where managers robotically follow a certain script that is offered when dealing with organizational problems. The creative solutions and the freedom to use them is recognition of the complexity of problems that do not easily respond to reductive and simplistic solutions.

Some researchers suggest that the decision-maker should identify at least three realistic alternative solutions before engaging in the implementation of their preferred solution (Parker et al., 2013; Parry et al., 2008; Patiar and Mia, 2009; Pavlatos and Paggios, 2009a, b). Indeed, existing literature has suggested certain methods for generating a broader list of possibilities based on the three realistic options that have been chosen by the decision-maker. One of the options for expanding the list of solution is brainstorming. This is a technique that allows for the exploration of various options regardless of how sensible they appear at the first glance. Brainstorming has the advantage of allowing the expression of various perspectives without censorship or premature evaluation of the options that have been presented. That means that every member of the team can explore the problem and suggest solutions based on their perspective and their experiences. Whereas brainstorming has been used in the classroom, it has recently been adapted for use in the corporate world. For example, team meetings that are dealing with contentious issues may use storming to elicit an open and frank discussion of the issue. In that sense, brainstorming is a participatory approach to problem-solving.

Another option involves expanding the list of options through changing the frame of reference for the problem that is being resolved (Jian Wang et al., 2010; John et al., 2014; Johnson and Clark, 2008; Jurevicius, 2016; Kabene et al., 2006). That officially means that the problem is re-orientated so that it opens the discussion. Alternative points of view will emerge when members of the team start perceiving the problem in different ways. It can be a very exciting exercise that elicits participation from even those members of the team that are naturally reluctant to engage. Managers use this technique to drive the conversation forward and prevent the naysayers from stifling debate. When undertaking this type of consultative exercise, it is important to make it clear that alternatives voices will be tolerated and even given the dignity of serious consideration. For the workers that engage in this process, the fact that they can participate and offer alternative opinions means that they perceived themselves to be part of the group. Hence, it is possible to build team spirit and morale.

Then there is the option of adopting a solution based on the resolution of a similar problem that was solved in the past (Stewart and Walsh, 1992; Stone et al., 2015; Stoorvogel et al., 2017; Storey et al., 2006; Subhas Chandra et al., 2010). Later in this book, we will explore this phenomenon in terms of the use of heuristics to solve problems. Of course, the use of heuristics can be problematic if they obscure any opportunities to perceive the problem in new and exciting ways. The fact that a similar problem was resolved using a specific method in the past does not necessarily imply that the same method will be successful in this new context. Indeed, one of the competencies of exceptional managers is that they can distinguish previous problems from current problems. The ability to link problems and reapply past solutions is also a skill in itself. The manager must straddle the balance between looking to the past and paying attention to the present or the future.

Once all the alternatives are generated, it is appropriate developed a full list of options and then reconsider them from the standpoint of a decision-maker that has access to knowledge (Stoorvogel et al., 2017; Storey et al., 2006; Subhas Chandra et al., 2010; Tarafdar et al., 2014; Thursfield and Grayley, 2016; Toner, 2015). Such an approach prevents the decision-maker from limiting the scope of their decision-making to only their first option. You should be able to reconsider the options available based on the research that you have undertaken and the various perspectives that have contributed to the list of options that you have. When evaluating the efficacy of various options, it is important to understand the level of effectiveness that is associated with any solution. This process does not detract from the creative aspects of the problem-solving process as demonstrated in Figure 2.6.

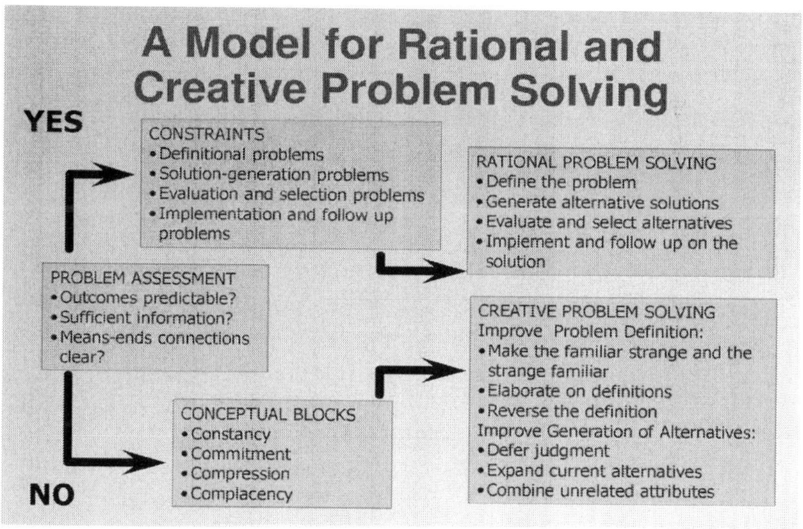

Figure 2.6. Creative problem-solving alternatives.

Source: Slide Player.

At the same time, you must also have a clear understanding of the costs that accrue because of selecting any of the options that have been presented (Storey et al., 2006; Subhas Chandra et al., 2010; Tarafdar et al., 2014; Thursfield and Grayley, 2016; Toner, 2015; Too and Weaver, 2014). In that sense, the evaluation exercise allows you to look at costs and the opportunity cost of the decision that you may eventually make. You must also be wary of options that appear to be simplistic and do not fit in with the complexity of the problem. For example, a solution may only consider the surface of the problem rather than the nuances of that problem. Clearly, such an option would not be appropriate because it is not delving into the reality of the problem. Rather, such a solution is superficial and ideally not be taken to be an indicator of possible success in the future.

In 1997, Bedell and Lennox proposed four criteria for evaluating the list of potential solutions that you may encounter as you deal with organizational problems (Milosevic et al., 2010; Min et al., 2008; Mitchell et al., 1997; Moore and Birtwistle, 2004; Moore and Doyle, 2010). The first question that you need to ask relates to the extent to which the proposed solution can satisfy the need or want that has been specified in the procedural statement of the problem. The second question that you will need to address is the level of sensitivity of the solution to the need that has been identified in the list. For example, it may be possible to balance different needs in the organization and examine the extent to which the proposed solution can deal with them. The third criteria are the question of whether the proposed solution is socially acceptable. In this respect, we also address the issue of legality. The business or organization must never allow itself to be placed in a situation where it is considering options that are illegal.

The decision-making process is a reflection of the norms and values of the society or context within which the organization is operating (Dumay et al., 2010; Dutse, 2013; DyReyes, 2008; Egan, 2009; Egloff and Bhalla, 2014; Evans, 2005; Farndale et al., 2008). Hence, there is an obligation to take note of the various roles and responsibilities that are attached to the corporate identity of the organization. This is where we speak of corporate social responsibility. The first and perhaps final consideration is the extent to which the organization and the decision-maker can execute the solution that has been proposed. This may turn out to be a question of power and authority. Managers must be particularly wary of making decisions that are above their responsibility. It is always better to consult than to make mistakes because of being overeager. Having written about the process of identifying alternatives, it is important to remember to evaluate them at the right time and not at the beginning of the process.

2.4. WHY SHOULD NOT EVALUATE ALTERNATIVES TO PROBLEMS IN THE INITIAL STAGES?

There is a tendency for managers to find solutions to organizational problems very quickly, and therefore managers may prematurely evaluate alternatives to problems in the initial stages (Ashton et al., 2010; Assink, 2006; Atkinson and Brander Brown, 2001; Atwal and Williams, 2009; Awadh and Saad, 2013). Clearly, this is not advisable because it stifles the creativity of the entire process. One of the problems with such an approach is that the decision-maker defines the criterion for evaluating the alternatives without fully understanding what the implications are for the organization. It is important that the evaluation and assessment process is based on experience and clear evidence of the effects associated with the options that have been proposed.

We have already indicated in previous parts of this book how essential it is to understand the problem before attempting to develop any solutions to it. Whereas the importance of understanding a problem seems obvious, this is an area often neglected by decision-makers (Nath, 2011; Newell and Simon, 1972; Nica, 2015; Obeidat, 2012; Odrakiewicz, 2012; Okotoni and Erero, 2005). For example, some decision-makers are looking for simplistic solutions to problems that they consider simple, yet the depth of the issue may necessitate more reflection. Then there are those that consider the problem statement as a box-ticking exercise. This means that they do not give it the attention and importance that it ought to have. A superficial consideration of organizational problems does not elicit long-lasting or effective solutions.

When trying to solve organizational problems, it is important to consider four major pillars of the organization's activities (Chevalier and Mazzalovo, 2008; Chung, 2015; Clegg and Palmer, 1996; Cold Cafe, 2018; Cole and Dawson, 2010). The first considerations are the customers or clients who purchase goods and services from the organization. In the public sector, the client is members of society who access public services or social services. The second pillar of the organization is the management or leadership team. These are the people that provide direction to the organization and will ultimately make decisions about which options are to be used for resolving organizational problems. Indeed, the managers will be actively involved in the alternative evaluation (see Figure 2.7), that is an essential aspect of the problem-solving process in organizations.

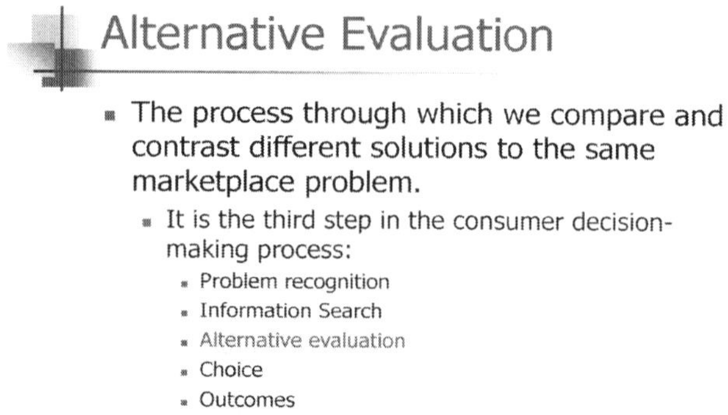

Figure 2.7. Alternative evaluation and choice.

Source: Dog publishing (2002) via Slide Player.

The third pillar comprises the perspectives or experiences of frontline staff members who may have critical insights into the problem (Maneesh et al., 2009; Manzoor, 2011; Matías-Reche et al., 2009; McGill and Wooten, 1975; Memili and Welsh, 2012). It is imperative to adopt an inclusive and participatory approach that calls for different opinion and perspective on the issue at hand. The fourth and perhaps last pillar of the organization is the marketing strategy. Ultimately, organizations rise or fall because they are able or unable to market their products effectively. A solution that negatively impacts on the marketing strategy should be reconsidered carefully. Indeed, the management team should ensure that such a problematic solution does not ultimately threaten the survival the organization itself.

If the decision-maker evaluates potential solutions in the early stages, they reduce the opportunities to ask pertinent questions (Schuler, 1989; Sedmak and Longhurst, 2010; Sendawula et al., 2018; Supply Chain Management and Logistics: Zara, 2013). You should always be asking questions which are addressed to the people that are involved in the problem or the structures that are affected by the problem. For example, you should ask what the problem really is and the implications that it has for the organization. You should be trying to understand how the problem has arisen. Think about all resources that you really need to resolve the problem. In thinking about the solutions, you need to have a very clear explanation as to why you need a specific resource. This is almost akin to making a business case for the various solutions that have been proposed for dealing with the problem. In other words, do not solve organizational problems before properly defining them.

Whereas it is generally recommended to make a brief problem statement, such an approach can necessarily limit you when you are trying to understand the problem (Rasim, 2008; Rose Ragins, 2004; Rosenthal, 2013; Rosser and Eccleston, 2011; Saenz and Pérez-Bouvier, 2014; Saji and Ellingstad, 2004). There is evidence that unusually narrowly stated problems limit access to alternative solutions. Clearly that is an approach that is undesirable because it does not get to the heart on the problem. Likewise, you should avoid making vague statements that do not provide sufficient guidance to the decision-maker. The most successful organizations are the ones that define their problems in terms of operational capacity and the ability to maintain their customer base. This is a good starting point and should provide you guidance for your own problem-solving process. Figure 2.8 highlights an example of a framework for evaluating solutions to organizational problems. Of course, organizations are not under obligation to follow specific formulas. However, these formulas provide useful guidance when faced with complex organizational problems.

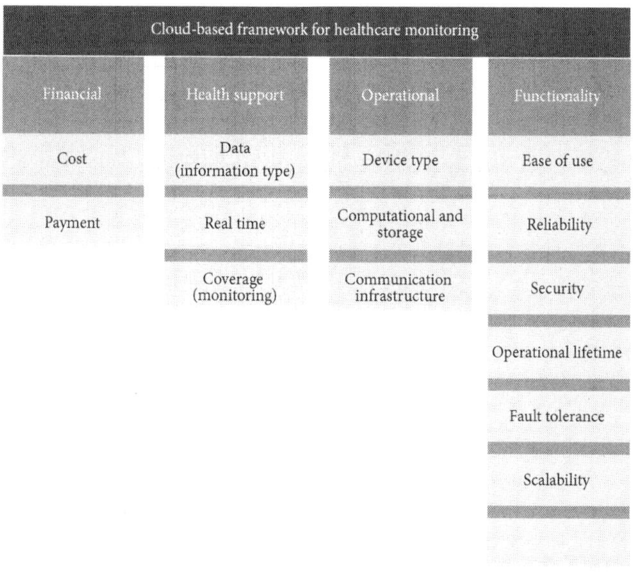

Figure 2.8. Evaluation criteria regarding the three solutions.

Source: AL-Qurishi et al. (2015).

It is advisable that organizations tease out the priorities when solving organizational problems and avoid wasting resources on side issues and distractions (Arthur and Dworkin, 1991; Ashton et al., 2010; Assink, 2006; Atkinson and Brander Brown, 2001; Atwal and Williams, 2009). There is a lot of hard work that goes into developing a problem statement. This is not just a summary that provides a skeleton overview the entire problem. Rather, it is a specific and technical description of a gap the organization's operations that must be addressed. If there is no clarity in the problem statement, it becomes very difficult to design and implement workable solutions. That is why the problem-solving process must be subjected to quality controls and checks. The result of these checks and balances might be that decision-makers are given further training and guidance when doing their work in solving organizational problems.

In fact, the problem-solving process maybe nothing more than narrowing the options to the ones that are most acceptable, least costly, and most effective (Guest et al., 2003; Hansen and Wernerfelt, 1989; Hansen and Olsson, 2011; Harney and Dundon, 2006; Harris and Brown, 1998). One of the key aspects of problem solving is to weed out any solutions that are clearly not appropriate for the context. You will then have a predetermined set of alternatives which are weighted against a pre-agreed selection criterion. For a complete and comprehensive comparative analysis, it is important to include specific minimum requirements within the description of an option. For example, you might include a cost and benefits analysis. It is also imperative to describe, in very clear terms, the merits and demerits of the option. Moreover, you will want to ensure that option is fully aligned with the preferences that are set out by the organization in its mission statement and vision during the planning processes.

Extensive and complex facets of solutions can make it difficult for the decision-maker to evaluate the alternatives in an objective way (Harney and Dundon, 2006; Harris and Brown, 1998; Harrison and Lock, 2004; Hartmann, 2014; Haworth and Hughes, 2015). This is typical when looking at the strengths and weaknesses of any given alternative. There will be many factors to consider, and the decision-maker may be confused by the sheer amount of information that is available to them. That is why it makes sense to narrow down the options to the most appropriate and workable ones. This ensures that the decision-maker is not overwhelmed. If the complexity of the problem requires significant information flows, it may be appropriate to provide additional support to the decision-maker. A case in point is where the responsibility is granted to a committee rather than an individual.

Alternatively, the organization may institution a clear review process so that the decision-maker is not the final arbitrator of their own sense of judgment.

The process of choosing from the different alternative can be negatively impacted by a series of externalities and biases (Kluike, 2015; De Kok et al., 2006; Korczynski, 2002; Kotas, 2014; Köllen, 2013; Lashley and Burgess, 2007; Le, 2017). Example, the decision-maker may be pressurized through time limits that mean that they must make a decision very quickly. At other times the decision-maker may be biased through the exercise and indulgence in personal emotions. That is why the decision-maker must be trained extensively to ensure that they can act in an objective and professional manner. Organizations should give the decision-maker as much time as they need to engage in deliberations. They need to ensure that the information-gathering process is extensive, and that the decision-maker is granted additional time because there may be certain issues that emerge during the data collection process that need to be considered in a much more critical way. In other words, the decision-maker must feel that they are fully prepared and equipped to deal with the monumental task at hand. Besides, the decision-maker must ensure that they prioritize those alternatives that are consistent with the strategic goals of the organization.

2.5. WHY YOU SHOULD FOCUS ON ALTERNATIVES THAT ARE CONSISTENT STRATEGIC GOALS?

As a general principle, solutions to organization of problems must be consistent with the strategic plan (Connell et al., 2009; Cooke, 2003; Cox et al., 2021; Cox, 1999; Crane, 2013; Crawford, 2016; Cunniff and Mostert, 2012). That means prioritizing those options that appear to adhere the goals and objectives that are set out in the strategic plan. In fact, the strategic plan is an important reference point for any decision-maker within the organization. An organization is only good at solving its problems if it has a coherent response to changes in the environment. Research has shown that many executives are neither consistent nor competent in resolving organizational problems. The result is that many organizations are failing at their inception or within two years of being formed. This has been a critical failing for small and family businesses. The customer is particularly important when making these decisions (see Figure 2.9 for an example of a strategic plan that is customer-focused).

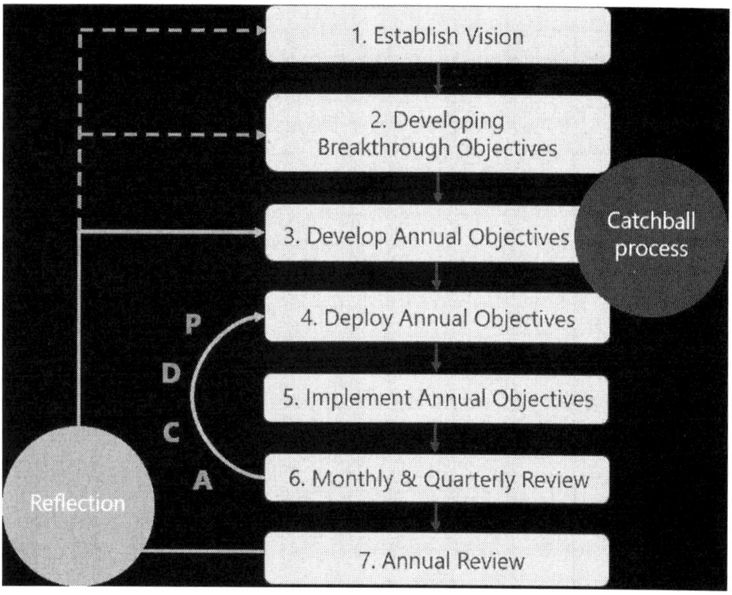

Figure 2.9. Strategic planning model for the customer-focused businesses.

Source: HubSpot Blog.

The statistics are not encouraging in terms of the ability of managers and senior executives to fully understand the problem-solving process (Dartey-Baah and Amoako, 2011; Day and Schoenrade, 2000; Deery and Nath, 2013; Dumay et al., 2010; Dutse, 2013). For instance, recent surveys have shown that nearly 85% executives agree or strongly agree that their employers are not good at solving problems; let alone diagnosing them. A similar proportion of executives agree that this flaw has significant cost implications for the organization. It is however not clear that these organizations are taking positive steps to ensure that they can tackle the various problems that they face. If the most senior people in an organization do not understand how to resolve its problems, then that organization faces an existential threat. More so, if the environment within which the organization is operating is constantly changing and becoming more competitive.

Because managers are under enormous pressure to deliver results, there is an incentive to search for quick solutions that may be inappropriate (Nagasawa and Fukunaga, 2015; Najam, 2000; Nath, 2011; Newell and Simon, 1972; Nica, 2015; Obeidat, 2012). That means that managers quickly switch to a resolution mode instead of checking the context and realities of the problems that they are tasked with resolving. This is despite the extensive literature and theory that is meant to guide the problem-solving process. For example, nearly four decades ago Mihaly Csikszentmihalyi and Jacob Getzels suggested that creativity is a critical resource when solving organizational problems. One of their important postulates is that the way in which a problem is framed has a significant impact on the possibilities of its resolution. However, the control that is exercised by organizations can stifle this creativity in favor of formulaic solutions that do not work.

Nevertheless, the urgency of successfully resolving organizational problems remains (Mosher, 2013; Mujeeb and Ahmad, 2011; Nagalakhmi and Trivedi, 2015; Nagasawa and Fukunaga, 2015; Najam, 2000). Existing literature strongly suggests that being passive is not an appropriate strategy for any organization in the face of a dynamic internal and external environment. For example, several philosophers including Albert Einstein to Peter Drucker have emphasized the importance of solving problems rather than ignoring them and hoping that they will resolve themselves. Unfortunately, some organizations are not willing to invest in the problem-solving process. Hence, they either pretend that the problems do not exist or that they do not significantly impact on the operations and external relations of the organization. These actions are unacceptable in a more competitive corporate world where company and public sector institutions must engage with an open market. In fact, the reality is that markets are very unforgiving for those organizations that are not willing to respond to change.

There are several reasons why managers and organizations struggle to resolve problems (Ahmad and Schroeder, 2003; Alshallah, 2004; Alvesson et al., 2011; Amos et al., 2008; Anckar et al., 2002). The first problem is related to over-engineering which means that there is a reductive approach to complexity. Organizations prefer to simply problems because that tends to elicit simple solutions. Yet, this approach ignores the nuance and complexity of the ecology of business and the public sector. The second problem relates to the diagnostic tools and frameworks that organizations choose to deploy when faced with problems. Existing literature has provided some popular formulas but some of these are falling out of fashion because they have not caught up with the modern corporate world. Other existing frameworks are not as comprehensive as they should be. Examples include TRIZ, Six Sigma, and Scrum which have become synonymous with management practice. Indeed, there is evidence that many new managers are not conversant with all these frameworks to start off with. Making strategy use of them becomes a challenge in these circumstances.

That is not to say that models and fearing that are currently being taught in schools of management are not effective. Existing research has shown that they can be effective in the right circumstances with the right people (Moore and Doyle, 2010; Morrison and Milliken, 2003; Mosher, 2013; Mujeeb and Ahmad, 2011; Nagalakhmi and Trivedi, 2015). The problem is related to the inability to accurately and appropriately apply these models which are in effect merely tools for achieving the goals of an organization. Many managers have complained that the models which are recommended in existing literature are so extensive, diverse, and complex that it becomes a time-consuming exercise to apply them completely on a regular basis. Managers are looking for solution that can be applied on a regular workday without having to expend inordinate resources. It is also important to ensure that the proposed solutions are contextually relevant. This can be a challenge when the context of the problem is markedly different from that in which the pre-existing models and theories were developed. For example, there may be cultural dynamics that do not fit into the Eurocentric focus of the models in existing literature.

Organizations have developed certain institutions and processes for improving the problem-solving process (Too and Weaver, 2014; Torre Edoardo and Luca, 2013; Turyakira, 2018a, b; Visser, 2012; WHO, 2018). For example, there are organizations that will hold annual strategy seminars that will incorporate the perspectives of line managers, supervisors, and frontline members of staff. These meetings can offer an opportunity to explore the tools that are currently used and then make selections based on the findings of the conference. Of course, some of the attendees on these conferences do not take them as seriously as they should. This should be treated as a performance management issue. Learning is part of the problem-solving process, and the problem-solving process also contributes to learning in turn.

Generally, the recommendation in existing literature is that the decision-makers in organizations should select options that are less disruptive, more efficient, and demonstrably effective (Rosenthal, 2013; Rosser and Eccleston, 2011; Saenz and Pérez-Bouvier, 2014; Saji and Ellingstad, 2004). It does not follow, however, that simplistic solutions are always the better solutions. If anything, simplistic solutions are never the answer to complex questions in the organization. There are several problem-diagnosis frameworks that can be used as an acceptable shortcut when dealing with relatively straightforward problems. A case in point is the use of a root cause analysis. Another option that is becoming popular is the use of five questions based on "why." These questions are rhetorical but seek to understand the nature and context of the organizational problems. It is akin to Socratic Questioning which has been popularized in pedagogy and coaching.

Looking at organizational problems in different ways can be useful when trying to generate a range of possible solutions (Bilson et al., 2013; Bjerregaard, 2011; Black, 2005; Brandsen and Pestoff, 2006; Bruce and Daly, 2006; Calabrese, 1997). For example, it has been suggested in existing literature that reframing the problem is one of the best solutions for organizations that are struggling to find a way out of their problems. This can be applied within the narrow context of organizational change. However, that must account for the possibility that there will be some resistance to organizational change. The work of change champions will come into play at this point. These change champions will ensure that members of the organization fully understand the need and urgency of the change. The rationale is that understanding is part of the journey towards embracing and accepting change. Change can be turned into goals, such as the ones demonstrated in Figure 2.10. These are then converted into objectives that seek to resolve the known problems in the organization.

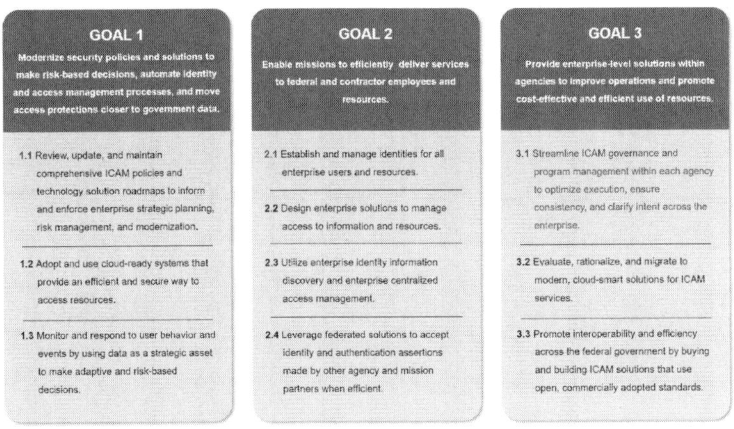

Figure 2.10. Examples of goals turned into objectives.

Source: FICAM Playbooks.

There are broadly seven interventions that might be used to improve the efficacy and relevance on the problem-solving process (Leary, 2001; Lee and Park, 2009; Leggett, 2007; Lengnick-Hall et al., 2009; Leuenberger, 2006; Leung et al., 2015). The first issue to be addressed is the legitimacy of the process itself and the people that are going to run the process. For instance, you might need to ensure this everyone that is affected or involved fully understands the methodology that is being used. Extensive discussions are not counterproductive if they are controlled and directed towards the resolution of the problem. The second issue that you will need to address is the need to have alternative perspectives from Outsiders. These are voices that are likely to think outside the box. You may need creative and unorthodox solutions that could be gleaned from the perspectives of those that do not always tow the line.

The third consideration is the proper and accurate memorialization of the various aspects of the problem-solving process (Awadh and Saad, 2013; BIS, 2015; Baker and Esherick, 2013; Bannò and Sgobbi, 2016; Barry et al., 2000; Bekker, 2014). That means putting everything in writing. By insisting on a requirement to write down opinions and perspectives, you ensure that contributors are not flippantly giving options that are likely to fail. Contributors must consider all the options that are presented to the committee or decision-maker. This can go some way towards ensuring accountability for opinions that eventually have to be supported by facts before they are presented. The fourth requirement is to always inquire about those aspects of the problem description that are missing. Do not take the problem statement at face value. Be inquisitive and explore its implications. Sometimes what is implied but not said is more important than what is said but not implied. The presenting problem is not always the actual problem, and it requires some investigation to get to the bottom of the problematic areas.

The fifth aspect to address is the need to consider multiple categories (Toner, 2015; Too and Weaver, 2014; Torre Edoardo and Luca, 2013; Turyakira, 2018a, b). Research has shown that powerful change can arrive when you transform the perceptions of people. This type of paradigm shift occurs when you trigger the curiosity of the contributors to the debate. For example, you may invite employees to identify specific categories that they think the problem emanates from. Examples include incentive issues, expectations, attitudes, and behavior. If possible, allow employees to expand the category list so that you have a wide lens insight into the problem. This is an established mechanism for encouraging participation and engaging with all segments of the organization. It is through these actions that you can ensure that solutions are comprehensive and well-directed towards the real problem that the organization is facing.

The sixth consideration is that of the positive exceptions that ought to be analyzed (Najam, 2000; Nath, 2011; Newell and Simon, 1972; Nica, 2015; Obeidat, 2012; Odrakiewicz, 2012; Okotoni and Erero, 2005). For example, you should look for instances when the problem that you are facing now did not occur. You should ask what was different between the previous situations on the current situation. Such questions will allow contributors to consider positive exemptions and the lessons that they provide will then be useful when trying to deal with the current problem. Some literature refers to this as the bright spot of the narrative. You may find that there are hidden factors which may have been ignored in the group setting. When you look back at the situations that went well, you may be able to glean insights into the solutions to the current problem. Of course, such retrospective inflection should not be too indulgent that it allows for lazy assumptions that try to over-simply the current problem. Even worse, are the situations where managers and opinion leaders attempt to create similarities and equivalences where they do not exists.

The final consideration is questioning the objective of the entire exercise (Haworth and Hughes, 2015; Hennigs et al., 2013; Hermansson, 2020; Hopkin et al., 1979; Hunter and Katz, 2012). There will be underlying goals and motivations from the diverse perspectives of the contributors to the decision-making process. These can be expressed as interest groups, although that term has developed negative political connotations. As a decision-maker, you should be able to separate the interests of the contributors and the objective value of their contribution. Trying to harmonize the various perspectives is part of the management process when resolving problems. Harmonization does not necessarily mean that you force consensus where it cannot and should not occur. Rather, you should be stimulating debate and then arriving at conclusions that are properly supported by evidence.

Chapter 2 Summary

This chapter has explored the processes of solving problems in organizations. It has shown that specificity and consultation are key ingredients in understanding and resolving organizational problems. All the relevant decisions should be based on accurate and timely information to improve the quality of the outcomes. This calls for a careful consideration of various solutions and evaluating them against the strategic plan and values of the commissioning organization. Chapter 3 tries to incorporate the value-base and culture of the organization into the problem-solving process.

CHAPTER 3

AN ORGANIZATION'S VALUES AND THE PROBLEM-SOLVING PROCESS

CONTENTS

This chapter builds on the work of Chapters 1 and 2 by highlighting the importance of values when making decisions about the problem-solving process. This chapter highlights the differences between a short-term and long-term outlook. It introduces the use of brainstorming as an instrumentality of generating ideas. Moreover, the chapter emphasizes specificity in linking solutions to problems. There is an introductory view of the evaluation process of different options or solutions. For example, the relative standard is explored as a tool of comparative analysis. We ought to begin this discussion by distinguishing the immediacy of the problem from its future implications.

3.1. THE DIFFERENCE BETWEEN SHORT-TERM AND LONG-TERM SOLUTIONS TO PROBLEMS

There is a clear difference between short-term planning and long-term planning when dealing with organizational problems (Chen et al., 2011; Chevalier and Mazzalovo, 2008; Chung, 2015; Clegg and Palmer, 1996; Cold Cafe, 2018). This distinction is particularly important when solving organizational problems with a mixture of short-term implication and long-term effects. One of the challenges that managers will face is the lack of accurate and timely information about the circumstances that they are trying to resolve. In the short run, the manager will stick to manage a crisis and prevent it from escalating. However, in the long-term the decision-maker will try to ensure that the circumstances that led to a crisis do not occur and do not have a significant negative effect on the operations of the organization. Managers who are dealing with short-term and long-term problems must be wary of relying too much on "hot advice" as opposed to "cold advice" (see Figure 3.1).

Cold advice	Hot Advice
Information-based	Relies on fragmented information, gossip
Research used	Opinion/ideologically based
Independent/neutral and problem-solving	Partisan/biased and about winning
Long-term	Short-term
Proactive and anticipatory	Reactive/crisis-driven
Strategic and wide range/systematic	Single issue
Idealistic	Pragmatic
Public interest focus	Electoral gain oriented
Open process	Secret/deal-making
Objective clarity	Ambiguity/overlapping
Seek/propose the best solution	Consensus solution

Figure 3.1. Differences between hot and cold advice.

Source: Jacob Endiartia (2020).

Planning can become a form of estimation and often outright guesswork when dealing with several unknowns concerning the organizational problem at hand (Mujeeb and Ahmad, 2011; Nagalakhmi and Trivedi, 2015; Nagasawa and Fukunaga, 2015; Najam, 2000; Nath, 2011). Several obstacles may conspire to make the decision-making process even more difficult than it already is. In that sense, it is important for decision-makers to be given as much information as possible about the problem that they are trying to resolve. Moreover, the planner may face a reduction in resources that are available for the resolution of the problem. Some organizations are not effective in prioritizing the management of their portfolio of problems. Other leaders suffer from a lack of vision and that means that they do not have clear values and priorities that guide their problem-solving process. Hence, it makes sense to only hire leaders who have a demonstrable capability to conceive and communicate an effective vision as well as the accompanying strategy.

The starting point is often the most difficult one because the decision-maker must define the terms of reference (DyReyes, 2008; Egan, 2009; Egloff and Bhalla, 2014; Evans, 2005; Farndale et al., 2008; Fetscherin and Heinrich, 2014). In some organizations, the terms of reference are predetermined and provide guidance to whoever is given the task of resolving an organizational problem. Managers are expected to set goals and objectives based on the strategic plan that will have been communicated to them through the leadership team. Additionally, decision-makers should be aware that there is a lot of unpredictability in the market and the ecology within which the institution of business operates. Hence, the need for dynamic planning and responses even as the organization scans its internal and external environment.

The problem-solving process calls for a combination of short-term thinking and long-term planning (Haworth and Hughes, 2015; Hennigs et al., 2013; Hermansson, 2020; Hopkin et al., 1979; Hunter and Katz, 2012). The trick is to get the balance right. In the short-term, the priority is to get rid of the crisis and protect the assets of the organization. In the long-term, the priority is to ensure the survival of the business model and to prevent the crisis from rising again. Some experts have advocated for the use of medium-term planning to bridge the gap between short-term solution and long-term solutions. However, the medium-term is not fully understood and therefore its application can be sporadic. Some managers prefer a clearcut between short-term and long-term planning rather than having any interim measures.

Regardless of the planning modality that is chosen, each of the options will have certain characteristics that allow it to achieve its aims and objectives (Argenti, 1996; Arthur and Dworkin, 1991; Ashton et al., 2010; Assink, 2006; Atkinson and Brander Brown, 2001). The short-term plan is not likely to last more than 12 months or a year. You can include a series of monitoring and evaluation milestone that can occur on a daily, weekly, monthly, quarterly, or annual basis. The literature accompanying the short-term goals will be referenced on a regular basis. It will incorporate certain steppingstones towards the overall larger goals in the organization. Hence, one way of looking at short-term planning is to think of it as the small goals that will contribute towards the bigger goal in the future.

In short-term, planning you need to look at the current situation and fix any potential issues that might arise from it within one year (Cold Cafe, 2018; Cole and Dawson, 2010; Collinson and Hearn, 1994; Connell et al., 2009; Cooke, 2003; Cox et al., 2021). The deadlines for short-term goals are necessarily very tight and can be as little as an hour or day. The complexity of the issue will determine the extent to which you rely on short-term solutions. However, every organization must think of the long term because the reality of development and growth. Inevitably the present problem will turn into a future headache unless it is addressed right from its root causes. This is despite the clear distinctions between short-term and long-term planning (see Figure 3.2).

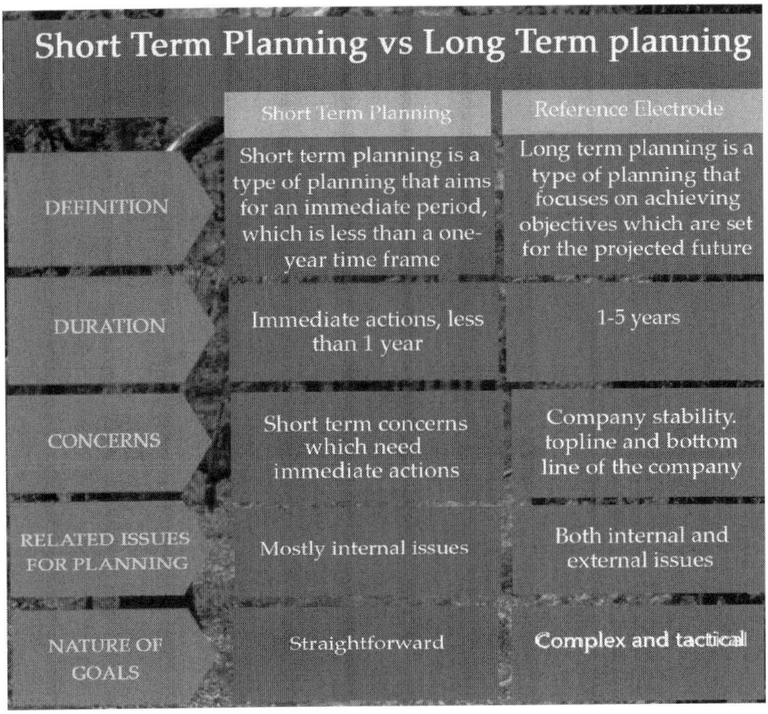

Figure 3.2. Short-term and long-term planning.

Source:Piyu via Difference Between.

The medium-term planning is the interim period before you transition to the bigger goals (Ifinedo, 2016; Ismail et al., 2005; Jansen et al., 2008; Jian Wang et al., 2010; John et al., 2014; Johnson and Clark, 2008). In other words, this can be defined as the intermediate goals or medium goals that can link the small objective to the larger long-term goals. In effect, you are looking for semi-permanent solutions to short-term problems. It may also incorporate a series of procedures and policies to ensure that the short-term problems that you are currently facing do not occur again. Of course, some problems are cyclical and therefore require a long-term solution. There is some level of investment in the medium-term which is higher than what you might need for a short-term plan. This is the priority that the organization must face as a matter of course if the problem lies between the short and long run. In any case, there should be sufficient investment in the processes and protocols of resolving organizational problems.

The long-term plan requires big thinking and will entail significant investment (Kerzner, 2003; Khan et al., 2011; King et al., 2000; Klikauer, 2014; Kluike, 2015; De Kok et al., 2006; Korczynski, 2002). It is for this reason that some small and family-owned businesses have sidestepped the important requirement to engage in long-term planning. Some even assume that they are bound to fail so do not spend time looking beyond five years. This is a mistake because it stifles the opportunities for growth and development in the organization. The organization might be restructured as part of a long-term strategy. Typically, the long-term plan is triggered because a problem is very significant and has not been resolved by either the short-term plans or the medium-term plans. There is no upper limit on the length a long time. For example, there are organizations that plan 50 years ahead.

It is important not to neglect short-term and medium-term goals wild assuming that the long-term goals will resolve all the problems (Li, 2009; Li et al., 2006, 2013; Lock, 2007; Loorbach, 2010; Lorenzo-Romero et al., 2013; Loundes, 2001). There may be a crisis within the organization that requires immediate attention. In such a case, it would be foolhardy to assume that a long-term plan will successfully resolve a short-term crisis. Ingvar Kamprad (IKEA pioneer) famously noted that we must think about where we will be in 200 years. Others have long term plans that are no more than 5 years in duration. It is about finding the right balance for the organization and problem you are facing.

Long-term plans are evidently complex because they deal with complex problems that have troubled the organization for a significant period (McGill and Wooten, 1975; Memili and Welsh, 2012; Menke et al., 2007; Meyer-Sahling et al., 2018; Mia and Patiar, 2001). Hence, long-term planning is a highly strategic endeavor which considers bigger issues within the organization. There is a lot of tactical awareness and positioning involved in long-term planning. Additionally, there will be certain technical processes and procedures that must be adhered to in the long-term plan. By way of contrast, the short-term plan is relatively straightforward. It deals with immediate problems that could be easily resolved with a short-term plan.

Over time, a dichotomy of planning has emerged in which short-term goals mostly focus internal issues or the internal environment (Atkinson and Brander Brown, 2001; Atwal and Williams, 2009; Awadh and Saad, 2013; BIS, 2015). Meanwhile, the long-term plans focus on the external ecology within which the organization operates. Medium term planning will focus on both the internal and external environment. Examples of internal issues that might be resolved by short-term planning include customer complaints about the quality of service or products that are being put on the market. An example of a long-term issue that might require long-term planning is a change in government regulation that might render the current business model legal.

That dichotomy of long-term and short-term planning should not be assumed to be mutually exclusive (Farndale et al., 2008; Fetscherin and Heinrich, 2014; Finkelstein et al., 2007; Gil-Pareja et al., 2007; Gruman and Saks, 2011). As you engage in long-term planning, you should also consider that short-term issues. Similarly, as we engage in short-term planning you should have some vision of the future and the bigger issues that the organization is facing. There are also macro issues such a change in the political, social, and economic climate which informs both your short-term and long-term planning. One of the techniques that have become popular in problem-solving is brainstorming.

3.2. WHY AND HOW DO WE BRAINSTORM WHEN SOLVING PROBLEMS?

One of the most popular techniques for generating ideas during the problem-solving process is the use of brainstorming (Saenz and Pérez-Bouvier, 2014; Saji and Ellingstad, 2004; Sakuramoto, 2005; Samah et al., 2013; Schlögl, 2005). The advantage of brainstorming is that it generates unique ideas from within a range of contributors in an organizational setting. This technique has been used extensively in teaching. However, it is now becoming increasingly popular in the corporate world. In fact, the popularity of brainstorming is such that it has been used interchangeably to mean problem-solving (Figure 3.3).

Figure 3.3. From brainstorming and towards solutions.

Source: Dreamstime.

Generally, brainstorming remains an important modality for generating ideas (Hunter and Katz, 2012; Huselid, 1995; Ibrahim and Zailani, 2010; Ichniowski et al., 1997; Ifinedo, 2016; Ismail et al., 2005). This is true, even though there is no systematic body of literature that has comprehensively explained the mechanisms underpinning brainstorming. The lack of such theories and models may be a failing of intellectual interest as opposed to the modality lacking in any disciplinary content. Nevertheless, corporate actors continue to use brainstorming as a means of extending the problem-solving process by generating new and interesting ideas from within a set working group. As a starting point, you need to have a very specific problem that is clearly defined before you can start brainstorming around it. However, some teams may use the brainstorming technique the things about the problem in depth. To make brainstorming effective, you must have a protocol for recording the various ideas that have been generated from different members of the working group.

The brainstorming technique calls for the free flow information (Li et al., 2006, 2013; Lock, 2007; Loorbach, 2010; Lorenzo-Romero et al., 2013; Loundes, 2001; Lycett et al., 2004). This means that you must resist any temptation to censor the various contributors to the debate. Unfortunately, the hierarchical corporate world tends to favor control over creativity.

That means that many managers are conditioned to expect obedience and orderliness from the working group as opposed to working in a truly collegiate way. For the most part, brainstorming is a creativity technique that is inclusive and participatory. Hence, the need to diversify the membership of the working group as much as possible. There will be a handful of team members that are responsible for generating potential solutions to a specific problem. These will be organized into a working group which allows for the free exchange of ideas. One of the starting goals for the group is that everyone should have the time and space to express their perspectives on the issue at hand.

The current team members will be laid by a director or a facilitator (Arbulú et al., 2015; Argenti, 1996; Arthur and Dworkin, 1991; Ashton et al., 2010; Assink, 2006; Atkinson and Brander Brown, 2001). The role of this leadership task is not to prevent the exchange of unwanted ideas, but rather to ensure that there is even more engagement from all members of the team. That means prompting and caring to elicit further clarifications of the ideas that are being presented. The engagement and prompting must be sensitive so that it does not come across as directing the contributors towards a certain perspective. In some cases, the facilitator may not even offer any opinions so that they are not privileged over the other contributions from the team. It is imperative that there is an ongoing flow of ideas from diverse voices even if it means that those voices are contradicting each other. Similarly, there should be an initial acceptance of ideas that may otherwise be considered unworkable. The brainstorming exercise is never about streamlining ideas but rather, expanding them to the maximum.

Inevitably, the ideas that emanate from brainstorming sessions are likely to be fuzzy and will therefore luck the finesse of carefully curated report (Chen et al., 2011; Chevalier and Mazzalovo, 2008; Chung, 2015; Clegg and Palmer, 1996; Cold Cafe, 2018; Cole and Dawson, 2010). In effect, they must be refined at a later stage. Leaders should resist the temptation to prematurely sieve out ideas that they consider to be undesirable or unworkable. This is a modality that encourages engagement and participation. The fact that the ideas are random and very extensive should not discourage managers from using brainstorming. After all, the intention is to improve our understanding of the problem and the potential solutions to it. These aspects are included in the comprehensive guide to brainstorming that is demonstrated in Figure 3.4.

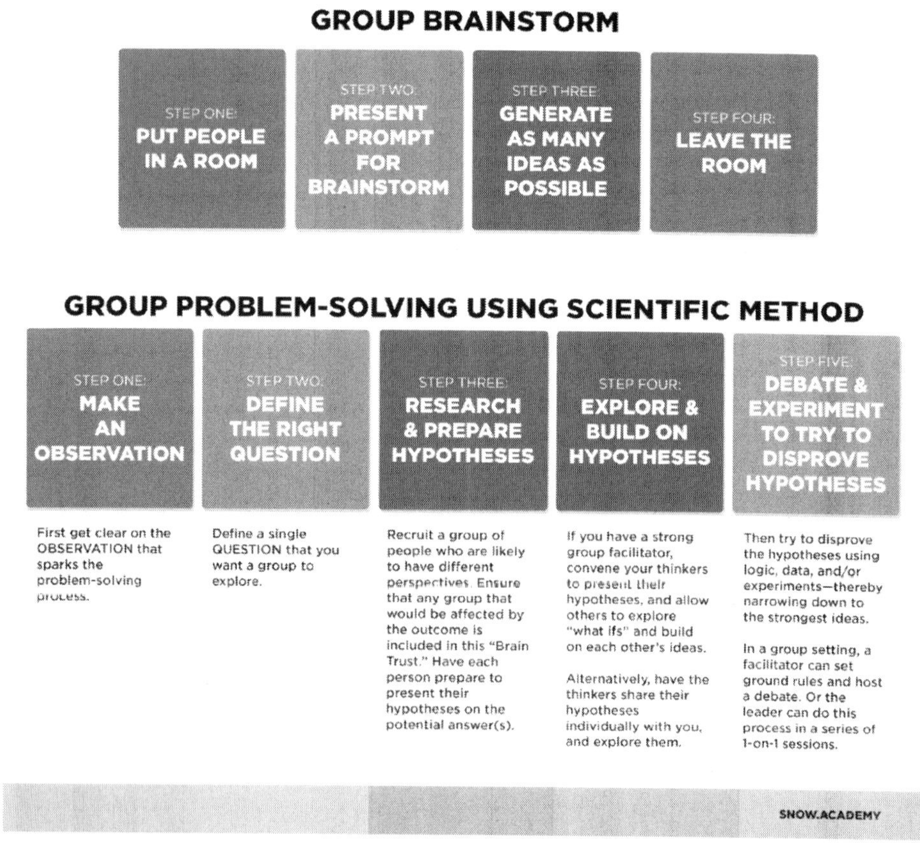

Figure 3.4. Ultimate guide to brainstorming.

Source: Shane Snow.

The origins of brainstorming as a problem-solving technique are deeply steeped in the tradition or the corporate world (Jian Wang et al., 2010; John et al., 2014; Johnson and Clark, 2008; Jurevicius, 2016; Kabene et al., 2006; Kasperk et al., 2011). The originator was Alex Osborne who started using the term as far back as 1939. This pioneer was frustrated that his team was unable to generate new ideas even after significant prompting. Hence, the development of new creative ways of eliciting participation and contributions from members of the team who would otherwise be reluctant to engage. This is a team-based approach that calls for social interaction. The origins of the technique also included group-thinking sessions. Anecdotal evidence shows that brainstorming can lead to the generation of a high quality and quantity of new ideas. This is particularly important for decision-makers when they are solving problems with limited information.

The emphasis during brainstorming is on the collection of a range of ideas rather than the strictness with which the group principles and protocols are adhered to (Huselid, 1995; Ibrahim and Zailani, 2010; Ichniowski et al., 1997; Ifinedo, 2016; Ismail et al., 2005; Jansen et al., 2008). Hence, it is much more important for all members of the team to produce at least one idea at the very least, as opposed to focusing on ensuring that there are strict protocols for engaging in the discussion. Some critics have argued that brainstorming tends to produce many ideas of a poor quality. Hence, those that are looking for quick solutions are bound to be disappointed with the outcomes from a brainstorming session. Nevertheless, the primary purpose of the brainstorming session is to generate ideas and not necessarily to refine them. However, it is always important to remember that the alternatives selected eventually must substantially or wholly resolve the specific problems that have been identified in the organization.

3.3. SELECTING ALTERNATIVES THAT RESOLVE SPECIFIC AND RELEVANT PROBLEMS

The exercise of choice is a major sticking point for managers and other decision-makers within the organization (Leuenberger, 2006; Leung et al., 2015; Li, 2009; Li et al., 2006, 2013; Lock, 2007; Loorbach, 2010). That is why excessive choice has been deemed undesirable when trying to solve organizational problems. Managers are sometimes conditioned to look for the simplest choices and will be alarmed by the existence of significant data volumes. Nevertheless, it is appropriate to consider a range of policy options when facing a challenge in the ecology of an organization or a business. Ideally, the focus should be on the stated goals or objectives of the problem-solving process. In that way, there are opportunities to prioritize the most important aspects of the problem and solution.

The alternatives that are presented as possibilities should include substantially different approaches to the problem (Patiar and Mia, 2009; Pavlatos and Paggios, 2009a, b; Peng and Huiling Chen, 2011; Phillips and Gully, 2014). There is no point in securing so many alternatives that are manifestly or latently like each other. Having diversity in the options that are presented for consideration will significantly improve the quality of the ultimate decision. Moreover, the options that are presented to the decision-maker should address the problem in real terms rather than focusing on surface issues which do not deal with the real issue. Managers prefer precision when making decisions. This is particularly true when managers are facing complex options whose clarity may not be as obvious as the decision-maker may desire.

It is true that you cannot arrive at good solutions if you do not have good alternatives (Steers et al., 2004; Stevens, 2002; Stewart and Walsh, 1992; Stone et al., 2015; Stoorvogel et al., 2017). Therefore, the quality of alternatives that are presented during the problem-solving process will have a significant impact on the outcomes. One of the mistakes that managers make is to focus on one solution that they believe will resolve the problem without opening their mind to alternatives that could be more efficient and even more appropriate for the circumstances. The advice and support from technical team can be invaluable when considering options. These technical advisors will highlight advantages and disadvantages of the different options without necessarily interfering in the final decision-making process. It is usually unacceptable for the technical team to become the decision-maker by default. Figure 3.5 sets out the minimum tasks or activities that are required when selecting alternative solutions to an organizational problem.

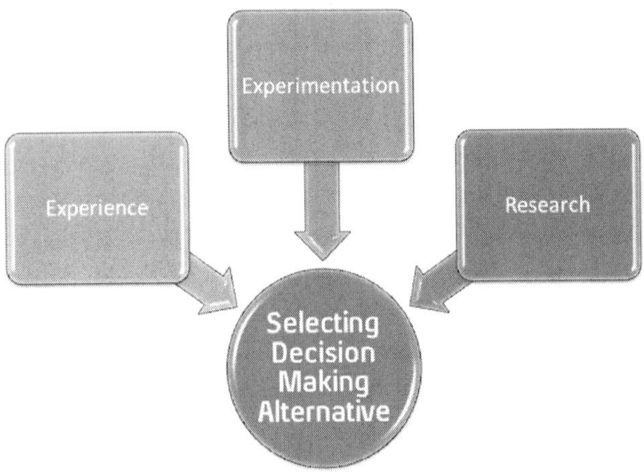

Figure 3.5. Choose best alternative in decision making.

Source: iEduNote.

The decision-makers must be aware that recommendations necessarily reflect the value judgments of the various actors within the core team that has been appointed to generate these options (Thursfield and Grayley,

2016; Toner, 2015; Too and Weaver, 2014; Torre Edoardo and Luca, 2013; Turyakira, 2018a). There is a tendency to prioritize the value judgments that are made by the decision-maker because they are ultimately responsible for the outcome. The technicians have professional expertise which they bring to bear on the decision-making process, but they are crucially not accountable for the final decision. It is important not to restrict the decision-making process to a subset of options that are initially perceived to be advantageous or appropriate for the situation. This is because the narrow scope of the limited selection does not allow for the possibilities of expanding the capabilities of the organization to deal with the problem in the short-term, medium term, and long-term.

The differences between the various options can be presented as trade-offs or the opportunity cost when making any selection (Ashton et al., 2010; Assink, 2006; Atkinson and Brander Brown, 2001; Atwal and Williams, 2009; Awadh and Saad, 2013). Moreover, the decision-maker will be keenly aware of the consequences of any selection that they make. Good information is at a premium and the organization should invest extensively in generating this information within the confines of the remit of the steering committee. Consultation with the various stakeholders is an important milestone in the problem-solving process. There should be clear documentation of this consultation and the outcomes so that any arbitrator who is reviewing the decision will have clear background information before they arrive at their own decision.

It could be argued that the generation of alternatives must really borrow ideas from the value perspective and technical perspective (Rosser and Eccleston, 2011; Saenz and Pérez-Bouvier, 2014; Saji and Ellingstad, 2004; Sakuramoto, 2005; Samah et al., 2013). This is particularly important if the technical perspective is outsourced. The teams that are coming in to provide support to the decision-maker may not be grounded in the norms and values of the organization. Yet, it is very clear that the decision-making process and the problem-solving processes must adhere to the norms and values of the organization that is the commissioning agent. In other words, the employer must ensure that the goals and strategies of the organization are part of the procedures that are followed when dealing with challenges that may occur in the organization. Such an approach allows for better alignment so that the solutions that are selected do not put the organization out of balance.

The alternative itself is not necessarily a single action or idea (Songa et al., 2012; Sparrow and Makram, 2015; Speer and Potter, 2000; Steers et al., 2004; Stevens, 2002; Stewart and Walsh, 1992). Instead, it comprises a portfolio of actions and justifications for those actions that may provide a holistic view of the solution that has been proposed. The decision-maker is when armed with a complete view of any option which they can compare against each other before they arrived at their final decision. That is why some literature speaks of strategy, portfolios, or packages when referring to the alternative solutions that have been presented to the decision-maker when generating potential solutions to problems. It reflects the comprehensiveness and completeness of the options that are posited. In the same vein, options that are half-backed are likely to lead to poor decision-making that does not resolve the urgent problems within the organization or the ecology surrounding it.

There are certain characteristics that are associated with a good alternative in the problem-solving process (Baker and Esherick, 2013; Bannò and Sgobbi, 2016; Barry et al., 2000; Bekker, 2014; Bell et al., 2011; Bercu, 2012). The first characteristic is that the option emanates from a screening process that builds specificity from generality. For example, it would be inappropriate to simply present the ideas that have arisen through a brainstorming session. You must curate those ideas and make selections so that the decision maker has a high-quality summary from which they can pick the optimum alternative. The technical descriptions of the alternative must also include the cost implications and the opportunity cost that are attached to the option. Proper decisions cannot be made without this crucial information. This is very similar to the process that is used in managerial economics (see Figure 3.6).

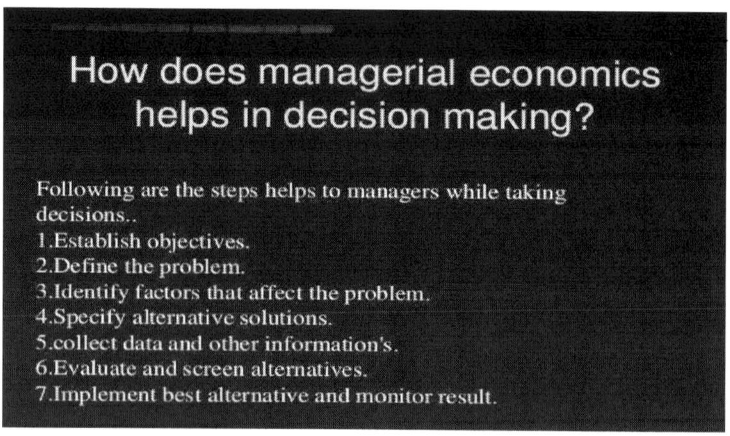

Figure 3.6. Managerial economics and decision-making.

Source: Ram Naresh Jha via Quora.

The evaluation process for each of the alternative is deliberate and focuses on a combination of internal consistency and external validation (Anwar and Sun, 2013; Anyim et al., 2011; Arbulú et al., 2015; Argenti, 1996; Arthur and Dworkin, 1991; Ashton et al., 2010). So, the option must make sense itself and make sense when compared to the ecological reality that the organization will be facing as it resolves the problem. There are situations where it is possible to identify joint gains in the options where a combination of alternatives creates advantages that are far greater than the individual advantages that may arise if one of the options is selected. If it is within the remit of the decision-maker and makes sense in terms of the use of resources, it may be possible to combine more than one alternative. You have a solution that is a package of responses rather than a disparate series of measures that may not work on their own.

The alternatives should be clearly defined and comprehensive in their description (Harris and Brown, 1998; Harrison and Lock, 2004; Hartmann, 2014; Haworth and Hughes, 2015; Hennigs et al., 2013). Moreover, these alternatives should be mutually exclusive so that there is no repetition. The decision-maker may have to commission an administrative process that seeks to reconcile the various alternatives to ensure that they meet the minimum standards that have been set by the organization. By engaging in extensive analysis, the decision-maker better understands the real decision that must be made rather than masking the problems that are associated with any option. This is how real choices are presented to the decision-maker and hence supporting them towards outcomes. It is an important stage in the evaluation process of alternatives.

3.4. THE EVALUATION PROCESS OF ALTERNATIVES WHEN SOLVING PROBLEMS

Organizational managers require specific guidelines on how to evaluate the various options that have been presented as part of the problem-solving process (Bannò and Sgobbi, 2016; Barry et al., 2000; Bekker, 2014; Bell et al., 2011; Bercu, 2012; Bernini and Cracolici, 2015). It is important to have established methods and criteria to explore the variance in the scoring of options that are laid before the decision-maker. There are several processes and procedures that must be considered as a matter of course. One of them is the analysis of the problem and the solution itself. Then there is the discussion about the various elements that comprise the alternative solutions that has been suggested. Afterwards, there is a review of the entire process to ensure that the critical aspects have been given due credence. Figure 3.7 is an example of a process for evaluating the various options for solving an organizational problem.

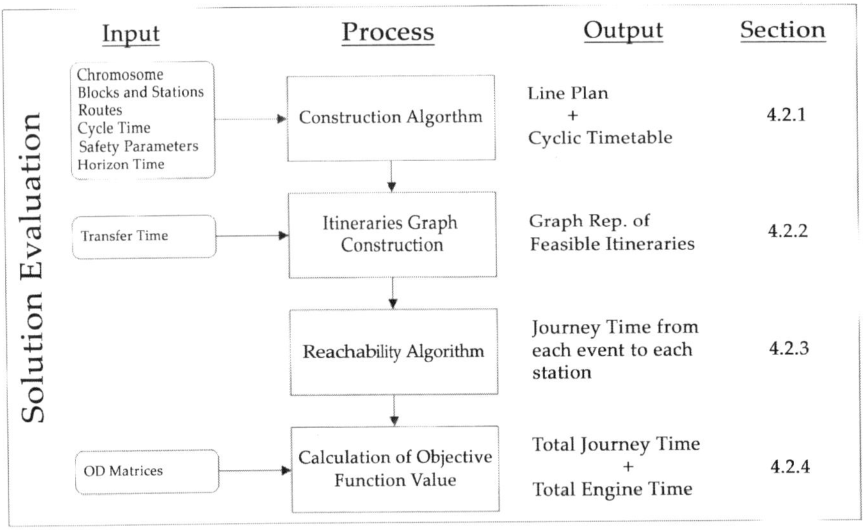

Figure 3.7. Example of a solution evaluation process.

Source: Kaspi and Raviv (2013).

Existing literature has shown that there is a need for iterative cycles of analysis during the problem-solving process (Odrakiewicz, 2012; Okotoni and Erero, 2005; Onyx and Maclean, 1996; Ozturk and Rumens, 2014; Papasolomou and Melanthiou, 2012). The reasons why these cycles are incorporated into the problem-solving process are that they can support the analytical processes as well as helping in the experimentation of different alternatives. The organization should facilitate the use of prototypes which are part of a pilot scheme. During the experimentation, there should be stimulation of the live environment to understand the ways in which the various solutions function within the context of an organizational structure. The scoring framework that has been adopted by the decision-maker must be substantiated with evidence. Hence, the conclusions that emanate from meat are supported extensively.

Existing literature has shown that the importance of the criteria and its descriptions are often imprecise (Brandsen and Pestoff, 2006; Bruce and Daly, 2006; Calabrese, 1997; Capko, 2003; Carraher, 2013; Chang et al.,

2006). That means that the total effect or impact of the solution is not fully understood and the time that the decision is made. It is important to have some analysis which will highlight some of the difficulties that may be faced when implementing a given solution. In some cases, the resulting scores during the analysis only differ by small margins when compared to the estimations. If the differences between the solutions are not clear-cut, it becomes difficult to make a decision because the committee is unable to clearly identify which of the options is optimal. At this point, it is recommended that the assumptions that underpin the descriptions of the options are interrogated. The criteria will have to go through a secondary evaluation process to ensure that the decision-maker has a clear understanding of the implications if they decided to go with that option.

There are several sub practices that are encouraged during the problem-solving process because they allow for a more thorough review of the criterion as well as the outcome (BIS, 2015; Baker and Esherick, 2013; Bannò and Sgobbi, 2016; Barry et al., 2000; Bekker, 2014; Bell et al., 2011). It is for this reason that the organization is encouraged to establish methodologies and criterion that can guide the committee when evaluating the different options. The agreement on this criterion is a separate process that must be thorough as well. It is useful to document the selection methods so that they can inform future managers, decision-makers, or committees that are resolving problems. This is particularly true of situations where the problems are like each other. Later in this book, we will explore how heuristics often fail because the criterion used to resolve previous projects is not fully or extensively documented.

There are three principal modalities of evaluation that must be accomplished as a matter of course (Lycett et al., 2004; Maneesh et al., 2009; Manzoor, 2011; Matías-Reche et al., 2009; McGill and Wooten, 1975). The first is the evaluation of the proposed alternatives or solutions in terms of establishing a clear criteria and methodology. The second issue to be addressed is the evaluation of the assumptions that underpin the process and as well as the options that were proposed. In this case, you are evaluating the criteria and evidence that support the assumptions. The third consideration involves evaluating the extent to which the uncertainties in the values for alternative solutions affects the evaluation self. To that end, you may need to address these uncertainties as appropriate, given all the information that is available to the decision-maker.

It helps if there is a distinction and consideration of the internal perspective as well as the external perspective in the problem-solving process (Ahimbisibwe and Nkundabanyanga, 2016; Ahmad and Schroeder, 2003; Alshallah, 2004; Alvesson et al., 2011). These are not necessarily competing forces, but a source of complementarity when evaluating potential solutions to problems. Figure 3.8 shows how these two facets of the ecology can impact on decision-making processes. Some organizations prefer to focus on the external perspective because that is where they interact with their customers. However, it can be impossible to meet the demands and expectations of customers if the internal environment is not well controlled. An effective solution to a problem will therefore combine an external and internal perspective.

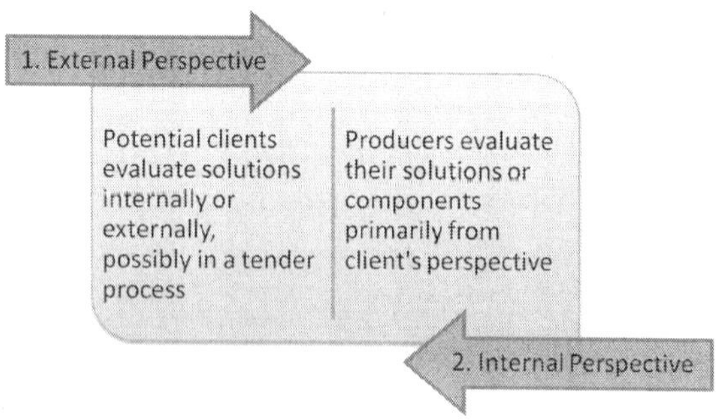

Figure 3.8. The solution evaluation in business analysis.

Source: microTOOL Blog.

We may consider an example open evaluation process to fully understand how the Criterion is supposed to be applied. For instance, a manager or any other decision-maker may be presented with differences between two values for different options based on the methodology that has been agreed. They will then have to make a decision whether the difference is significant enough to warrant further investigation or comparative analysis (Le, 2017; Leary, 2001; Lee and Park, 2009; Leggett, 2007; Lengnick-Hall et al., 2009; Leuenberger, 2006). Where there is little difference between the values, it makes it infinitely more difficult to choose. It is also important to consider whether the variation in scores represents a high-impact risk. There will be risk differential depending on the options that have been presented. The priority should be given to examining those high-risk situations that may render an option unworkable. During the resolution process, you may have to run simulations to understand how the various aspects of the solutions will change the outcomes for the organization. Therefore, the decision maker has always been given the option of modifying the criterion if they are unable to make a clear-cut decision.

The performance of a simulation is an important aspect of the decision-making process and some literature considered it to be the fourth criterion that must be included in the evaluation process as a requirement (Cox, 1999; Crane, 2013; Crawford, 2016; Cunniff and Mostert, 2012; Cunningham, 2011; D'Ippolito and Timpano, 2016). The simulations lead to several additional processes that are important including the modeling of the various options contributed to the solution. The modeling allows you to mimic the live environment without the risk harming the operational capabilities of the organization through inappropriate and untimely implementations of untested possibilities. To that end, the pilot scheme will inform the organization about potential problems without running the risk of expending significant resources on projects that are bound to fail. Indeed, it is a requirement in many projects to have some pilot scheme to ensure that all the aspects of the project are tested.

Managers should avoid restricting themselves to one option and failing to explore the alternatives fully (Leung et al., 2015; Li, 2009; Li et al., 2006, 2013; Lock, 2007; Loorbach, 2010; Lorenzo-Romero et al., 2013). The value of simulations and experimentations is that they offer new opportunities to define alternative options and solutions in a relatively safe environment. This is a process that should be allowed as much time as is required to get the right outcome when solving an organizational problem. Where the proposed alternatives are not testing well, it is acceptable to identify any alternative. This is the leeway that is provided to the decision-maker so that they can account for the dynamism of the problem-solving process. Additionally, the methodology can be reviewed and changed if the decision-maker is not getting a clear-cut outcome.

At each stage of the evaluation process, there should be clear protocols for documenting procedures and outcomes (Singh and Masuku, 2014; Singh et al., 2016; Slack et al., 2006; Songa et al., 2012; Sparrow and Makram, 2015). This can act as a reference point when reviewing the decisions at a later stage. Moreover, the alternatives should be presented and justified following the same stringent evaluation procedures. These are lessons that can make heuristics more reliable if a similar problem is encountered in the future. The question that remains for managers is how to retain high quality throughout the process. This is when the value of relative standards comes into play.

3.5. SETTING A RELATIVE STANDARD WHEN EVALUATING SOLUTIONS TO PROBLEMS

Setting standards is an important aspect of organizational practice (Ahmad and Schroeder, 2003; Alshallah, 2004; Alvesson et al., 2011; Amos et al., 2008; Anckar et al., 2002). Standardization allows for the evaluation of practice and performance within a framework that aims to achieve the goals of the organization. The standards are often prepared in a written document that can be shared by different decision-makers as they trawl through different alternatives. In that sense, the standards are a performance management tool that improves the practice of employees and teams across the organization. The standards may be written as rules and guidelines that ought to be followed by decision-makers. However, some organizations provide their managers with discretion or leeway to adjust certain criterion depending on the levels of seniority that have been achieved by that manager. Figure 3.9 is an example of a quality management standard that could be used as a reference point for certain organizations.

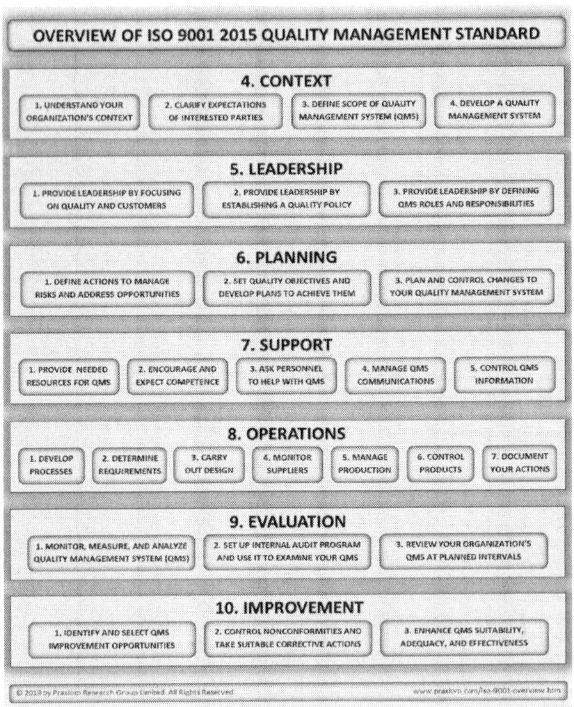

Figure 3.9. Example of a quality standards framework.

Source: Praxiom.

The standards that are written within the document can be complemented with a description of certain processes that are involved in the decision-making process (Parry et al., 2008; Patiar and Mia, 2009; Pavlatos and Paggios, 2009a, b; Peng and Huiling Chen, 2011). It can also incorporate products and services that comprise the core output. All the stakeholders should be consulted as well as benefiting from the expertise of frontline members of staff that will have unique insight into the working environment. Having obtained consensus, it is important to accredit the standard and there are many professional bodies that will assist in this process. The purpose of standards is to optimize order in a range of contexts within which organizational of problems may occur. Hence, the lack of standards can lead to chaotic and unstable performance.

The process of formulating, issuing, and implementing organizational standards is known as standardization in existing literature (Cox et al., 2021; Cox, 1999; Crane, 2013; Crawford, 2016; Cunniff and Mostert, 2012; Cunningham, 2011). The standardization process has several aims. The first objective of the standardization process is to ensure that all options are fit for purpose. This fitness for purpose must be proved in a range of context and must be relevant to the problem that is being dealt with. The stakeholders that are using the product or the employees that are working with the options will have an opportunity to highlight their perspectives and even evaluate the product. Stakeholders include customers, employees, supervisors, managers, Executives, owners, and the organization itself.

When paying attention to the expectations of the stakeholders, it is important to understand their expectation may not fit in with the needs of the organization (Huselid, 1995; Ibrahim and Zailani, 2010; Ichniowski et al., 1997; Ifinedo, 2016; Ismail et al., 2005; Jansen et al., 2008). Besides, the expectations that are expressed by the various stakeholders may not address the problem as conceived by the decision-maker. The service users may not understand the complexities of the organization and how it runs its businesses. That means that they will require such guidance to fully appreciate the context of the problem. Indeed, one of the senior managers can be deployed to explain the nuances of the problem so that the stakeholders can provide an informed perspective on it.

It is important to understand that standards are not limited to the operations of the organization (Nica, 2015; Obeidat, 2012; Odrakiewicz, 2012; Okotoni and Erero, 2005; Onyx and Maclean, 1996; Ozturk and Rumens, 2014). Some of the standards that must be considered emanate from outside the organization. For example, the regulator may stipulate that a certain minimum standard must be met on any solution that is proposed for problems within the organization. Typically, the regulator will use the threat of a fine or other legal sanctions to ensure that decision-makers within the organization are always following the minimum standards that have been set. Indeed, the society itself will use community sanction to control the behavior of organizations directly or indirectly. For example, community sanction may be withdrawn for the organizations that are operating outside the parameters or standards that are set by society. Therefore, the decision-making process is a reflection of the values and principles that are prevailing within the context that the organization is operating in.

From a technical perspective, standards may be incorporated into the problem-solving process because the market expects certain performance achievements within the production process (Sedmak and Longhurst, 2010; Sendawula et al., 2018; Supply chain Management and Logistics: Zara, 2013; Sharma and Upneja, 2005). For example, when producing medicine and other potentially dangerous chemicals it is imperative that the guidance provided by the regulator is meticulously followed. Many organizations depend on community sanction because it is an indirect determinant of popularity with customers. That community will be repulsed if the organization is not reflecting the norms and values of the society when managing its problems. A brand that repulses potential customers is not going to last long. The industry may also create certain standards that ensure that the reputation of that segment or niche is not threatened by businesses or organizations that are trying to cut corners. A cost of quality diagram (such as the one displayed in Figure 3.10) may be used to remind everybody what is at stake.

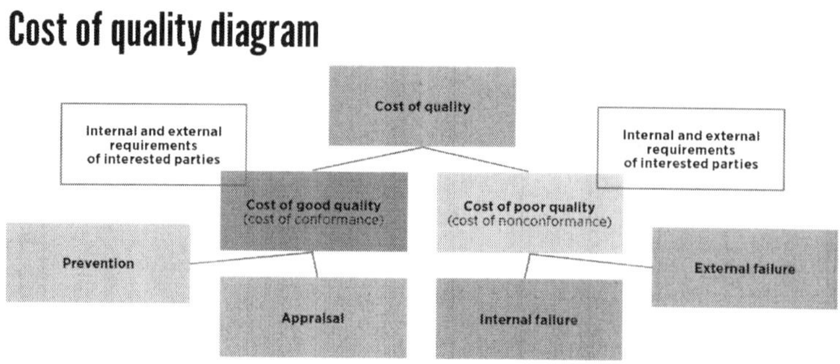

Figure 3.10. Example of a cost of quality diagram.

Source: Denise Robitaille (2019).

The wide selection of choices when resolving problem will increase the discretion of the decision-maker (Loorbach, 2010; Lorenzo-Romero et al., 2013; Loundes, 2001; Lycett et al., 2004; Maneesh et al., 2009; Manzoor, 2011). This is ultimately the aim of the organization when they constitute a committee or appoint a representative that is supposed to curate and evaluate the various options that are possible for dealing with a specific problem. If possible, make sure that the experts are the ones that inform decision-makers about the qualities of the various options that have been presented to them. These experts have the advantage of familiarity with the intricacies of the options from a technical perspective. You may source the expertise from within the organization or hired it from outside to operate as consultants. Outsourcing this function will have cost implications that are included in the consideration for the various options when dealing with an organizational problem.

Standards can help to remove the arbitrariness of the decision-making process (Anwar and Sun, 2013; Anyim et al., 2011; Arbulú et al., 2015; Argenti, 1996; Arthur and Dworkin, 1991). Many managers use their discretion in ways that are neither rational nor beneficial to the organization. Through standardization it is possible to control the activities of these potentially rogue managers. Standardization has been a benefit to organizations that seek homogeneity in their operations. For instance, the standardization means that services, projects, and processes are interchangeable in case there is a need. Crisis points within the life cycle of the organization may require the exchange or interchange of all or various options that have been proposed for the problem-solving process. This is the flexibility that is valued in the corporate world and standardization can be part of the process towards that goal.

Standards can also be a marketing ploy for organizations that rely on their reputation to navigate a competitive market (Jansen et al., 2008; Jian Wang et al., 2010; John et al., 2014; Johnson and Clark, 2008; Jurevicius, 2016; Kabene et al., 2006). Customers are always looking for the best quality of service or product on the market. The existence of standards ensures that customers can be reasonably sure that the product that they are purchasing is of a suitably high standard. Hence, there are brands the prize themselves on the provision of products that have gone through a rigorous standard. In fact, these organizations will create a summary of the standards that they are following and place them on the labels for the product. Hence, the fact that an organization is compliant with certain standards will become a marketing tool. Ideally, the organization should invest in ensuring that it is following the standards that have been agreed and publicized. Once expectations are raised with the public, they must be met. One of the worst occurrences that can occur is where the organization has set standards that are so high that it is unable to achieve them. The failure to achieve these self-imposed standards can be catastrophic for the market positioning of that brand or organization.

For the public sector, the organizations that fall within this category are obliged to follow certain standards (DyReyes, 2008; Egan, 2009; Egloff and Bhalla, 2014; Evans, 2005; Farndale et al., 2008; Fetscherin and Heinrich, 2014; Finkelstein et al., 2007). This is not just about buying and selling products; but also ensuring that the personnel policies of an organization are in line with employment law. The human resource management team will be one of the contact points for issues relating to industrialization and the treatment of employees. Likewise, the public sector organizations are under a certain obligation to provide minimum standards to the public in a way that is socially acceptable. For example, a public sector organization will lose community sanction if it is providing services on a discriminatory basis or is otherwise corrupt. The significant media interest in the public sector organizations means that standardization is not an option but a reality for all the actors within the sector.

Chapter 3 Summary

This chapter has explored the ways in which values and principles can be brought to bear on the decision-making process. For instance, values may determine whether short term or longer-term decisions are made today to resolve problems. The chapter has also introduced brainstorming as a tool to find alternative to solutions that could reflect the various perspectives within the organization. Perhaps, one of the most important aspects of this chapter is an examination of the evaluation process when making decisions about options for solving organizational problems. The chapter concludes with some discussion about the usefulness of standards beyond compliance. As we speak of values and perspectives, the issue of bias is never far behind and that is the concern for Chapter 4 in this book.

CHAPTER 4

AVOIDING BIAS WHEN DEALING WITH ORGANIZATIONAL PROBLEMS

CONTENTS

Bias is part of human nature because our perspectives when dealing with problems impact on our decisions. Organizations and researchers have sought different tools for reducing bias including randomization and systems. This chapter explores some of the ways in which one can avoid bias when solving organizational problems. The discussion is based on the assumption that bias necessarily prevents the decision-maker from accessing and using the best information for the decision. This chapter will explore validity or reliability tests, the typologies of bias, linkages between organizational goals and objectives, possible or proven solutions, and the definitional advantages of being explicit in explaining problems. As a starting point for this chapter, we might consider validity and reliability means for an organization when it is trying to resolve problems.

4.1. TESTING THE VALIDITY AND RELIABILITY OF THE PROBLEM-SOLVING PROCESS

One way of looking at the problem-solving process is to perceive it as a question of applying an intervention into a situation or circumstances which require some change to allow operations to continue (Lock, 2007; Loorbach, 2010; Lorenzo-Romero et al., 2013; Loundes, 2001; Lycett et al., 2004; Maneesh et al., 2009). Hence, it makes sense to ensure that the intervention being recommended for the problem is both reliable and valid. The concepts known as "reliability" and "validity" are gleaned from research methodology. Validity refers to the extent to which an instrument does what it purports to do. For example, if you have a scale that measures happiness; the validity of that scale is the extent to which it explains or highlights the happiness of the respondents to which it is applied. In contrast, reliability refers to the extent to which the same result will be elicited regardless of how many times the instrument or intervention is applied. For example, if research shows that taking an antihistamine reduces the symptoms of an allergic reaction; the reliability of that intervention will be demonstrated by an improvement in the condition of various people that have a logic reaction and take the antihistamine.

Referencing the validity and reliability of interventions in the problem-solving process is important because it improves the quality of the outcome (Kabene et al., 2006; Kasperk et al., 2011; Kay et al., 1994; Kerzner, 2003; Khan et al., 2011; King et al., 2000; Klikauer, 2014). An organization that does not invest in the exploration of the validity and reliability of the interventions that it recommends for dealing with problems will find that it has more misses than hits. Using a strict research methodology will improve the possibilities of achieving a positive outcome when an intervention is applied to a problematic situation. It will also reduce the amount of time that is wasted on interventions that clearly do not deal with the problem. Of course, the validity and reliability of the information can only be explored and confirmed through experimentation. This is a process that has been identified as being important particularly when the organization is relying on heuristics to solve problems.

Because of its association with research, the business world has been slow to engage in systematic tests of validity and reliability when designing interventions (John et al., 2014; Johnson and Clark, 2008; Jurevicius, 2016; Kabene et al., 2006; Kasperk et al., 2011; Kay et al., 1994). The paradigm that is required to incorporate this into the decision-making process is to look at problem-solving as the application of an instrument that must be valid and reliable. In the corporate world, it is not just about measuring the extent of the problem but also ensuring that there are appropriate solutions to that problem. Figure 4.1 highlights the quantitative and qualitative aspects of validity and reliability in research.

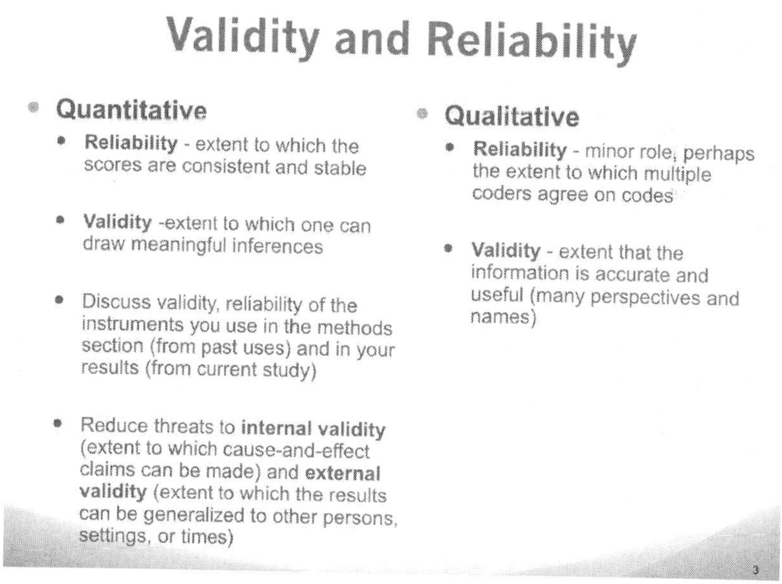

Figure 4.1. Meaning of validity and reliability.

Source: UMich Mixed Methods.

In research, development, and reliability of an instrument is known as its psychometric properties. This is a prerequisite to research and the resultant findings can be discarded if there are no references to the validity and reliability of the instrumentation that has been used. There is extensive literature on the development of reliability and validity testing for a range of instruments that are used in research. However, there is a dearth of research concerning the validity and reliability of interventions that are applied to organizational problems (Dartey-Baah and Amoako, 2011; Day and Schoenrade, 2000; Deery and Nath, 2013; Dumay et al., 2010; Dutse, 2013). This is despite these tests being implicit in the problem-solving process. That is why there is an explosion in pseudoscience which is based on anecdotal evidence as well as a gut instinct. In the absence of clear standards, various actors within the organization will come up with interventions that are not tested. Although this may be encouraged as part of an experimental process, it can lead to problems if it means the wastage of resources of unworkable interventions. Pilot scheme is the best environment for experimentation rather than wasting the sources of the organization on innervations that are not backed up by aby empirical evidence.

A decision-maker in the organization will need to have a clear idea of what a good intervention is and what it is not (Bercu, 2012; Bernini and Cracolici, 2015; Berthon et al., 2009; Bilson et al., 2013; Bjerregaard, 2011; Black, 2005). It is important to address certain questions that will inevitably highlight issues of validity and reliability. The first question that you must answer is the extent to which the intervention is relevant to the problem. A good intervention will resolve the problem in the shortest amount of time possible with the least resources possible. Hence, that the intervention is demonstrably successful and appropriate. This is what some managers refer to as efficiency. If the correct procedures have been followed when evaluating the various options, it is likely that the instrument will be valid because there will be extensive experimentation and evaluation throughout the process.

The decision-maker has been diligent; they will be able to answer the question as to what makes a good intervention for a particular problem in the organization (Bjerregaard, 2011; Black, 2005; Brandsen and Pestoff, 2006; Bruce and Daly, 2006; Calabrese, 1997; Capko, 2003). This is the information that will inform future decision-makers and the organization. In effect, it is a template of a mechanism for dealing with problems that occur in a cyclical pattern. When organizations speak of learning lessons from mistakes, they are referring to this documentation and experimentation that arises from the problems that have been resolved in the past. Unfortunately, this approach may be risky for the organization because the customers are very sensitive to disruptive interventions or deterioration in the quality of product that they are receiving on the market. The organization must develop a mechanism for evaluating interventions on a generic model. Of course, there will be specific advantages for the intervention in specific problems. However, the organization will have an overarching tool that can be used as a starting point in the analysis.

An effective intervention will have certain qualities that can be identified at every stage of its development (Milosevic et al., 2010; Min et al., 2008; Mitchell et al., 1997; Moore and Birtwistle, 2004; Moore and Doyle, 2010; Morrison and Milliken, 2003). First, the effective intervention will be able to highlight the problem and target the specific contributors to the problem in an efficient way. The impact will be consistent such that if the same circumstances were replicated, the intervention will work in pretty much the same way. The organization needs stability and those interventions that lead to stability will be preferred to those that cause chaos. Decision-makers should be careful about adopting interventions that are not appropriate for specific problems. For example, there is the temptation to throw money a problem in the hope that an increase in investment will necessarily deal with the issues that have caused the problem. However, research has shown that they are problems which are resolved by alternative means and some of those problems are made worse by the injection of money.

So, why do companies consider the validity and reliability of their interventions? Figure 4.2 is a graphic representation of validity and reliability which somehow demonstrates some of the reasons why organizations should ensure that their interventions are valid and reliable. An unreliable intervention does not hit the mark and will not resolve the problem in any meaningful way (Carraher, 2013; Chang et al., 2006; Chen et al., 2011; Chevalier and Mazzalovo, 2008; Chung, 2015; Clegg and Palmer, 1996). By contrast, an unreliable intervention may be valid, but its results will be inconsistent such that the organization has to think twice before using it again just in case things do not go according to plan. The worst intervention is with low validity but high reliability. This means that you will always get it wrong when you utilize this option. At least with an invalid and unreliable intervention, there is a high probability that it may not do any harm on some occasions. Organizations that simply implement interventions without subjecting them to validity and reliability tests are not doing any favors to themselves.

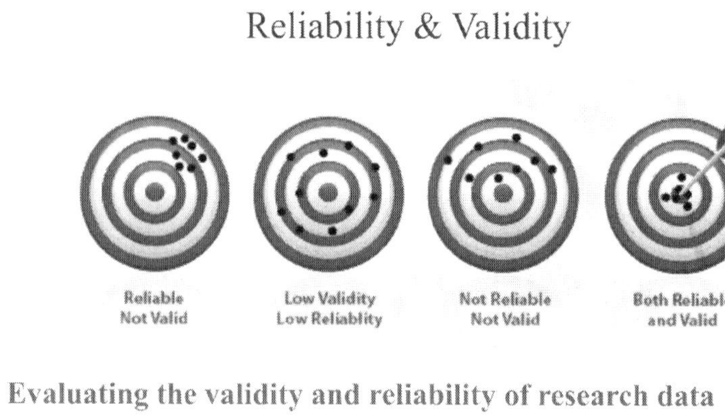

Figure 4.2. Graphical demonstration of validity and reliability.

Source: Assignment help.

The ideal intervention is one which is relevant to the situation and the organization (Samah et al., 2013; Schlögl, 2005; Schmid and Adams, 2008; Schuler, 1989; Sedmak and Longhurst, 2010; Sendawula et al., 2018). Typically, these interventions are consistent with the norms and values of the organization. At the same time these interventions make business sense because they cost less than the benefits that they bring to the organization. The organization must consider acceptability of the intervention. There are interventions that are effective but the cost of those interventions in terms of harmonization of work practices may be too high for them to be implemented. The ability to manage and reduce resistance to the necessary change following a specific intervention can be one of the considerations when solving problems.

Organizations must select interventions that are uniquely suited for their circumstances (Morrison and Milliken, 2003; Mosher, 2013; Mujeeb and Ahmad, 2011; Nagalakhmi and Trivedi, 2015; Nagasawa and Fukunaga, 2015). One of the problems associated with relying on selected formulas is the fact that has been applied in other circumstances and there is a possibility that this formula is not appropriate for the organization. For example, they may cause significant disruption, or they may require resources that are not available to the organization at this time. This has emerged as one of the problems of outsourcing because the consultants that are hired to give their perspective on the development of the organization may not have an understanding of the key structures and the principles that underpin the operations of that organization. Therefore, there is a likelihood that these consultants will rely on models that have been tested and approved in alternative circumstances. Organizations differ from each other, and the problem-solving process must recognize this diversity to be effective.

It is also important to remember that validity and reliability are not static concepts (Assink, 2006; Atkinson and Brander Brown, 2001; Atwal and Williams, 2009; Awadh and Saad, 2013; BIS, 2015). They change with time. What was valid and reliable 10 years ago may be invalid and unreliable today. The organization must engage in continuous research and development process that targets the changes in the market and practices so that the organization is not behind. The problem-solving process is an evolution, and it can become cyclical in its responses when required. At the same time, the organization must recognize that there are problems that require one intervention that will never be repeated. The organization will use the available information including big data to find out how it resolved previous problems. It will also scan by environment to get an insight into the ways in which its competitors and partners are resolving their own problems. Being in the business world or the corporate world requires the flexibility to learn from mistakes and to learn from the experiences of other people who are sharing business ecology with your organization. One of the key areas that will have to be addressed is the risk of bias in the problem-solving process.

4.2. WHAT ARE THE DIFFERENT TYPES OF BIAS WHEN SOLVING PROBLEMS?

To be biased is to be human. The decision-makers in an organization are necessarily biased by their experiences, perceptions, and personalities (Berthon et al., 2009; Bilson et al., 2013; Bjerregaard, 2011; Black, 2005; Brandsen and Pestoff, 2006; Bruce and Daly, 2006). Sometimes the bias is professional and arises through the socialization of various members of the team. The organization may develop a certain culture that elicits biases towards or against specific problems. The decision-making employee must be aware of their own biases and the biases that emanate from within the environment. When working in an organization, it may also be necessary to understand how the cultural dynamics that are embedded within that organization will impact on the perceptions of a problem and the selection of an option to deal with that problem.

There are several major biases that would hinder the problem-solving process in an organization (McGill and Wooten, 1975; Memili and Welsh, 2012; Menke et al., 2007; Meyer-Sahling et al., 2018; Mia and Patiar, 2001). One of those biases is simply being aware of certain shortcuts that might be used to deal with a problem. This is a historical issue that might arise out of an over-reliance on heuristics. The decision-maker must be aware that situations vary, and it is important not to make assumptions about the similarities between and among circumstances when evaluating the seriousness and implications of a problem. Figure 4.3 highlights some of the biases that we may experience in our personal and professional life. Cognition is an important determinant of these biases and hence the solutions must also consider the option of addressing cognitive deficits that are controllable.

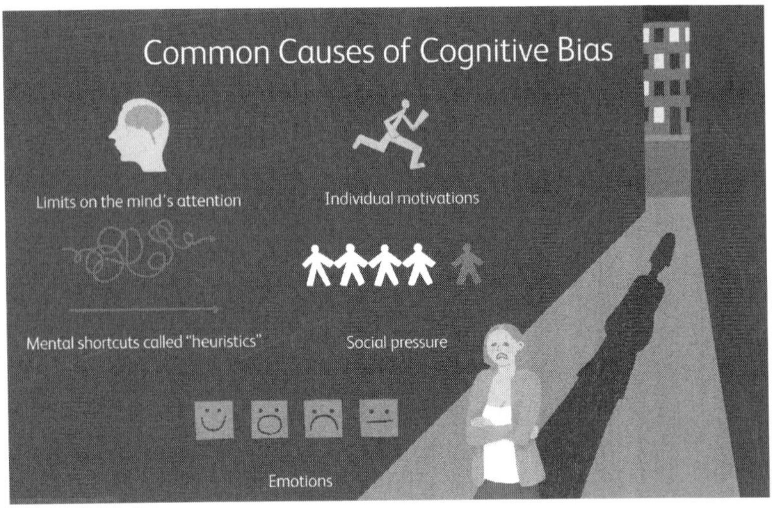

Figure 4.3. Common causes of cognitive biases.

Source: Very well Mind.

The assumptions that underpin the thinking of the decision maker may prevent them from considering options that would otherwise be realistic and appropriate (Klikauer, 2014; Kluike, 2015; de Kok et al., 2006; Korczynski, 2002; Kotas, 2014; Köllen, 2013; Lashley and Burgess, 2007). That is why it is important to have an open mind when dealing with problems, particularly if those problems are new in some way. Some decision-makers are so confident of their judgment that they failed to understand the true impact of their cognitive biases. Psychology has provided a framework through which we can understand the major biases that arise in decision-making. This is important for organizations that routinely must deal with crises and must reference a range of opinions to come to a firm conclusion. A multidisciplinary lens might be appropriate in this respect since a lot of management science is informed by psychology.

Having biases is not restricted to uneducated or inexperienced members of staff (Sendawula et al., 2018; Supply chain Management and Logistics: Zara, 2013; Sharma and Upneja, 2005). Even the FBI has spoken of mental biases that impact on the decision-making of high-ranking officers with significant experience in the field. The consequences of following a bias when making decisions can be deadly for the organization. For example, the organization may reject opportunities that would improve its standing in the market. Alternatively, the organization may take on responsibilities and options that damage its standing. A biased decision-maker is dangerous for the organization because they open the possibilities of legal sanctions and making blatant mistakes which will take a long time to correct.

The information processing strategies that we adopt when making decisions will determine the extent to which we are biased (WHO, 2018; Wilkinson, 1997; Williamson, 2008; Willmott, 1993; Wysocki, 2013; Yang and Chen, 2006; Zhang and Wen, 2008). Sometimes it is a question of oversimplifying a complex situation. At other times, it is a question of using our own experiences in ways that are inappropriate. Then we make assumptions about the variables within the problem and the failure to check those assumptions means that the final decision that we make will not be able to deal with the problem. Where the organization must go back and correct the mistakes of the decision-maker, biases will add to the operation costs of the organization and threaten its very existence.

The first major type of bias that is known in existing literature is that of confirmation bias (Atwal and Williams, 2009; Awadh and Saad, 2013; BIS, 2015; Baker and Esherick, 2013; Bannò and Sgobbi, 2016). Here, the decision-maker will favor information that confirms their own perspectives, and they will neglect information that disagrees with their pre-existing perspectives. To that end, the decision-maker seeks information that confirms their own views whilst simultaneously rejecting any information that might challenge their preconceptions. We have seen this pattern in elections where groups of people will form a bubble which is impenetrable in terms of providing alternative opinion. When the reality of the election results appears, the group will not believe that members have been wrong all along. Indeed, the media often uses this type of confirmation bias to drive narratives among selective groupings.

The second form of bias that may impact on the decision-making process in an organization is known as the recency bias (Mitchell et al., 1997; Moore and Birtwistle, 2004; Moore and Doyle, 2010; Morrison and Milliken, 2003; Mosher, 2013). Under this Paradigm, the decision-maker will give precedence and priority to information that is newly arrived. By the same token, the decision-maker will ignore or marginalize information that was received earlier. The effect is that decisions are made without adequate access to the right information. We know that you need a significant knowledge of the past before you can use it to predict the future. Ignoring the old past is a foolhardy strategy or a sign of negligence by the decision-maker. We have seen this type of bias in the financial sector where the analysts will consider recent trends while ignoring the history or the larger patterns. Yet, it is very large, overarching, and historical patterns that are the key to managing the financial sector. Organizations that are inundated with significant amounts of information have a high risk of this bias because it seems easier to pay attention to information that has just coming rather than going back to historical records. This bias is slightly different from but also related to the cognitive biases (see Figure 4.4) that are emphasized by psychologists.

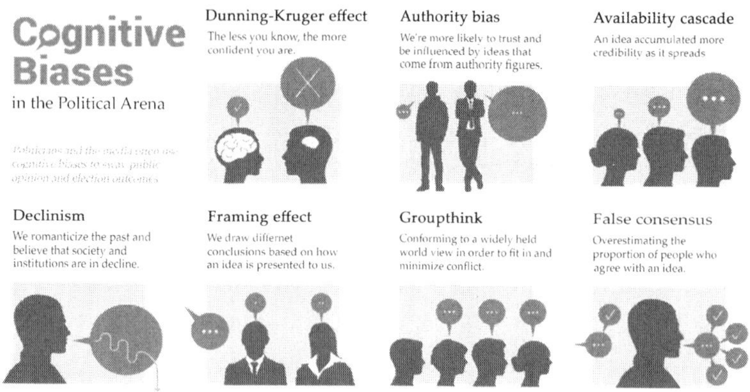

Figure 4.4. Cognitive biases that influence political outcomes.

Source: Visual capitalist.

The third major bias that decision-makers must be wary of is the framing bias (Willmott, 1993; Wysocki, 2013; Yang and Chen, 2006; Zhang and Wen, 2008; Zheng, 2017). Under this paradigm, the decision-maker is concerned about how the ultimate option is presented and its reception within the organization. Moreover, the decision-maker will be influenced by the way in which the information is presented. Hence, a skilled presenter can possibly manipulate a susceptible decision-maker to accept an option that is inferior simply because that option has been presented professionally and in an attractive way. This is a tactic medics often are used in marketing where the positive aspects of the products are presented while the negative ones are minimized. Saying that a product is 90% fat-free is a really good way of saying that product has 10% fat content. So, for the consumer, the presentation is meant to manipulate them into believing that the product is an advantage when that product is dangerous to their health. Decision-makers must be wary of manipulators and clever marketing agencies which are experienced in the presentation of bad information in such a way that it is attractive to those that hold power within an organization.

There are other forms of biases that decision-makers will meet from time to time (Ozturk and Rumens, 2014; Papasolomou and Melanthiou, 2012; Parker et al., 2013; Parry et al., 2008; Patiar and Mia, 2009). This may include an ignorance of the absence where the decision-maker will not consider information that has not been included in the information that is presented to them. Another bias is the bandwagon fallacy where the decision-maker will try to follow trends regardless of whether those trends are suitable for that problem that is being solved. Then there is the planning fallacy and the gambler's fallacy. The planning fallacy emanates from our own optimism about the amount of time it takes to accomplish tasks. Hence, the decision may confidently assume that it is going to take a much shorter period to accomplish the goals have set than the reality. The gambler's fallacy is whereby the decision-maker assumes that the patterns of the past are more likely to happen than they really are. Indeed, this is the fallacy that drives people into addiction. They will participate in gambling in the hope that eventually they will win when the chances of winning a very low.

There is no final and ultimate remedy for the biases that we have discussed (Menke et al., 2007; Meyer-Sahling et al., 2018; Mia and Patiar, 2001; Milosevic et al., 2010; Min et al., 2008). Instead, the decision-maker must be wary because they accept the reality of bias. It is important to understand that human beings are frail, and they make mistakes. Listen to alternative voices and if possible, make sure that the decision is made by a diverse group or committee that can bring different voices. This does not mean that you ignore the perspectives of frontline members of staff members who may not necessarily have elevated qualifications or hierarchical power;

but will nonetheless have a significant insight into the problem. Extensive consultation and testing can help to identify biases. Therefore, if there is a pilot scheme or a review process it is possible for the biases to be picked up and for a senior team to ensure that the final decision that is taken is objective. If the decision-maker does not check the origins of their perceptions, there is a very high likelihood that they will be biased. Having dealt with bias, the decision-maker will need to ensure that organizational goals and objectives are linked to the problem-solving process.

4.3. LINKING ORGANIZATIONAL GOALS AND OBJECTIVES TO PROBLEMS

Through the process of setting goals, the organization can ensure that its strategic plan is linked to all the activities that take place in the organization including the problem-solving process (Leggett, 2007; Lengnick-Hall et al., 2009; Leuenberger, 2006; Leung et al., 2015; Li, 2009; Li et al., 2013). Alignment is a critical objective when resolving issues in the organization. It is not appropriate that solutions are implemented which are contrary to the needs of the organization or its values. The process of setting goals can also be used to motivate employees and orientate their practice towards achieving the strategic plan. Through this process, it is possible to integrate the interests of the organization with those of the individuals that work within it. The successful management of the organization relies on this alignment for the most part. However, there must be a balance struck between individual needs of the workers and the interests of the organization. Otherwise, employees will no longer be useful to the organization and the organization will no longer be useful to them in turn.

Work environments that are supportive of staff and partners are productive because they are not hindered by ongoing resistance to change (Korczynski, 2002; Kotas, 2014; Köllen, 2013; Lashley and Burgess, 2007; Le, 2017; Leary, 2001; Lee and Park, 2009). By way of contrast, those organizations that violate the rights and expectations of their employees will face resistance. Alternatively, employees that experience cognitive dissonance and disillusionment may decide to abandon the organization in search of better opportunities that align with their own value system. The use of competency management frameworks can help to improve the alignment and to understand the needs of frontline members of staff (see Figure 4.5). Best practices across the industry can also be used as reference points.

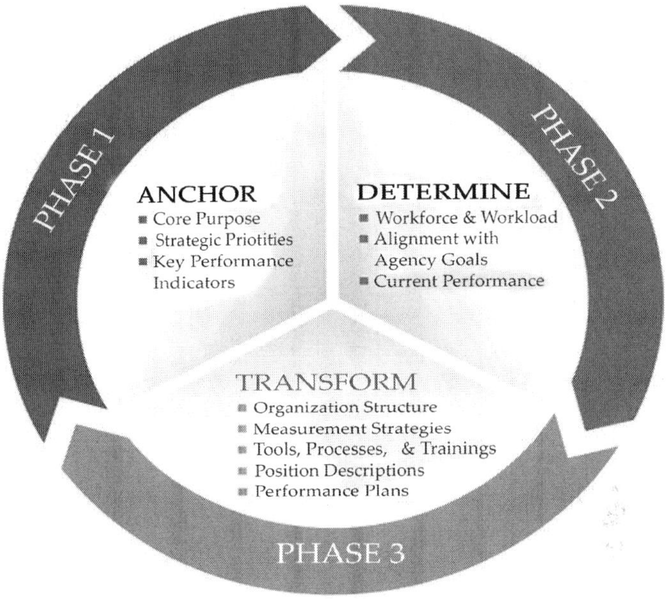

Figure 4.5. Performance management and performance alignment.

Source: OPM.

It is not always the case that the goals of an organization can cascade gracefully from the top of that institution to the frontline members of staff (Barry et al., 2000; Bekker, 2014; Bell et al., 2011; Bercu, 2012; Bernini and Cracolici, 2015; Berthon et al., 2009). In fact, there may be many obstacles to the goals as they descend from the corporate office to the teams that are supposed to contribute towards achieving them. That is why it is very important to align the goals and values of the staff members that are responsible for these tasks. One of the problems that will arise if the alignment has not been achieved is the possibility of overlapping accountabilities. This can be very confusing to staff members who are looking for clarity and predictability in their work roles.

The failure to properly align goals with personal and team goals has been associated with redundancies (Chung, 2015; Clegg and Palmer, 1996; Cold Cafe, 2018; Cole and Dawson, 2010; Collinson and Hearn, 1994). Workers will therefore engage in activities that conflict with each other and which do not achieve the objectives that were set for them. The annual strategic planning session is not sufficient to ensure this alignment. Similarly, it is not enough to simply communicate the decisions of the top executive team in a general meeting. These strategies must be reintegrated into objectives and work plans that can be implemented at the team and individual level. By achieving transparency and alignment, the organization will ensure that every member of the team understands their responsibilities and can consequently take responsibility for their day-to-day activities. Organizations sometimes fail because nobody seems to be in charge or responsible for any of the decisions that are taken.

Cascading goals throughout the organization can help to manage progress so that it is beneficial to the organization as well as the people that work for it (Okotoni and Erero, 2005; Onyx and Maclean, 1996; Ozturk and Rumens, 2014; Papasolomou and Melanthiou, 2012; Parker et al., 2013). This is a precursor to continuous Improvement and personal development. Indeed, the better organizations ensure that the personal development plan references the strategic goals as a matter of course. Figure 4.6 shows an example of an alignment framework for performance at work. One of the notable features is the way in which the individual efforts of employees translate into organizational success. At the same time, the organizational success that is experienced at the strategic level is translated into better performance by individual teams and workers. It is almost akin to a two-way feedback process in which performance and accountability are the messages.

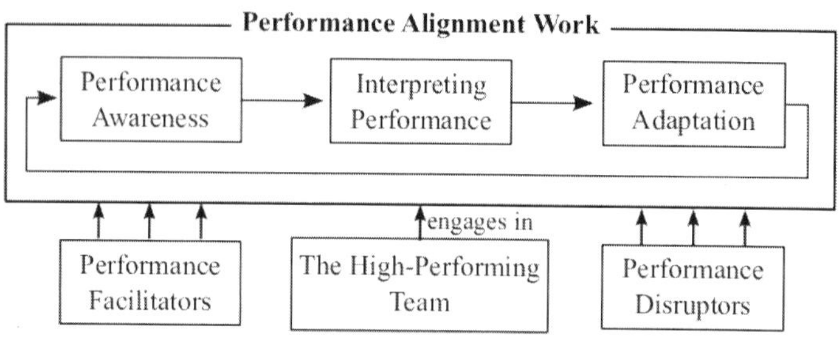

Figure 4.6. Performance alignment at work.

Source: Fagerholm et al. (2016).

It is the case that there a mutuality of influence between the organization and employees (Shatte et al., 2014; Sinclaire and Vogus, 2011; Singh and Masuku, 2014; Singh et al., 2016; Slack et al., 2006). The workplace is a place of interaction, and it is expected that such interaction will lead to an exchange of values, behavior, perceptions, and even practices. The strategy of the organization is also informed by the personal values of the individuals that work in an organization. It has been assumed in the past that it is only the organization that will determine the progress of values and norms in its structures. However, research has shown the workers including frontline members of staff have an important role in progressing the ways in which the organization performs its functions. This is where the culture of the organization is so important. Indeed, there have been extensive studies on how the culture of an organization is determined and its influences on the people that are employed by it.

Existing literature has identified a process for aligning various strategies goals to the individual practice of employees (Cole and Dawson, 2010; Collinson and Hearn, 1994; Connell et al., 2009; Cooke, 2003; Cox et al., 2021; Cox, 1999). The first task is to develop goals that can be achieved within a reasonable period. This is typically a year or thereabouts. The number of strategic goals must be restricted to no more than five and no fewer than three. The reasons for this restriction are based on the need to ensure that the organizational can focus on a limited number of goals and achieve them in the most efficient manner possible. It is a very different proposition from circumstances where the organization has too many goals to achieve within a limited period. A process of alignment and consolidation might ensure that certain goals are combined because they are similar. At other times, the organization may seek differentiation between and among goals because the aims call for such an approach. Regardless of the approach and changes that occur, it is important that they are communicated to every member of staff so that they are fully integrated within the operations of that organization.

The nature of the organizational goal and the ways in which it is presented can have an impact on the possibilities of integration (Shatte et al., 2014; Sinclaire and Vogus, 2011; Singh and Masuku, 2014; Singh et al., 2016; Slack et al., 2006). For example, the goal should be measurable and aligned to the overarching aims of the organization. There is always a reason why an organization or a company has been established. The workers in the organization must continuously reference that original purpose when they are developing strategic goals. So, it begins from the general and moves towards the specific. As one travels towards the lower echelons of the organization, it becomes clear that the goals are turning into objectives which a far clearer and more specific than the overarching aim of the organization. This structure and approach mean that the organization can answer questions about strategy and specific practices with reference to existing procedures. The resultant explanations will be as general or as specific as required because all members of the organization have the information they need about its direction.

Additionally, the goals must be managed on an ongoing basis based on the information that is been gleaned from the operations of the company or organization (Lorenzo-Romero et al., 2013; Loundes, 2001; Lycett et al., 2004; Maneesh et al., 2009; Manzoor, 2011; Matías-Reche et al., 2009). This is an acknowledgment that goals are not static and that they can change with the environment. Indeed, it is important to understand the ecology within which the institution operates because it will have a significant impact on the progress of the goals. Monitoring and evaluation is therefore part of that process. The leaders, managers, and supervisors within the organization will ensure that from time to time they check the progress of the goals. They may even request that the goals are modified considering the information that is coming from the environment. These issues that is interlinked because scanning the internal and external environment is a critical aspect of organizational management. Even as goals are being aligned, the organization and its decision-makers must distinguish between possible and proven solutions when solving problems.

4.4. THE DIFFERENCE BETWEEN POSSIBLE AND PROVEN SOLUTIONS

One of the distinctions that will be made when solving the problem is that between solutions that are proven and those that are possible (Onyx and Maclean, 1996; Ozturk and Rumens, 2014; Papasolomou and Melanthiou, 2012; Parker et al., 2013; Parry et al., 2008). Just because a solution is possible does not necessarily mean that it is workable or is backed by proof. Many organizations are prioritizing evidence-based problem-solving. Hence, they will research the problem and the solutions that are presented for resolving that problem. The ones that are supported by facts and figures and experience will be selected. Those decisions that are based on intuition alone cannot be supported by evidence unless there is previous or subsequent research that seeks to understand the ways in which the solution will work. Figure 4.7 is an example of an evidence-based approach to finding solutions to organizational problems.

Model	Description	Advantages for OpusCapita	Disadvantages for OpusCapita
License reseller	Sell licenses for RPA solutions, bundled with standard process libraries. Pay-per-license.	- Easy to enter the market early on. - No special expertise related to RPA is required. - No development, maintenance, or customization costs.	- No long-term business. - Low profit margins. - Low threshold for competition.
Value-added consultant/reseller	In addition to selling licenses for RPA solutions, offer implementation consultation and support. Pay-per-implementation.	- Provide unique value to the client. - Competitive advantage through automation expertise. - Cumulative knowledge base in the long term.	- Limited business opportunity after implementation is complete. - Limited opportunity to innovate in process redesign. - Limited control over software tools. - Fairly low threshold for competition.

Figure 4.7. Possible business models for robotic process automation.

Source: Asatiani and Penttinen (2016).

Solutions must transform a problematic situation into one in which clear goals and objectives are achieved (Ibrahim and Zailani, 2010; Ichniowski et al., 1997; Ifinedo, 2016; Ismail et al., 2005; Jansen et al., 2008; Jian Wang et al., 2010). This is akin to a diagnostic process in which the manager or decision-maker can understand why there are problems in the organization. They will create templates of a possible solution based on a framework for evaluating those solutions before arriving at a conclusion which selects the ideal solution. This is an optimization process for potential solutions to problems regardless of the sector that they impact on. The distinctions between what is proved and what is possible will be a critical consideration. It turns the speculative into the actual and practical.

Further analysis may be required beyond that which is given when recommending a specific solution (Crane, 2013; Crawford, 2016; Cunniff and Mostert, 2012; Cunningham, 2011; D'Ippolito and Timpano, 2016). Managers can be skeptical about solutions before they are convinced through evidence and explanations. This is a natural progression and is indicators of the managers are not willing to accept advice at face value without understanding how the advice has been constructed and evaluated.

Indeed, this is a critical aspect of the decision-making process. Otherwise, it becomes nothing more than a rubber-stamping exercise. Organizations with a detailed and deliberate problem-solving process are more likely to be successful than those that adopt a perfunctory and superficial stance.

The more complex a problem is, the more likely it is that he will require extensive analysis before you can select any solution (Manzoor, 2011; Matías-Reche et al., 2009; McGill and Wooten, 1975; Memili and Welsh, 2012; Menke et al., 2007). However, it is always advisable to investigate the problem further to understand its origin and the potential Solutions. There is some overlap between the various stages of identifying the problem and solution. Hence, you should not expect a linear outcome which progresses from cause, effect, and consequence. There will be instances of progress and retreat from time to time. The possible solutions are the one which the experts consider to be viable based on models that may be theoretical, or alternatively referenced heuristics. Theory and modeling are not enough because you need to move to the next stage which is gathering evidence about the applicability and internal consistency of the solution that has been recommended.

Another step within the decision-making process is to evaluate the solution against criterion that is established in the ecology within which the organization operates (Singh et al., 2016; Slack et al., 2006; Songa et al., 2012; Sparrow and Makram, 2015; Speer and Potter, 2000). To make the distinction between possible and proven solutions, you may have to go through five stages that are explored in established literature. The first stage is identifying all the information that is relevant to the problem and solution. This is a research process that must be as extensive and as rigorous as would be when making the final decision. Cast the net as wide as possible to let you get a rich narrative of information about the problem that you are trying to resolve. At the same time, you should consider quantitative elements that may reference statistical data. This is a combination of objective and subjective perspective on the problem provides a rich overview for purposes open solving that problem. Some organizations refer to it as a holistic diagnosis of the problem and the identification of whole solutions. Figure 4.8 is an example of a solution model for the problem of urban youth unemployment that is based on a combination of possible solutions that are turned into proven solutions.

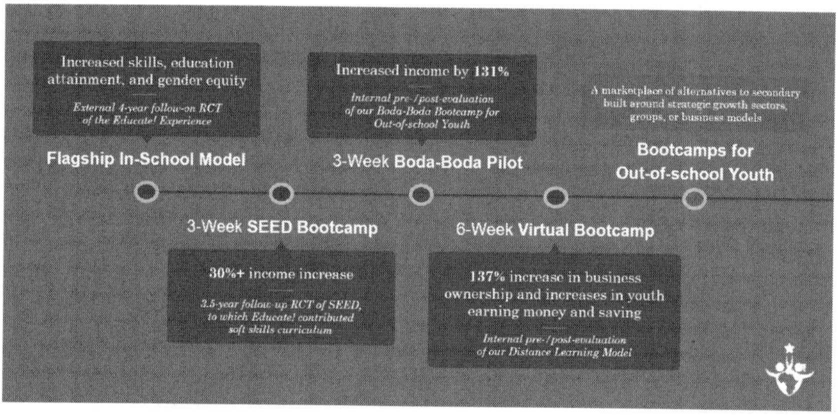

Figure 4.8. Solutions for out-of-school youth in Africa.

Source: Educate.

Having gathered information about the problem or solution, the next stage is to collect and record the information that you have identified (Morrison and Milliken, 2003; Mosher, 2013; Mujeeb and Ahmad, 2011; Nagalakhmi and Trivedi, 2015; Nagasawa and Fukunaga, 2015). This is a critical stage for evidencing and rationalizing the decision. Any entity that will be reviewing the decision may reference the information that has been collected. Hence, it is necessary to ensure that the collection process is rigorous and reliable. There will be certain company guidelines on how long the information can be used and the access protocols under the data protection legislation in the jurisdiction. Information that is recorded can be durable depending on how it is stored and accessed. However, the decision-maker must be aware that information may be fragile and could become outdated. Nevertheless, it is also appropriate to be wary of the recency bias which means that only the latest updates of information are given credence whilst ignoring older information. Initially, all information may be relevant. However, with time there will be a process of evaluation and exclusion such that you remain with only the information that is specifically relevant to the problem that you are trying to resolve.

The next stage in the process is presenting the information in a way that is persuasive to the audience for which it is intended (Jurevicius, 2016; Kabene et al., 2006; Kasperk et al., 2011; Kay et al., 1994; Kerzner, 2003; Khan et al., 2011). This is not about masking the figures or exploiting the science of presentation. Rather, it is a question of ensuring but those that need information to make decisions can access it in ways that are convenient for them. Some of the information that comes to the organization will be in formats that are not clear enough in terms of relating it to a specific organizational problem. Therefore, the organization must develop protocols for presenting information in ways that are suitable. These protocols are unique, but they are also adjustable depending on the circumstances. The organization should not be afraid to make adjustments where they are necessary. However, any adjustments should be made following extensive consultation with the stakeholders and those that are affected by the problem in some way. Of course, some problems are so technical that they require a consultancy to provide ongoing support. The resultant advice must be considered carefully before being integrated into the operations of the organization if appropriate.

The fourth stage is the evaluation of the effectiveness of the criterion that is used to decide between solutions that are possible and those that are backed by proof (Khan et al., 2011; King et al., 2000; Klikauer, 2014; Kluike, 2015; de Kok et al., 2006; Korczynski, 2002; Kotas, 2014). The possibility of a solution is based on experimentation and hypotheses that are developed through research. However, it is important to remember that these assumptions and models must be tested in a live environment before making a conclusion as to whether they are workable. The live environment can be problematic and expensive to execute. Therefore, the organization may routinely organize some experiments or pilot schemes which allow it to test the variables in a way that is not excessively expensive. Moreover, those solutions that have been tested extensively in existing literature may be assumed to be workable. These initial assumptions must then be tested against empirical evidence that is specifically related to the problem. That is how you transition from a solvable problem to one that is solved using proof and evidence. In other words, the organization is trying to test existing theories and models within its own environment with reference to a specific problem.

The fifth and final stage is the construction of a course of action that will resolve the problem (Willmott, 1993; Wysocki, 2013; Yang and Chen, 2006; Zhang and Wen, 2008; Zheng, 2017). When constructing a course of action, one must understand the nature of the solutions that have been recommended and accepted. Yet, there is an additional research process that focuses on the nature and application of the solution in terms of its variables and the ideal environment for its application. It may be necessary and appropriate to adjust some of the organization's operations and staff members to ensure that the organization can implement a certain solution. There are solutions that require an overall transition of the organization. Others merely target specific parts of the organization that have been found to be problematic. Ultimately, a proposed solution is turned into a solution that works and helps to resolve a specific problem in the organization. All these aspects discussed in the chapter are part of the process of explicitly defining organizational problems.

4.5. THE IMPORTANCE OF EXPLICITLY DEFINING ORGANIZATIONAL PROBLEMS

This book has already hinted at the importance of specificity when defining and resolving organizational problems (Pavlatos and Paggios, 2009b; Peng and Huiling Chen, 2011; Phillips and Gully, 2014; Pitts, 2009; Podoshen et al., 2015). It is a topic worth emphasizing, given the fact that many organizations have failed to fully resolve problems because of a lack of specificity or clarity in their definitions. The linkages between strategy and objectives also rely on this specificity. If the problem is only vaguely defined, then there is every chance that the solution will not hit the market. Specificity may call for a full explanation of the departments, segments, or personnel that are affected by the problem. Hence, the solution is likely to address all those parts of the organization as part of a comprehensive resolution. If those details are not specified, then there is a high likelihood that something important will be missed. Figure 4.9 is an example of how a structural approach might be used to achieve specificity in the problem definition.

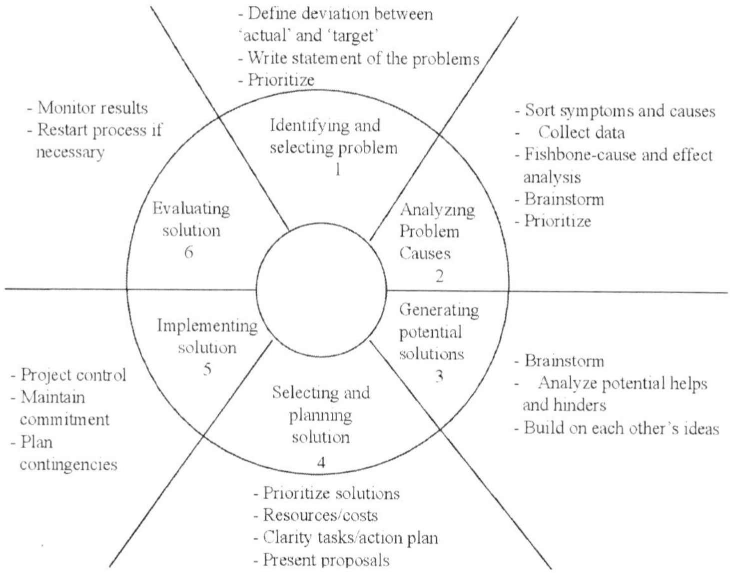

Figure 4.9. Example of a structural approach to problem definition.

Source: Elsaid et al. (2013).

The notion of specificity is borrowed from mathematics (Alvesson et al., 2011; Amos et al., 2008; Anckar et al., 2002; Anwar and Sun, 2013; Anyim et al., 2011). It helps to describe the accuracy of tests and reports. However, in the business context specificity relates to the accuracy of the intervention that is meant to solve a problem. Where a true condition is reported, mathematics refers to it as the Gold Standard Test. When this test is applied, there is a positive and negative result for the issue. A decision-maker in an organizational context would be interested in the extent to which the application of the recommended solution results in a positive change in the circumstances that are being addressed.

The related concept of "sensitivity" is used in a similar way (Memili and Welsh, 2012; Menke et al., 2007; Meyer-Sahling et al., 2018; Mia and Patiar, 2001; Milosevic et al., 2010). In mathematics, it refers to the probability that a positive test which is conditioned on a certain outcome during the gold standard test is true. Moreover, sensitivity accounts for the unknown responses or results in the experimental environment. For business or organizational purposes, it is imperative to ascertain the extent to which the intervention that is deemed to be positive results in positive outcomes. This bears in mind the possibility of the law of diminishing returns. Hence, it could be argued that the relevance and effectiveness of the intervention itself is under scrutiny during the problem-solving process. The organization should not be investing in interventions that are demonstrably ineffective or ones whose outcomes are relatively unknown.

One of the challenges that organizations have faced over time is the tendency to throw good money after bad (Bekker, 2014; Bell et al., 2011; Bercu, 2012; Bernini and Cracolici, 2015; Berthon et al., 2009; Bilson et al., 2013). This is based on the often-erroneous assumption that organizational problems can be resolved by money alone; or at least that money will make such a positive impact the problem will no longer have a sufficiently negative effect to hinder the operational efficiency of the establishment. The details processes of the problem-solving strategy are designed to capture all the nuances of the challenges that the team or individual is facing during the work. Money is not always the answer. If anything, excessive application of money to problems can condition the organization define all its challenges in monetary terms.

When you speak of specificity in management practice, we mean that the interventions that are used to deal with problems in the organization must be directly linked to the problem that they are meant to be addressing (Kasperk et al., 2011; Kay et al., 1994; Kerzner, 2003; Khan et al., 2011; King et al., 2000; Klikauer, 2014; Kluike, 2015). It goes back to the requirement for reliability and validity when selecting interventions. This is a scientific process that requires irrefutable evidence or a significantly weighty balance of probabilities that the organization can be certain that once the intervention is implemented it can lead to an improvement in operations. The lack of specificity in defining a problem and solution may indicate that there has not been sufficient research into the issues that the organization is facing. If that was the case, the organization should be reluctant to invest in a direction that is not clear or supported by research.

In the search for easy solutions, managers sometimes make the mistake of ignoring the nuances for the difficulties of the operational challenges that they encounter (Alshallah, 2004; Alvesson et al., 2011; Amos et al., 2008; Anckar et al., 2002; Anwar and Sun, 2013). For example, the manager may use a reductive approach that does not consider the subjectivity of the experiences of the teams that are dealing with a problem. These situations where the leadership team will elicit significance swathe of data which do not address the problem or explain what is going on in the organization. Then there is the risk of going into formulas that have been used before and are recommended by managers in the same mindset without looking for creative solution that might deal with the challenges that the organization is facing. A sense of imagination and embracing creativity is essential when trying to develop solutions to a complex environment that will change from time to time. The organization may develop an over-arching theory such as total quality management to ensure that all employees take a comprehensive and holistic view of problems. Figure 4.10 showcases an example of how a total quality management approach can be used to deal with problems of safety in the workplace.

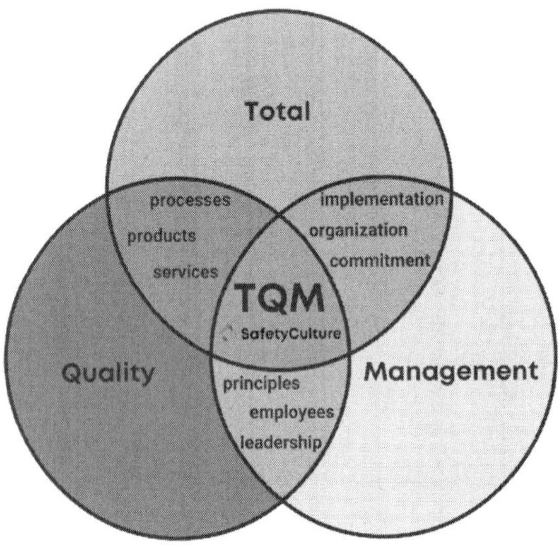

Figure 4.10. The principles of total quality management.

Source: Safety Culture.

There are other problems that are associated with a lack of specificity when defining or addressing organizational problems (Aboulian et al., 2008; Abramovsky et al., 2004; Abu-Saifan, 2012; Ahimbisibwe and Nkundabanyanga, 2016). For example, if a problem is vaguely defined it means that sponsors and other supporters that might help are unaware of or unclear about their requirements. Sometimes the organization will lose out on possible resources or support because it has not clearly defined what the problem is. For instance, there are donors that are very clear about the criteria for their funding priorities. If the organization cannot describe its problems in ways that are consistent with the priorities of the funder, then there is the possibility that they will not be able to qualify for that package of assistance.

Indeed, even the national budget is based on priorities that target specific issues within organizations and sectors. That is why the problem statement must be very specific and clear; not only for purposes of internal assessment and responses, but also to engage with external support mechanisms.

Chapter 4 Summary

This chapter has considered bias as an underlying problem when solving organizational problems. To that end, the chapter has introduced validity and reliability testing from a research perspective to help managers refine their own decision-making mindset. In that sense, this can be pathway to linking the strategic goals of the organization to all the activities that resolve problems. The chapter has explored the ways of distinguishing possible problems from ones that are proven in their effectiveness. To close, the chapter has reiterated the importance of specificity in problem definition. Chapter 5 moves on to the requirements when implement solutions to organizational problems.

CHAPTER 5

IMPLEMENTING SOLUTIONS WHEN SOLVING PROBLEMS

CONTENTS

Implementing solutions to problems is a key aspect of the problem-solving process. After all, it does not make sense to engage in all the research and testing that has been described in Chapters 1–4 without achieving any tangible outcome. This chapter explores a range of issues related to implementation including pilot schemes, feedback, acceptance, consensus, monitoring, evaluation, and the embedding of agreed solutions. This phase of the problem-solving process will typically begin with some sort of experiment or pilot scheme, particularly if the organization is cautious about expending resources on schemes without a realistic chance of success.

5.1. HOW TO SELECT AND ORGANIZE PILOT SCHEMES FOR SOLUTIONS?

The pilot scheme is an experimental modality that allows the organization to assess the efficacy and applicability of a solution to a problem (Gil-Pareja et al., 2007; Gruman and Saks, 2011; Guest et al., 2003; Hansen and Wernerfelt, 1989; Hansen and Olsson, 2011). The question then remains how to organize such a pilot scheme in a way that is fruitful and appropriate. A good pilot scheme should be reflecting the reality of the circumstances in which the solution will be implemented within the organization. It must also be efficient because the organization has a limited number of resources to expend on solutions. Moreover, the solution must be safe, and the experimental environment will attest to this. Pilot schemes must be smart in terms of focusing on those aspects of the model that are most important to the problem situation.

When undertaking a pilot scheme, it is important to have developed a prototype or use the advanced model to have emerged from the search exercise (Clegg and Palmer, 1996; Cold Cafe, 2018; Cole and Dawson, 2010; Collinson and Hearn, 1994; Connell et al., 2009). This must be advanced to an extent that it can be implemented on a trial basis. Once the pilot scheme has started, it does not make sense to go back into the research process. You would have to wait for the results of the pilot scheme before proceeding to engage in an extensive research process. You need garner enough information about the problem or potential solutions before moving on to the pilot scheme. The ideas and insights that are provided by the research committee or any other decision-maker will be scrutinized in the pilot scheme to see how applicable to a situation the intervention is. This is a precursor to the implementation of the solution on a bigger scale.

Leverage your access to the latest information when undertaking pilot scheme because it is likely that your competitors will not have knowledge of the research and the findings that you have generated unless your work is otherwise published (Harrison and Lock, 2004; Hartmann, 2014; Haworth and Hughes, 2015; Hennigs et al., 2013; Hermansson, 2020). However, for most organizations the pilot scheme will take place in the utmost secrecy and only those staff members that can guarantee a modicum of personal discretion will be allowed into the experimental environment. The reason for this protective approach is the risk that new ideas or innovations within the firm or company will be sold to other parties that may not have the interests of that organization at heart. This is particularly true of the technological industry in which innovation drives profitability. If an organization cannot secure its business secrets, it is likely to be driven out of the markets because competitors may steal or appropriate those ideas. To avoid some of these problems, organizations should try to learn from other pilot schemes. Figure 5.1 is an example of a well-planned pilot scheme in the open resource research and development niche.

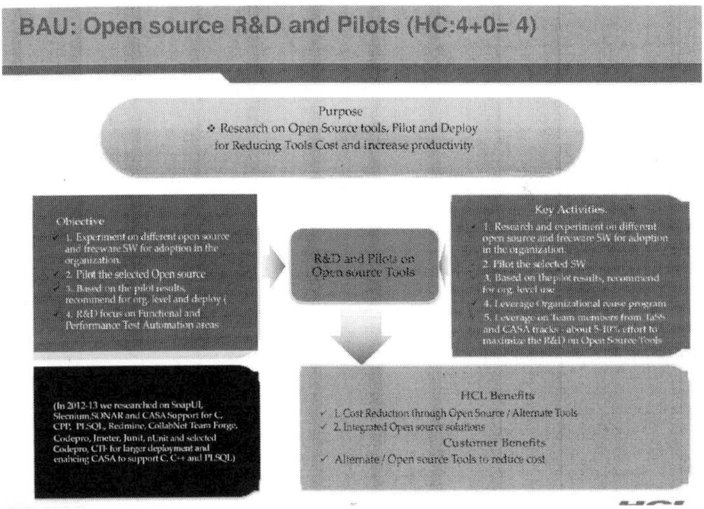

Figure 5.1. Example of an open-source research and development pilot scheme.

Source: Poppy gray.

There are certain products or projects within the organization or company which are of strategic importance and therefore require increased interest in terms of supervision and leadership to ensure their success (Evans, 2005;

Farndale et al., 2008; Fetscherin and Heinrich, 2014; Finkelstein et al., 2007; Gil-Pareja et al., 2007; Gruman and Saks, 2011). A pilot scheme may be carried out if there is a problem in these high-priority areas. However, there will be increased scrutiny of the experimental process and the records must be prepared in ways that are more detailed than would be the case which was a routine pilot scheme. It makes sense that the pilot scheme will also generate insight concerning the methodology that is used to identify solutions to problems. It can also be a diagnostic process in which ideas are tested before being fully operationalized. If the solution is not working, then it could be that there were issues with the identification of the problem, its definition, and the selection of the ultimate solution.

As a starting point, the organization needs to set out an environment that is a mini representation of the live environment within which the intervention will be integrated (Stevens, 2002; Stewart and Walsh, 1992; Stone et al., 2015; Stoorvogel et al., 2017; Storey et al., 2006; Subhas Chandra et al., 2010). Hence, the team allocated this task will be able to do the initial rollout of the system. The entire workforce should be warned so that there are no obstacles. However, there are some experiments in which the ignorance of the workforce will be of advantage because the solution depends on a lack of awareness on the part of the actors within the experimental environment. The organization must consider the ethics of the experiment as well as the pilot scheme. This is particularly important in the age of health and safety. Sufficient resources should be provided to allow the pilot scheme to go ahead without interruptions. That may mean changing the staff workplans and giving people some time off to be able to engage in the pilot scheme. Typically, only a few selected teams or individuals will be involved in the pilot scheme. Nevertheless, it is likely that the pilot scheme will cause some disruption to the operations of the organization.

The organization must set up a plan of work before the pilot scheme commences (Loundes, 2001; Lycett et al., 2004; Maneesh et al., 2009; Manzoor, 2011; Matías-Reche et al., 2009). This is important to ensure that every member of the team understands their role and responsibilities. At the same time, it is possible to identify the necessary resources for the pilot. This is the time to ensure that there are contingency plans can be triggered if there is any problem. Once the pilot has commenced, the team must do everything in its power to allow the experiments to continue unimpeded. However, the organization must be wary of piloting teams that have not yet been tested or do not have sufficient empirical evidence to back them up. This is a task that is undertaken when identifying solution, rather than repeating the preliminary research stages. The pilot scheme is subject to monitoring and evaluation to understand the progression of the intervention and how far it can address the issues that are raised in the initial assessment of the problem. These reports are reference points for decision-makers in the future. On the other hand, other manager that may rely on heuristics to make decisions, with specific reference to data that comes from pilots as well as the live situations.

The failure to plan properly for the pilot scheme can have catastrophic consequences for the entire intervention (Turyakira, 2018b; Visser, 2012; WHO, 2018; Wilkinson, 1997; Williamson, 2008; Willmott, 1993; Wysocki, 2013). If the pilot scheme is not providing accurate data, then it cannot be relied upon to make decisions about whether the potential solution can be implemented on a larger scale than the pilot scheme in the future. Indeed, the pilot scheme is like a protective mechanism for the organization so that it is not prematurely investing in ongoing experiments and findings that are half baked. Organizations ought to be protective of their resources in this way. Otherwise, a significant budget can be expended on activities that are bound to fail and do not significantly contribute to the survival or prosperity of the organization.

There are several reasons why a pilot scheme may not be as successful as the management team had anticipated (de Kok et al., 2006; Korczynski, 2002; Kotas, 2014; Köllen, 2013; Lashley and Burgess, 2007; Le, 2017; Leary, 2001). The main sticking point in these cases is often the schedule. We have already spoken about those over-ambitious or optimistic estimations in terms of how much time it takes to accomplish certain tasks or achieve certain goals. In certain cases, this can form a type of bias. If you do not give the pilot scheme sufficient time to be executed, then you are not likely to get the result that you are looking for, which understands the operation of the solution in a problem environment. Another potential issue occurs where the scope of the pilot is so narrow that it does not reflect the complexity of the problem situation. In that sense, you are experimenting with an environment that does not reflect the reality that will eventually determine the success or failure of the intervention.

Other pilot schemes stall because they lack the support from the key stakeholders or the staff members that are bound to eventually be utilizing the intervention (Johnson and Clark, 2008; Jurevicius, 2016; Kabene et al., 2006; Kasperk et al., 2011; Kay et al., 1994; Kerzner, 2003). This is a problem that ought to have been resolved during the consultation phase when the committee or decision-maker is trying to understand the nature of the problem and its impact in the organization. Additionally, it is important to involve all the stakeholders throughout the process because they then take ownership of the Intervention when it is being implemented. Where the pilot team does not have the right members, other issues may arise. It is important to assemble a comprehensive team that is representative of the final working groups that will utilize the intervention or solution.

Where there is the prestige that is attached to the project, it is possible that employees will engage in a game of one-upmanship in which only the favored workers will get access to the project (Sparrow and Makram, 2015; Speer and Potter, 2000; Steers et al., 2004; Stevens, 2002; Stewart and Walsh, 1992). Meanwhile, others that are not considered popular may not be given a chance to engage in the project. This is a subjective decision that is disastrous for the pilot scheme because it is not based on facts. The steering committee must ensure that the right people are part of the pilot scheme. By the right people, we are meaning those members of the staff teams that are going to use the intervention or are going to be affected in some way by the intervention itself. Whereas the pilot scheme is exclusive by its own definition, it must not be so exclusive that it does not include those people that matter in terms of the intervention and solving the problem.

Perhaps one of the biggest problems with pilot schemes are those situations where there is a lack of cooperation among various people, agencies, teams, or interest groups that are ostensibly engaged in the process (Visser, 2012; WHO, 2018; Wilkinson, 1997; Williamson, 2008; Willmott, 1993; Wysocki, 2013; Yang and Chen, 2006). Remember that you are effectively setting up a new mini-team. A collection of people that are newly put together for the pilot are likely to encounter certain problems, certainly during the initial stages. These are problems which are typical of a new team. Hence, the challenges of social and professional interaction within the teams must be given specific consideration during the risk assessment. The steering committee should watch out for internal politics which prevents the proper implementation of the pilot scheme. Government agencies are particularly prone to cronyism and all the forms of latent discrimination. Figure 5.2 highlights some of the key starting points when engaging in a pilot scheme. Many of these challenges should be addressed in the initial stages rather than waiting until they are a serious crisis.

Where To Start - Agile Pilot Project Selection
Agile Pilot Project Selection Framework

Based on our Agile Consulting experience, what we have learned is that we need to look at two major aspects while selecting pilotAgile projects:

- **Agile Benefits (Suitability):** This will cover the benefits that projects can derive or project challenges that will be addressed by adapting agile delivery. Projects with significant expected benefits should be considered for initial agile project adaption
- **Agile Readiness (Adaptability):**This will cover the parameters that are critical for successful agile delivery. Since Agile needs significant mindset change, strong organization support is required forpilot agile projects

Figure 5.2. Example of a starting point for an agile pilot scheme.

Source: Technology business (2013).

You may have to do some form of housekeeping by looking at the ways in which the pilot scheme is administered (Cunningham, 2011; D'Ippolito and Timpano, 2016; Dartey-Baah and Amoako, 2011; Day and Schoenrade, 2000; Deery and Nath, 2013). This is a separate issue from the merits of the intervention itself. In other words, you are looking at the ways in which the team members are communicating with each other and relaying critical messages for the success of the pilot scheme. Ensure that everyone in the pilot scheme has sufficient training in the interventions and understands how it is going to impact on the work plans. Think about issues of visibility and branding so that there is no backlash against the pilot scheme. One of the problematic areas maybe if members of the piloting scheme are given benefits over and above what are the members of the organization receiving. This can lead to petty jealousy and other problems of social interaction. A dysfunctional pilot scheme is not going to give you the results that you are looking for.

Other problems that might negatively impact on the pilot scheme include issues of documentation, particularly where critical records are missing (Collinson and Hearn, 1994; Connell et al., 2009; Cooke, 2003; Cox et al., 2021; Cox, 1999; Crane, 2013). You must ensure that there is a supervisory team that deals with the administrative requirements of the pilot scheme. Having terms of reference will ensure that you can bring about accountability in the running of the scheme. Monitor progress on a regular basis and provide feedback to those that are working on the pilot so that any issues are addressed before they turn into crises. The monitoring and evaluation process might also highlight the negative influence of external factors or third parties who have an interest in making the entire pilot scheme fail. Do not allow anyone or anything to derail the objective of the scheme which is to understand the ways in which the intervention is working. Have an open mind and expect that the pilot scheme might or might not work. Additionally, there should be contingency plans in case there are crisis or the risks that have been estimated in the assessment turn out to be true. The operations of the organization should not come to a standstill because the pilot scheme is not working as expected.

Another issue that you might pay attention to is any regulatory requirements particularly if you are working with sensitive materials or people (Finkelstein et al., 2007; Gil-Pareja et al., 2007; Gruman and Saks, 2011; Guest et al., 2003; Hansen and Wernerfelt, 1989). It is important to get your vendors or people in the supply chain to buy into the pilot scheme so that they are not confused by any changes in the normal routines. At the same time, it is important to be clear that the pilot scheme is nothing more than an experiment. Therefore, there is no guarantee the variables and interventions will be adopted eventually. Sometimes the participants in the pilot scheme become so excited by the first problem that is resolved that they immediately assume that the scheme is going to be implemented in full. Indeed, there may be additional problems of unauthorized premature communication such an internal leak (of information) that is so destructive if the scheme is not adopted. Do not over-promise and under-deliver. It is far to under-promise and over-deliver if you cannot achieve accuracy in your predictions. Outside the pilot scheme, it is always a good idea to establish channels for gathering feedback.

5.2. THE IMPORTANCE OF GATHERING FEEDBACK FROM AFFECTED PARTIES

Feedback is an essential aspect of the problem-solving process (Cole and Dawson, 2010; Collinson and Hearn, 1994; Connell et al., 2009; Cooke, 2003; Cox et al., 2021; Cox, 1999). It is a term that is used to describe any information which is helpful or a form of criticism about behavior or an intervention. Typically, feedback occurs retrospectively. Hence, if the feedback is negative, a mistake or a problem will already have occurred. This is the reason why some people are reluctant to take feedback because it is an implicit criticism of their activities or behavior. Nevertheless, feedback is critical for understanding the extent to which interventions in an organizational problem are effective or otherwise.

The decision-makers should be prepared to accept positive and negative feedback because it is part of their growth and development (Bruce and Daly, 2006; Calabrese, 1997; Capko, 2003; Carraher, 2013; Chang et al., 2006; Chen et al., 2011). It also means that feedback helps to improve the information available concerning an intervention because it highlights areas that require further work. Hence, it can be argued that feedback is helpful regardless of whether it is positive or negative. This feedback must be communicated in some way before it becomes useful since it is virtually impossible to work out what the human mind is processing unless the individual explains. That is why organization must create feedback loops that allow various actors within the organization to provide a perspective on how well an intervention is helping to resolve an organizational problem. In large-scale projects such as the one summarized in Figure 5.3, feedback is a precursor and consequence of stakeholder engagement.

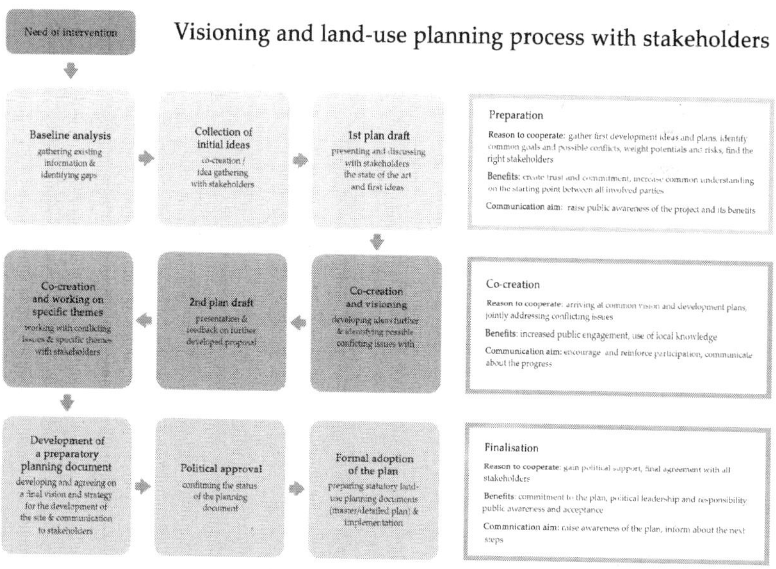

Figure 5.3. Integrated planning and partnerships.

Source: Baltic Urban Lab.

Unless feedback is acted upon in terms of changing of course of action or behavior modality, it becomes redundant (Supply chain Management and Logistics: Zara, 2013; Sharma and Upneja, 2005; Shatte et al., 2014; Sinclaire and Vogus, 2011; Singh and Masuku, 2014). Therefore, it is imperative that the decision-maker analyzes and evaluates the feedback to make a decision as to whether they are going to modify the intervention in some way. Feedback is not an instruction, and the decision-maker is at liberty to ignore those aspects that are not appropriate. For example, the feedback may exaggerate problems that can easily be resolved without overhauling the entire exercise. At other times, the feedback may be overly optimistic meaning that a decision-maker must take things much more seriously than the messages that they are receiving from the environment. It is important not to miss key pointers that may explain why and how an intervention is working or not working.

In some ways, it could be argued that feedback is a reaction from the environment when an intervention is deployed (Slack et al., 2006; Songa et al., 2012; Sparrow and Makram, 2015; Speer and Potter, 2000; Steers et al., 2004). The classic case in point is where customers provide feedback on a new product that has been launched or a service modality that is new. The organization has not had the opportunity to understand the perspectives of service users unless it encourages feedback. The way in which the organization responds to feedback, particularly if the feedback is negative, will determine if there is future feedback. Organizations that are overwhelmingly negative about feedback will discourage other people from giving their perspectives on interventions. This is the problem from a personnel management point of view because it means that members of staff are no longer confident to critique the actions that are taking the organization. Hence, the organization will no longer be learning, growing, or developing.

Ideally, feedback should form a loop in which there is an exchange of information that travels along either side of the loop (Brandsen and Pestoff, 2006; Bruce and Daly, 2006; Calabrese, 1997; Capko, 2003; Carraher, 2013; Chang et al., 2006). It is not enough for one side to continuously provide criticism while the other side is merely reacting to that criticism. Indeed, there can be situations in which the modality and quality of feedback is questioned. Nevertheless, the organization must endeavor to understand the message and move beyond critiquing the messenger. In any case, it is good practice to encourage as much feedback as possible even if that feedback is not always acted upon. At the very least, the organization will have good sources of information that can be relied upon to better understand the problem and the solutions to it.

Extensive research has shown that feedback has a positive effect on the performance of the organization and can motivate workers to become even more effective in their job roles (Hermansson, 2020; Hopkin et al., 1979; Hunter and Katz, 2012; Huselid, 1995; Ibrahim and Zailani, 2010; Ichniowski et al., 1997). However, feedback that is unclear or excessively negative can discourage employees and prevent them from undertaking the basic tasks that comprise their job. Managers must be wary of providing feedback in ways that are discouraging and prevent growth. That is why a distinction is made between general feedback and constructive feedback. The key aspect of constructive feedback is that it aims to improve the performance of the individual and to improve the level of effectiveness of the operational teams in the organization. Constructive feedback is not meant to discourage or demotivate people. It is never provided out of malice, but concern for improvement.

The feedback is obtained from a range of sources and not just restricted by internal team that is piloting the solution (Loundes, 2001; Lycett et al., 2004; Maneesh et al., 2009; Manzoor, 2011; Matías-Reche et al., 2009). For example, you may obtain feedback from employees, customers, owners, members of the supply chain, and even competitors in the industry. This type of wide-ranging feedback will give you a holistic view of the problem and the solution that you are trying to implement. Whenever possible, try to ensure that the feedback is focused and is relevant to the problem that you are trying to resolve. Giving feedback is not just about complaining. It is also about providing potential solutions and suggesting ways of doing things better. Through feedback the organization will make better-informed decisions throughout its activities. A case in point is the continuous engagement that takes place during consultations with stakeholders, which improves the relevance and effectiveness of change projects. Figure 5.4 demonstrates an example of such an approach.

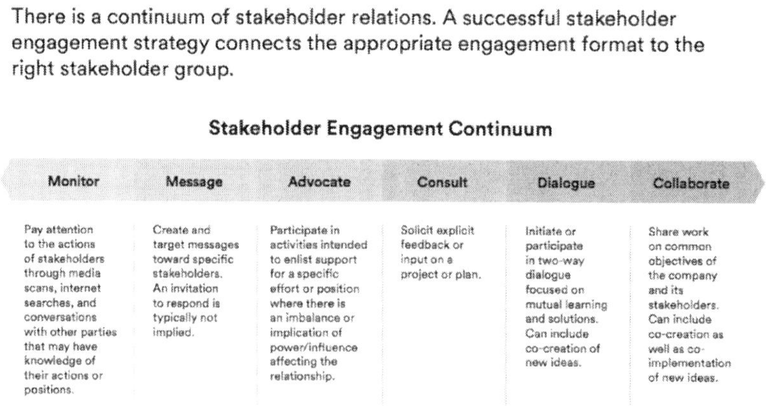

Figure 5.4. A guide to stakeholder engagement for healthier communities.

Source: Martin Lemos via BSR.

Research has shown that the best-performing businesses are the ones that encourage ongoing feedback in their decision-making process (Torre Edoardo and Luca, 2013; Turyakira, 2018a, b; Visser, 2012; WHO, 2018; Wilkinson, 1997). They can identify the most optimal responses to problems within the corporate ecology. However, those businesses and organizations that are excessively defensive about feedback may never realize that they are not doing the right things. That means that they invest their resources in projects and activities that are bound to fail. The mission of an effective management is the willingness to accept and deal with feedback without losing equanimity. The top companies are always looking for continuous improvement, which is the direct consequence of a feedback loop. The conscientious organization will actively seek information from the environment about its performance and then uses that information to make improvements that, in turn, improve the rating feedback from the environment. It is an ongoing and symbiotic process that is critical for organizational growth and development.

That is not to say that all feedback is useful (Köllen, 2013; Lashley and Burgess, 2007; Le, 2017; Leary, 2001; Lee and Park, 2009; Leggett, 2007; Lengnick-Hall et al., 2009). There are certain forms of feedback that are not constructive and merely work to depress the workforce or its motivation. The manager must ensure that they have a clear criterion for separating constructive feedback from mere negative complaints. Of course, the privilege of customers is that they can provide feedback in a negative way and remain very much part of the demand chain. The customer is always right in this instance. The business must separate the modality of providing feedback from the content of that feedback. For example, a customer may have a genuine complaint but then raise it in ways that are damaging to the organization. Whereas the organization will take steps to protect its staff members from harassment, the feedback will be valid, nonetheless. Hence, the organization must take steps to ensure that the issues that have been highlighted are addressed or corrected as appropriate. This is very typical in the hospitality sector where customers are willing to highlight performance quality through tips, complaints, or ratings online. Unfortunately, some organizations are so desperate for positive feedback that they manipulate the ratings to ensure that they are ranked highly despises the clear issues that have been identified by customers. This is the wrong approach because an effective organization and its managers must ensure that the key issues that arise in the feedback loop are addressed at the earliest opportunity. Feedback may lead to changes. However, these changes must achieve consensus and acceptance to be fully integrated into the organization without significant resistance.

5.3. HOW TO ACHIEVE ACCEPTANCE AND CONSENSUS?

Once a decision has been taken to follow a certain solution when resolving an organizational problem, the new challenge is ensuring that there is broad-based acceptance of that decision (Bell et al., 2011; Bercu, 2012; Bernini and Cracolici, 2015; Berthon et al., 2009; Bilson et al., 2013; Bjerregaard, 2011). One of the ways in which acceptance might be achieved is operating in an environment that allows for participation and consensus, as opposed to merely imposing the will of the senior managers. This is an approach that has been used in politics, but also has relevance in business and the public sector. Consensus does not mean avoiding making difficult decisions. Rather, it means that all the members of the group or the team that has been selected to implement a resolution to a problem are actively involved in making a decision about which solution is going to be used. There will be many disagreements, but consensus allows for those disagreements to be harmonized and reconciled so that a final position from the decision-making body is presented without significant resistance from the constituent members.

Because consensus takes time and effort, managers that are looking for quick solutions will typically want to avoid it (Cooke, 2003; Cox et al., 2021; Cox, 1999; Crane, 2013; Crawford, 2016; Cunniff and Mostert, 2012; Cunningham, 2011). However, a dictatorial approach may win short-term gains but will not achieve change that is sustainable. Besides, a dictatorial approach tends to lead to resistance from the environment or the community that is affected by the solution. Rather than having to deal with clandestine resistance, the organization may invest in consensus-building. If consensus leads to acceptance, then people take ownership of their roles in implementing that decision. That is a much healthier and more efficient way of working then if there are members of the team that are aggrieved by the process through which the decision was arrived at. Some organizations have numerical determinants for when consensus has been achieved. For example, when there is an overall majority or a supermajority in the voting exercise consensus may deem to have been achieved. Alternatively, the organization may insist that all members of the steering committee are in agreement before consensus is achieved. Regardless of the modality or standards that are adopted, it is important to remain consistent. Figure 5.5 highlights some prerequisites for consensus to work best. The organization should try to mirror these prerequisites in areas such as shared values, information, communication, and commitment.

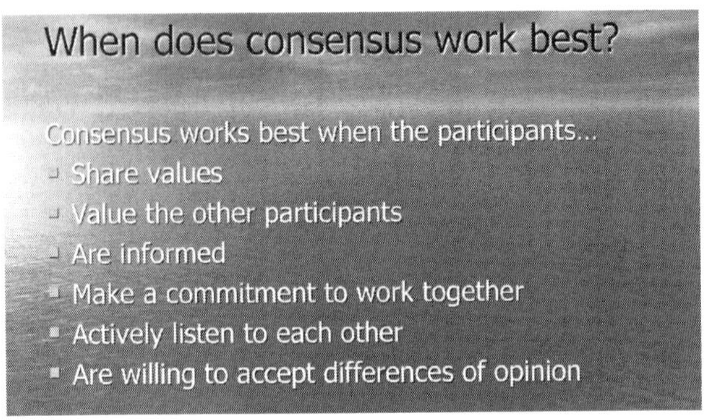

Figure 5.5. Key prerequisites for consensus.

Source: Shawn Sutton vid slide player.

There is a challenge of meetings that are unproductive because consensus is not being achieved and certain actors are refusing to engage in the process (Kasperk et al., 2011; Kay et al., 1994; Kerzner, 2003; Khan et al., 2011; King et al., 2000; Klikauer, 2014). The leader or key decision-maker may decide to ask for a majority decision before proceeding. A narrow majority is not an example of good consensus because it means that a significant number of the decision-making bodies are not in agreement. By way of contrast, a supermajority may indicate that the steering committee is nearly as a point where they can claim consensus. It is important to understand that consensus does not mean unanimity. Not everyone in the steering committee or the organization must agree before a decision can be deemed to have been achieved through consensus. For example, some member's main raise their objections but then agree that the majority decision is probably the right one. They may not want to interfere with the majority decision; yes, they continue to conscientiously object to it.

Consensus is not only a goal, but it is also a process regardless of the eventual disagreements between the different actors within the decision-making body (Aboulian et al., 2008; Abramovsky et al., 2004; Abu-Saifan, 2012; Ahimbisibwe and Nkundabanyanga, 2016). Hence, the fact that there has been extensive consultation is deemed to indicate consensus. A case in point is how ministers of state may have collective responsibility that allows them to object to decisions that are taken by the cabinet. Yet, these ministers will take overall or collective responsibility for the outcome of that decision. Indeed, it is the basis of democracy. Of course, democracy has also been criticized for becoming nothing more than a dictatorship of the majority. These are group dynamics that the decision-maker must be aware of. In other words, no one in the steering committee should feel aggrieved by the processes or even the outcomes of the decision-making process. Rather, most people in the steering committee should feel that they have contributed to the decision-making process; even if the final option was not the one they preferred. In fact, consensus is just one of many decision-making modalities (see Figure 5.6) including lotteries, unanimous votes, compromise, majorities, policy guidelines, expert committees, announcements, and historical precedents.

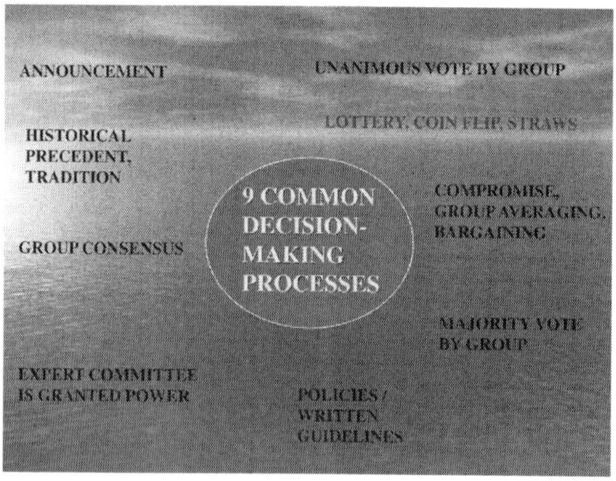

Figure 5.6. Nine examples of decision-making approaches.

Source: Shawn Sutton vid Slide Player.

There are certain characteristics that have been associated with decision-making processes that are based on consensus (Sinclaire and Vogus, 2011; Singh and Masuku, 2014; Singh et al., 2016; Slack et al., 2006; Songa et al., 2012; Sparrow and Makram, 2015). One of those characteristics is the existence of collaboration among members of the steering committee. In these cases, the participants will contribute towards a proposal and shape it along the way. Additionally, the concerns of different members of that group will be addressed and acknowledged with respect. Nobody will be treated as if they are a sideshow. Such experiences are positive and mean that members of the steering committee will have goodwill towards the eventual decision that is taken. That is not to say that consensus must comprehensively address all the concerns of all the members of the steering committee. For example, some suggestions may be unworkable or alternative be unacceptable because they go against the values and principles of the organization. The decision-maker will often be guided by the terms of reference and the guidelines are provided which impact on the decision-making process.

Cooperation is a very important aspect of consensus-building (Black, 2005; Brandsen and Pestoff, 2006; Bruce and Daly, 2006; Calabrese, 1997; Capko, 2003; Carraher, 2013). Everyone in the steering committee must be engaged in the task at hand. If there are stragglers or people that are disengaged from the process, consensus cannot be achieved. The leader or keep the steering committee will ensure that all the members of the team are involved and will prompt those that are reluctant to engage. Where a member of the team has shown a history of not cooperating in these meetings, it may turn out to be a disqualifying aspect when selecting the committee itself.

The steering group should operate on a basis of cooperation rather than each party forcing their views on others. The leaders should be wary of competing interests which stand in the way of attaining consensus. Never lose sight of the goal which is to resolve an organizational problem. Therefore, there may be instances where individual members of the decision-making body set aside their own prejudices in favor of a solution that has demonstrated the capability of resolving the problem at hand. Through training and development, it is possible to steer members of the team towards reflecting on their own prejudices as they make the decisions. Indeed, the organization might make it a priority to review the decision-making process so that any snags are identified and dealt with as soon as possible.

Consensus in decision-making necessarily calls for a certain level of egalitarianism (Collinson and Hearn, 1994; Connell et al., 2009; Cooke, 2003; Cox et al., 2021; Cox, 1999; Crane, 2013). The implication is that people are given opportunities that are equivalent to each other. Of course, there is the recognition that people are different. However, difference does not mean discrimination or marginalization. Managers should be particularly aware of minorities whose voices are often suppressed. Similarly, those that have unconventional opinions should be given a voice. We have already explored such considerations when discussing brainstorming as a decision-making modality. Hence, opportunities to present and contribute to the discussion should be open to all members of the team. Despite this inclusiveness, there should an appropriately critical review of opinions that are presented for consideration. For example, facts should be separated from fiction or intuition. The leader of the steering committee should also make a case that is backed by evidence rather than their own prejudices. If the steering committee has established a working environment that is led by respect, it is possible for people to disagree without becoming disagreeable. When opinions are shared and discussed, it should be possible to amend the proposal all the implementation program through the normal channels. However, all the objections and the resultant actions should be carefully documented in case the decision has to be reviewed at a later stage. This can feed into the process of monitoring and evaluation.

5.4. MONITORING AND EVALUATION OF SOLUTIONS TO PROBLEMS

Monitoring and evaluation are two of the most important aspects of project management (Cunningham, 2011; D'Ippolito and Timpano, 2016; Dartey-

Baah and Amoako, 2011; Day and Schoenrade, 2000; Deery and Nath, 2013). In some sense, the resolution of a problem in an organization closely resembles a project. These two modalities are critical for non-governmental organizations (NGOs) that need to learn lessons from the various solutions that they implement for their target populations. Typically, the monitoring and evaluation is oriented towards results. However, there is also an interest in the process of resolving the problem because it contains important lessons for the organization. Hence, the results-based framework must also pay attention to the procedures that are used to implement various solutions to a given organizational problem. The lessons are not just about the result, but also the journey towards the goal. Hence, it makes sense to have a strong mission statement that is complemented by detailed objectives.

It is also important to appreciate the fact that monitoring is an ongoing process whilst evaluation comes at the end (Visser, 2012; WHO, 2018; Wilkinson, 1997; Williamson, 2008; Willmott, 1993; Wysocki, 2013; Yang and Chen, 2006). That means that monitoring occurs in real-time whilst evaluation is retrospective. This can cause problems of coordination and diligence. The steering committee may be so taken up by the need to produce results that they forget to chart the development of the solution. Besides, it is imperative to acknowledge that the problem resolution is not always a linear process. Hence, there may be setbacks or developments that are unexpected. All these aspects of the trajectory should be noted because they can contribute to the decision-making process. The various employees that are given the responsibility for monitoring and evaluation should coordinate with each other so that there is consistency. An inconsistent set of procedures will not fully and appropriately inform the steering committee. To simply matters, some organizations have considered the use of modern technologies for monitoring and evaluation.

The use of technology in monitoring and evaluation is typical in many organizations (Sparrow and Makram, 2015; Speer and Potter, 2000; Steers et al., 2004; Stevens, 2002; Stewart and Walsh, 1992). However, technology cannot eliminate the power over the human touch. That is why human resources are critical to the resolution of problems in organization regardless of how advanced the technology being used. The monitoring and evaluation process will focus on activities and output which leads to results. These are based on the strategic plan of the organization. It may be possible to couple different programs on a strand of monitoring and evaluation which highlights the competencies of the staff within the organization as well as the effectiveness of the procedures that are being used. Technology will accomplish some of the administrative tasks that can be onerous for the steering committee and the other teams that are involved in the problem-solving project.

Project management has sometimes been prone to an estimation or overestimation of certain variables (Johnson and Clark, 2008; Jurevicius, 2016; Kabene et al., 2006; Kasperk et al., 2011; Kay et al., 1994; Kerzner, 2003). This is all part of the search for predictability when solving organizational problems. Moreover, modern project management techniques tend to reductive in nature. This approach then fails to appreciate some of the finer subjective issues that may determine whether a particular solution is appropriate for a specific problem. Figure 5.7 is an example of a framework that combines both qualitative and quantitative aspects to achieve a more comprehensive view of the problem and its solutions.

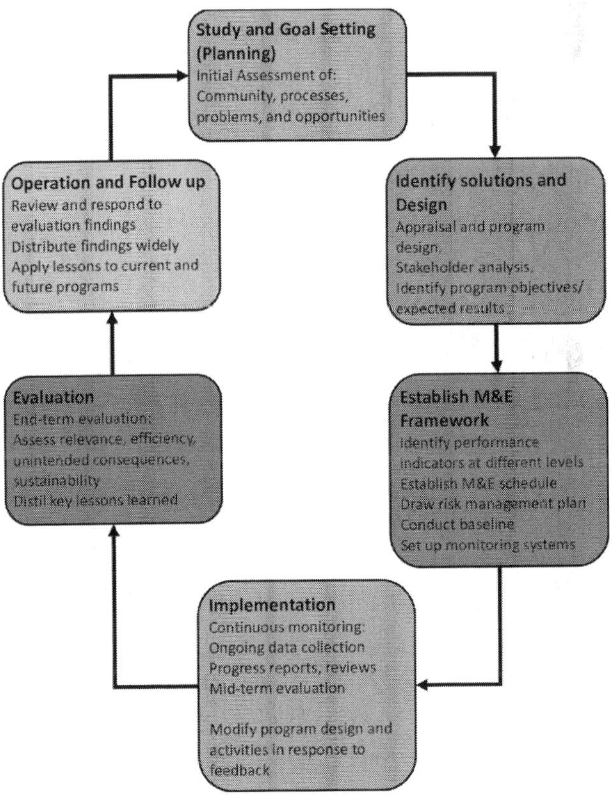

Figure 5.7. Example of a program monitoring and evaluation framework.

Source: Diwakar and Rao (2018).

It is important that project evaluation and monitoring moves beyond the simple exercise of data collection (De Kok et al., 2006; Korczynski, 2002; Kotas, 2014; Köllen, 2013; Lashley and Burgess, 2007; Le, 2017; Leary, 2001). The decision maker must understand how the data is collected and its impact on the outcome of the intervention that has been piloted. They must additionally understand the impact of the intervention on various job roles within the organization. The pilot team should aim to maintain high-quality records of the proceedings or the outcomes of the monitoring process so that future decision-makers can use it as a reference point. The success or failure of a project may not be immediately apparent, but time might reveal the real impact it has. The detailed records that are left behind by the steering committee will inform the future decision-makers when they are assessing the level of success that was achieved. This is not just about documentation but also visualization of the various aspects of the problem as well as the solution.

The more sophisticated solutions may require time before their results are fully understood (Turyakira, 2018b; Visser, 2012; WHO, 2018; Wilkinson, 1997; Williamson, 2008; Willmott, 1993; Wysocki, 2013). These complex implementation programs necessitate a monitoring and evaluation procedure that is highly attuned to the nuances of all the dynamics within the entire process. The complexity of the implementation process might mean that the monitoring and evaluation takes time to present. Indeed, there are situations where there are only partial results which do not reflect the full reality of the circumstances. Managers must watch out for the risk of failing to provide scalable solutions. These can easily aggregate the results that are needed for the monitoring and evaluation on a regular basis. In the absence of a simplistic solution, some organizations will appoint a team or an officer that is responsible for the documentation and the updates on the system.

During the implementation process, the steering committee will make a decision as to whether they are going to adopt a highly customized approach to monitoring and evaluation (Loundes, 2001; Lycett et al., 2004; Maneesh et al., 2009; Manzoor, 2011; Matías-Reche et al., 2009). The decision to have a standardized procedure is dependent on the circumstances of the project. Either way, it is imperative that the option that is selected is consistent with the values and norms of the organization. In the modern era, it is not advisable to have a lot of manual data aggregation. That is where technology comes into play because it takes on some of the more tedious tasks that are traditionally undertaken by human resources. Under the direction of an employee, the technology may make the process much quicker and predictable. Indeed, research has shown that organizations that use technology effectively to monitor and evaluate their projects are more likely to follow the standardized procedures for assisting the assessment of their projects.

There are several mistakes that can be committed during the monitoring and evaluation process (Stevens, 2002; Stewart and Walsh, 1992; Stone et al., 2015; Stoorvogel et al., 2017; Storey et al., 2006; Subhas Chandra et al., 2010). These are important because they can prevent the organization from fully understanding some of the challenges that have been made and the solutions that have been designed to address them. The first mistake that organizations could commit is to assume that monitoring and evaluation is a luxury that should not be included in the priority spending of the organization. We are living in a world where social impact is almost as important as brand identity. If you cannot identify the social impact of your intervention then you are likely to continue making mistakes that will make your brand less popular with the public. Social media is a brutal response mechanism for those brands that have failed to adhere to the expectation standards of performance with regard to corporate social responsibility. The monitoring and evaluation exercise can offer opportunities for learning and improving, as demonstrated in Figure 5.8.

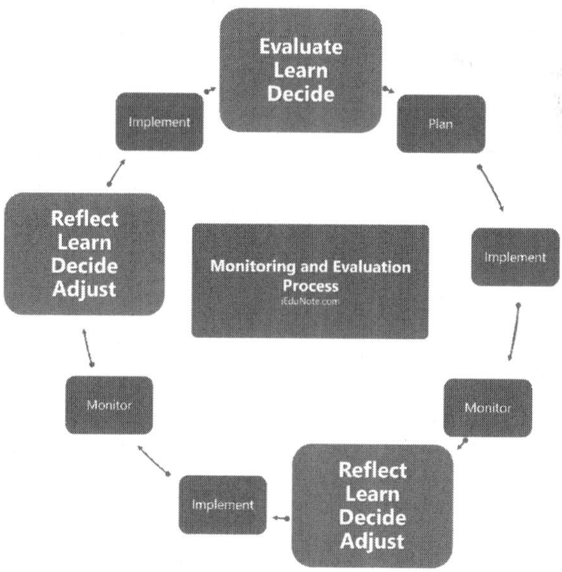

Figure 5.8. Conceptualization of monitoring and evaluation.

Source: iEduNote.

Another problem that routinely emerges is where there is a lack of trust in the data that has been presented for decision-making (Evans, 2005; Farndale et al., 2008; Fetscherin and Heinrich, 2014; Finkelstein et al., 2007; Gil-Pareja et al., 2007; Gruman and Saks, 2011). Hence, the manager will be suspicious that they are not being provided with a true and accurate picture of the situation on the ground. It does not help much that we live in an age of big data where there is a deluge of information that is not necessarily appropriate for specific problems in the organization. The decision-maker must evaluate the sources of feedback and the sources of primary data to ensure that they support their decision-making process. Otherwise, the entire procedure is at risk of being derailed by an infiltration of data that is not necessary for the decision-making process. Where there is a significant lack of trust in the data, leaders will be reluctant to make the necessary decisions to correct problems. Indeed, they may try to second-guess the responses of the various teams within the organization that are affected by the problem.

Then there is the problem of not have a robust theory of change that drives the data collection (Harrison and Lock, 2004; Hartmann, 2014; Haworth and Hughes, 2015; Hennigs et al., 2013; Hermansson, 2020). In such instances, the organization does not have a sound strategy to support its data collection and use. That means that monitoring and evaluation is not directed by clear rules that can assist those that are engaged in the process. When the decision-maker does not understand the assumptions underpinning the data collection process, it can be very difficult to evaluate the data that is presented. That is why it is advisable to have a primary mission that must be referenced at every stage of collecting and processing data. It is this theory that you also justify the results and resultant organizational change once the solution has been implemented. Additionally, the theory will inform the stakeholders who are part of the monitoring and evaluation process. Monitoring and evaluation are not enough to guarantee sustainable change. Rather, the organization must come up with strategies for embedding the adopted solutions in all its operations.

5.5. EMBEDDING FINAL SOLUTIONS INTO THE OPERATIONS OF THE ORGANIZATION

The initial introduction of a solution in an organization may turn out to be one of the easiest stages in the entire process (Clegg and Palmer, 1996; Cold Cafe, 2018; Cole and Dawson, 2010; Collinson and Hearn, 1994; Connell et al., 2009). The real challenge is in ensuring that the solution that has been introduced is sustainable in the long run. That means embedding that solution in all the operations of the organization. It also means ensuring that there is a good fit between the solution and the needs of the various teams or employees that are going to be affected by the new change. Of course, all this happens within an ecology that is continuously changing. The solutions that worked yesterday may not work today. The organization must be prepared to change course depending on the circumstances. This is the type of agile management that has become so prized today.

The culture of the organization will have a significant impact on the responses from the teams when new changes are introduced (Gil-Pareja et al., 2007; Gruman and Saks, 2011; Guest et al., 2003; Hansen and Wernerfelt, 1989; Hansen and Olsson, 2011). For example, there are organizations that are extremely conservative in their approaches to new Innovations. Hence, the members of staff will be socialized not to accept change easily. Others could resist the change because they think that it threatens their position. Certain organizations are plagued by difficulties of problematic employees that build small "empires" that they fiercely protect against any perceived or actual threat. Parts of the change will be to dismantle these small empires and ensure that the organization can continue to function with the new changes. There have been cases where the resistance to change has been so fierce and determined that the organization has had to dismiss certain employees. This might be a regrettable, but necessary, step to ensure that the organization continues to function well.

When implementing a solution in organization, the decision-maker must understand the requirements of all the key units that will be affected (Aboulian et al., 2008; Abramovsky et al., 2004; Abu-Saifan, 2012; Ahimbisibwe and Nkundabanyanga, 2016). This calls for an understanding of the entire structure that underpins the organization or company. Organizations will adopt new techniques and approaches as they engage with their ecology. Hence, the problem may have far-reaching consequences beyond early estimations. The real challenges may emerge later. When a solution is implemented, the organization must continuously monitor and evaluate progress to ensure that there are no serious issues that could impede future operations. Several ways of strengthening the change may be adopted, including the use of committees (see Figure 5.9 for an example in the World Bank).

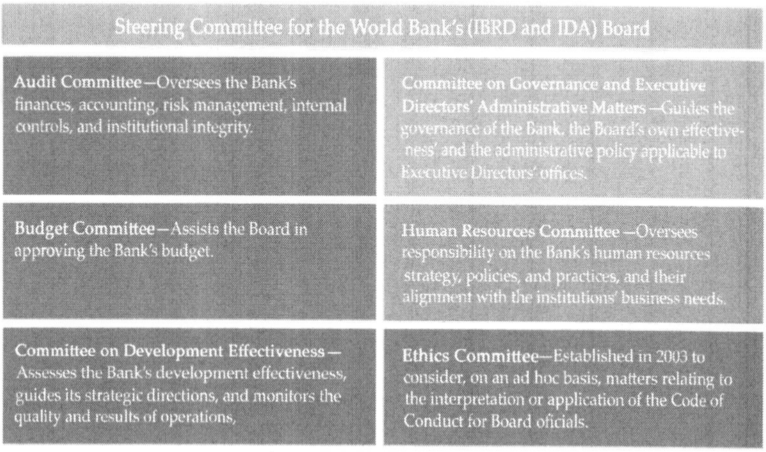

Figure 5.9. Example of strengthening through committees.

Source: World Bank Group.

The solution that is implemented will have to account for several dynamics or variables within the model that has been proposed (Alshallah, 2004; Alvesson et al., 2011; Amos et al., 2008; Anckar et al., 2002; Anwar and Sun, 2013). Many of these issues will be addressed during the pilot scheme. For example, the new solution may require changing technologies and techniques. That might necessitate additional training and development for members of staff. Another change that the organization may have to account for is the increase in the number of competitors or a challenging change in the strategies that are adopted by industry competitors. The organization is in a continual struggle to understand how the market is responding to any solutions that it implements in its operations. Part of the competency that is being constructed through the problem-solving process is learning from mistakes and adjusting quickly. The most dynamic corporate ecologies are highly dynamic and will quickly exclude organizations that cannot keep up with the demands of the market.

Public and state institutions have an interest in ensuring that business is consistent with the norms and values of a society (Kasperk et al., 2011; Kay et al., 1994; Kerzner, 2003; Khan et al., 2011; King et al., 2000; Klikauer, 2014; Kluike, 2015). The government or regulator has an interest in ensuring that the organization is following certain guidelines that are implemented as part of the licensing process. Change within the organization does not mean it can be absolved of its responsibilities under the law. Besides, the change that occurs in the organization is subject to the macro structures that underpin the economy. For example, the macroeconomic or political situation may impact on the ability of the organization to initiate and execute certain solutions to organizational problems. A case in point is where the organization has decided to offer redundancies to some of its employees. However, it may be government policy that redundancies ought to be avoided whenever possible. In this case, the organization will have to adhere to the rules that are set by the government. The power to offer and withdraw a trading license can be a strong incentive for organizations to comply with state regulations.

Change management remains one of the key challenges for all managers in all sorts of organizations (Bekker, 2014; Bell et al., 2011; Bercu, 2012; Bernini and Cracolici, 2015; Berthon et al., 2009; Bilson et al., 2013). The initial stages are relatively straightforward. However, the managers may soon find that there is an underlying resistance to the change. Those members of staff that do not want to embrace change may deploy clandestine and devastating tricks to ensure that progress does not occur. For example, someone employees adopt a work-to-rule approach which has been a key tactic in collective bargaining and industrial action. Other workers may decide to leave the organization entirely because they feel that the changes that are being implemented are contrary to their own values and aspirations. The organization can ill-afford high levels of turnover in a relatively short period.

Besides, the implementation of change is an unstable part of the business cycle which is necessarily delicate (Memili and Welsh, 2012; Menke et al., 2007; Meyer-Sahling et al., 2018; Mia and Patiar, 2001; Milosevic et al., 2010). The organization will take specific steps to ensure that disruption is minimized. Part of that response is to identify the challenges that employees face before taking concrete steps to ensure that the emerging concerns are properly addressed. When there are overarching issues that predetermine virtually all the activities of the organization, consideration should be given to using cultural transformation as an instrumentality for embedding the range of options that are selected. Figure 5.10 highlights such an example in the form of a "smart quality culture."

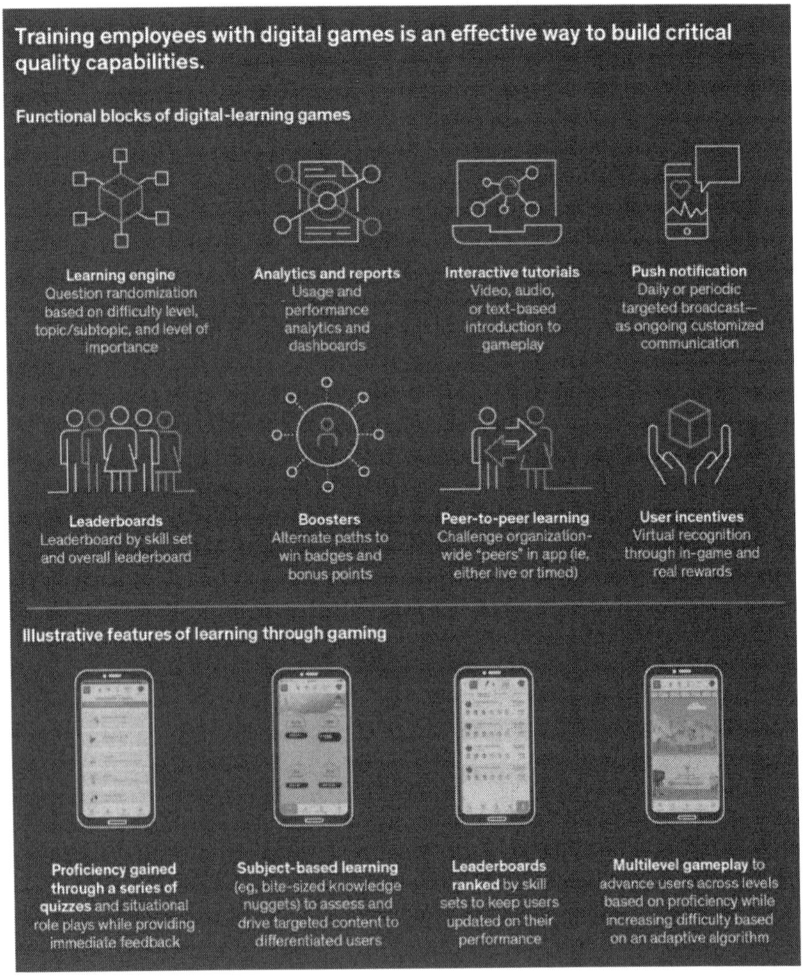

Figure 5.10. Embedding 'smart quality' culture and capabilities in the organization.

Source: McKinsey.

Implementing solutions to organizational problems requires sustainable change that can transform the fortunes of the organization (Alvesson et al., 2011; Amos et al., 2008; Anckar et al., 2002; Anwar and Sun, 2013; Anyim et al., 2011). This can be a tedious process that is fraught with difficulties. Some members of the team will find the new processes challenging and will require additional support from their supervisors. The organization itself runs the risk of competitors copying or adopting some of its ideas and then implementing them with possibly greater success. The transition period is quite challenging for the organization, and there is evidence that some organizations fail due to the inability to implement the appropriate changes when faced with problems.

Existing research has shown that one out of every two (50%) change-driven projects in organizations tend to fail. The reasons for this failure stem from the inability to sustain initial wins (Pavlatos and Paggios, 2009b; Peng and Huiling Chen, 2011; Phillips and Gully, 2014; Pitts, 2009; Podoshen et al., 2015). The organization may quickly implement change, having engaged in a detailed research process. However, there is always the risk that the problem will return. Indeed, some of the teams may initially accept the changes that have been implemented and yet still surreptitiously engage in activities that sabotage the entire process. That is why it is so important to gain acceptance and cooperation from all members of the team. If there are questions about the nature of the problem or the solution that has been suggested, there should be a senior manager on hand to provide the answers that employees and customers need.

It is tempting to have very high expectations of change (Willmott, 1993; Wysocki, 2013; Yang and Chen, 2006; Zhang and Wen, 2008; Zheng, 2017). This is particularly the case where the organization is looking for quick wins and has been dealing with a problem that is not easily resolved. That means that there is an overestimation of the capabilities of the various teams to deal with the new tasks and modalities that have been allocated to them. If the organizational capacity has not been reconstructed and brought up to the level where it can deal with the new change systems, the organization will not achieve all the targets that it has set. There must be coherence and logic in the ways that the problems are resolved. To gain more control, it is appropriate to understand some of the key problems that organization typically experience so that relevant protective mechanisms can be put in place. These problems will therefore be explored in Chapter 6.

Chapter 5 Summary

This chapter has explored the key considerations when solving problems and implementing certain options that have been selected. These issues include piloting projects, feedback, consensus, acceptance, cooperation, monitoring, and evaluation. Finally, the chapter provided some tips on embedding solutions for sustainability. In Chapter 6, we will briefly explore the problems that organizations can typically expect to deal with depending on their unique ecology.

CHAPTER 6

KEY PROBLEMS IN BUSINESS AND RESPONSES TO THEM

CONTENTS

This chapter is a brief overview of the potential problems in a range of corporate contexts. It is a learning experience for managers and decision-makers so that they are well-prepared for the reality of a dynamic and complex ecology. Some of the problem areas that will be explored include uncertainty, regulation, human resource management, technology, big data, and reputational risks. The starting point for this discussion is the instability and implicit uncertainty of market conditions today.

6.1. DEALING WITH UNCERTAINTY IN THE MARKET

The corporate world is fraught with uncertainty (Khan et al., 2011; King et al., 2000; Klikauer, 2014; Kluike, 2015; de Kok et al., 2006; Korczynski, 2002; Kotas, 2014). Most businesses have learned to live with the fact that the future of their enterprise is unpredictable. Indeed, some literature suggests that unpredictability can be a positive attribute because it inspires businesses to perform better. Rewards in entrepreneurship are associated with risk, and risk is one of the key features of uncertainty in the business world. The speculation and investment niche in the corporate world is specifically associated with uncertainty. Hence, speculators will predict the future in terms of the movement of prices. Those speculators whose predictions are accurate will win profits. Meanwhile, those speculators that get it wrong will lose a lot of money.

Leadership training often refers to responding to and managing uncertainty because it is an important quality for dealing with a changing corporate environment (Jurevicius, 2016; Kabene et al., 2006; Kasperk et al., 2011; Kay et al., 1994; Kerzner, 2003; Khan et al., 2011). Modern leadership training and socialization provides learners are with the competencies that are necessary to thrive even where the future is not clear. One of the strategies that might be adopted for uncertainty is for the business to ensure that its operational modalities are flexible enough to deal with changes in the markets. If you have sufficient capacity and ready flexibility, the uncertainty of the market will not have a significant impact as would be the case if you were an inflexible Enterprise. Indeed, it seems that there is no space for inflexible enterprises in the modern business world.

Understanding risk is just the beginning of the journey. A good leader should be able to manage risk in a sensible way whilst adhering the values and norms of the organization that they are working in (Morrison and

Milliken, 2003; Mosher, 2013; Mujeeb and Ahmad, 2011; Nagalakhmi and Trivedi, 2015; Nagasawa and Fukunaga, 2015). Taking too many risks that are not accounted for is a recipe for disaster. In fact, those leaders that are risking organizational assets without doing the proper risk assessment are likely losing their jobs. Calculated risk is important for profitability and leaders should not be discouraged from taking calculated risks. However, the process of evaluating risk and preparing contingency plans is as important. Modern managers must understand the dynamism of competitive markets and then respond accordingly, preferably with sufficient flexibility. The top organizations and companies in the economy will have an edge in dealing with uncertainty because they have built extensive capacity. Additionally, these big companies benefit from highly sophisticated contingency planning which significantly mitigates the risks that they face. This is a result of risk assessments that are fairly accurate and supported by significant investment. Such organizations have gradually moved away from a reductive factory model (see Figure 6.1) which failed to understand the nuances of risk.

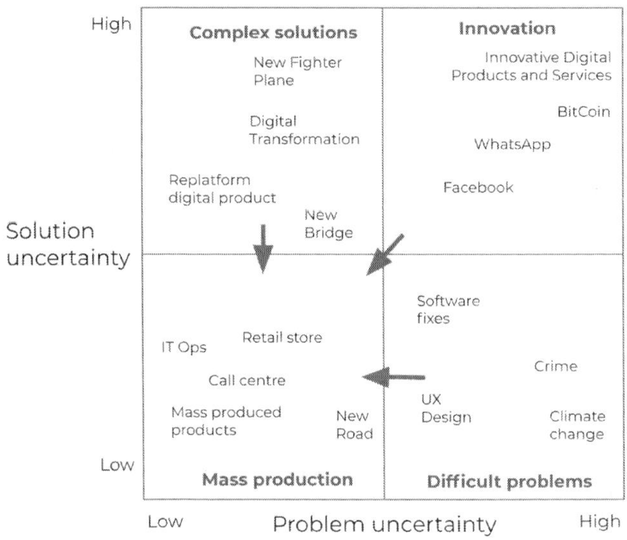

Figure 6.1. Failures of a factory model in an uncertain market.

Source: Murray Robinson (2021).

Once you have built flexibility within your business model, you should also consider being more transparent about the risks that you face (Singh et al., 2016; Slack et al., 2006; Songa et al., 2012; Sparrow and Makram, 2015;

Speer and Potter, 2000). This is particularly important when dealing with your supply chain and employees. These are people that rely on you for their business or wages. Therefore, it makes sense that you discuss with them any concerns about potential risks and the reaction that you would like present to the market if it is volatile. This is a formal consultation and engagement which will benefit the organization in the long run. You are in effect building and strengthening partnerships that can withstand the challenges that may arise during volatile times. Some Industries are so advanced in this cooperative approach that they develop an ecological network of social relationships that are symbiotic. Hence, the various actors within the industry will help each other in times of crisis. Recently, these industries have survived the worst effects of the Covid-19 pandemic despite the dire predictions of economic malaise.

Another response to uncertainty that an organization may consider is implementing solutions that are already significantly tested (Manzoor, 2011; Matías-Reche et al., 2009; McGill and Wooten, 1975; Memili and Welsh, 2012; Menke et al., 2007). That calls for a certain level of commitment. You should not be doing half measures if you realize that a particular solution is relevant to the problem that you are trying to deal with. When you fully committed to a solution and provide the appropriate resources, you will be rewarded in terms of resolving the problems that you are facing. Besides, the problem-solving process will act as a learning experience for the organization so that in the future the teams in the organization will be able to deal with similar problems. Additionally, it is expected that you will try to optimize each solution that you implement. It is not enough to simply implement a poor-quality version of the solution that you have chosen. Instead, you should foster the ideal conditions and recruit the ideal team to implement the solution. This will maximize the benefits that you possibly can garner from that solution.

The information that you will get in the problem-solving process may not be as clear as you would like it to be (Crane, 2013; Crawford, 2016; Cunniff and Mostert, 2012; Cunningham, 2011; D'Ippolito and Timpano, 2016). That is why it is advisable to embrace ambiguity in the data collection process. This is in effect acknowledging that the ecology within which you are operating is not linear. Rather than expending all your energies on complaining about the ambiguity within the information that you are getting, you should be seeking insights that provide you with the pathway to resolve the organizational problems you are facing. Curate a series of methodologies that work so that you can reuse them in the future.

This is the basis of heuristics. When faced with chaos and ambiguity, the methodologies that you have created will be important in developing some level of control. This is particularly important when you are dealing with ambiguous missions. Existing literature has identified certain models and methodologies that you may use including Six Sigma and the project management methodology. Focus on data-driven approaches and make good use of statistical information that can inform your decision-making process.

When you are trying to change an organization or a system, the change should start with yourself as the leader and then move on to the nearest team (Ibrahim and Zailani, 2010; Ichniowski et al., 1997; Ifinedo, 2016; Ismail et al., 2005; Jansen et al., 2008; Jian Wang et al., 2010). Once the benefits of the change are clear to everyone in the organization, you will not face as much resistance as if you are running an outfit that is disorganized. A changed leadership team inspires the rest of the workforce to follow the example that has been given. This is how transformations and revolutions begin. The conditions that the organization is encountering can be perceived as either negative situations that cannot be improved, or alternatively you can see them as opportunities for change. Reframe complexity as a challenge for your team to do better. Re-characterize the challenges that the organization is facing so that they turn into overarching goals that can inspire the rest of the team to achieve them. Figure 6.2 is an example of this type of response to strategic uncertainties.

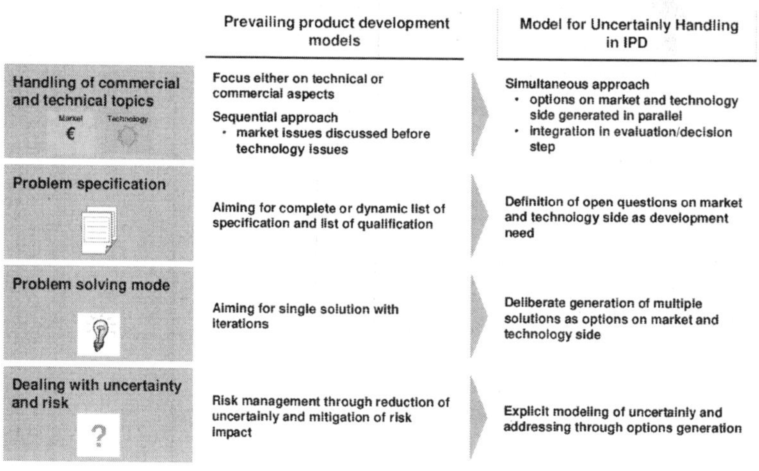

Figure 6.2. Example of responses to strategic uncertainties.

Source: Lorenz (2008).

Good communication skills are an essential asset when dealing with uncertainty in the markets (Onyx and Maclean, 1996; Ozturk and Rumens, 2014; Papasolomou and Melanthiou, 2012; Parker et al., 2013; Parry et al., 2008). The worst thing that can happen is where there is disorganized and unclear communication within the organization. Through communication, you can address problems before they become crises. During a crisis, the entire workforce is looking for certainty in terms of information that is credible and reliable. The organization should be the first point of contact and the information that is provided should be believable. The personal integrity of the leadership team in the change management group will be a critical determinant of the responses from the rest of the workforce. If the leaders are credible, it is likely that the change messages that are being communicated to the rest of the working group will be believed. This helps to establish mutual trust and cooperation. The communication should be candid and explain the reality of the problems rather than trying to hide behind technicalities. That does not imply that the business cannot have its own corporate secrets. Rather, it means that the communication that is released by the change management team is factual. You should not allow your teams to play games of manipulation.

The organization should renew and strengthen its leadership values and culture during periods of uncertainty (Lorenzo-Romero et al., 2013; Loundes, 2001; Lycett et al., 2004; Maneesh et al., 2009; Manzoor, 2011; Matías-Reche et al., 2009). If you are very clear about what you stand for as an organization, the ambiguity within the business sector or the industry will not have as much impact as if you are not certain of what you stand for. This is the process of developing business values and culture which is supportive towards achieving the goals of the organization. Culture is a gradual process that would emerge through continuous interaction and construction of ways of doing things that differentiates your business or organization from the rest of the industry. The leaders that you put in place will reflect your cultural values, and they must follow the norms that have been established within the organization. At the same time, you should be prepared to engage in self-criticism if there are cultures or practices that are inconsistent or unethical. Organizations that can reflect on their own practice are likely to grow and develop with time. This is a different proposition from an organization perceiving that everything going well and therefore sees no need to engage in self-reflection. Another problem that organizations are likely to face today is excessive regulation.

6.2. THE CHALLENGE OF EXCESSIVE REGULATION

Government regulation is meant to ensure that businesses follow the rules (Shatte et al., 2014; Sinclaire and Vogus, 2011; Singh and Masuku, 2014; Singh et al., 2016; Slack et al., 2006). These are rules that are designed to reflect the morals, values, and Norms of a society. Those organizations that break the rules will be punished in some way. The punishment might range from losing their license to practice and go right up to imprisonment in some extreme cases. Indeed, a business that complies with regulations may benefit from an improved reputation with members of the public. However, those businesses that do not comply with regulations on a regular basis may acquire a bad reputation and lose customers, therefore. The regulations that are put in place by the government may cover several issues, including the preservation of the value that shareholders invest in the organization. The regulations relating to the relationship between the organization and members of the public are enforced to prevent exploitation and unethical practices. For instance, public sector organizations are mandated to ensure that they deliver high-quality services to the public without unlawful discrimination.

Despite their benefits, some government regulations can be so onerous that they impact on the operational efficiency of a business (Cole and Dawson, 2010; Collinson and Hearn, 1994; Connell et al., 2009; Cooke, 2003; Cox et al., 2021; Cox, 1999). That is why countries are trying to control regulation and reduce its impact on small businesses. If the demands of the regulators are so onerous, it might mean the family-owned businesses and small enterprises can no longer engage in the commercial world. This has become a philosophical discussion with some experts arguing that government regulation harms business efficiency as a matter of course since it almost always adds layers of bureaucracy to the process of doing business.

Generally, excessive regulation means that businesses cannot compete effectively with other establishments that are based in locations that adopt a laissez-faire approach (Shatte et al., 2014; Sinclaire and Vogus, 2011; Singh and Masuku, 2014; Singh et al., 2016; Slack et al., 2006). In other words, it has been argued that the regulator must try to strike the right balance between regulating the sectors in the economy and ensuring that small businesses can survive. Of course, we have had examples of disastrous outcomes when there is a reduction in the regulatory framework that the state is imposing on its businesses. The financial crises of 2008 and 2009 emerged from the failure to regulate the housing sector in the USA. Many politicians were outraged that financial institutions were offering expensive loans to people who could clearly not afford them because of their poor credit ratings. Some critics have referred to historical data (see Figure 6.3 for an example) to argue that high regulation is associated with low economic growth.

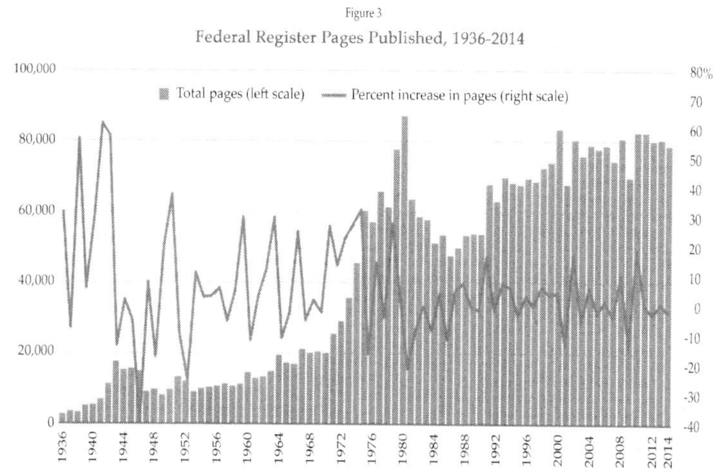

Figure 6.3. Regulation and the economy in the USA.

Source: Committee for Economic Development.

For a business or organization, the existence of regulation is a call to compliance (Okotoni and Erero, 2005; Onyx and Maclean, 1996; Ozturk and Rumens, 2014; Papasolomou and Melanthiou, 2012; Parker et al., 2013). Although there may be corners that can be cut, it is preferable to follow the rules and avoid the long arm of the law. The costs of being fined by the courts are so significant that any savings that were tentatively made from breaking the law become moot point. Compliance is not just about external concerns but can also the impact on internal efficiencies. A well-run business has benefits for its employees and other operational units. By way of contrast, a business that is engaging in illegal activity will end up harming everyone that associates with or works for it. Following regulations ensures that the business can maintain high standards. If there are issues with excessive regulation, the business or organization can join with other institutions in a similar situation and lobby the government to change the law. Indeed, many establishments lobby the government on a regular basis to ensure that there are no occurrences of over-regulation.

There are several options that might be pursued by organizations or business that are faced with excessive regulation (Chung, 2015; Clegg and Palmer, 1996; Cold Cafe, 2018; Cole and Dawson, 2010; Collinson and Hearn, 1994). The states will be aware of those options. Indeed, some governments take steps to pre-empt the decisions that are made by the organization in responding to a climate of excessive regulation. For example, in the USA, various states will differentiate the regulation from each other to increase their competitiveness within the country. Hence, a business can move away from the over-regulated states into ones with less regulation. A case in point is the Northern flight of businesses to the South, where limited government is preferred. However, that option is not always available to countries that are not federations. The regulation in the country may be so expensive than the business must consider the possibility of relocating to another area that is less regulated. We have seen these patterns in the labor force where businesses have outsourced certain functions in their organizational structure to developing countries because they have been discouraged by the excessive regulation that comes with employment law in the more industrialized nations.

That does not take away from the primary functions of government regulation (Barry et al., 2000; Bekker, 2014; Bell et al., 2011; Bercu, 2012; Bernini and Cracolici, 2015; Berthon et al., 2009). The functionalist perspective is that the regulations must serve a useful societal function. Otherwise, they would have been repealed. Indeed, there have been examples of economies that have faced significant challenges because of relaxing regulatory regimes. The function of the regulation is to control natural monopolies. Research has shown that businesses that are in monopoly situations tend to abuse this position. For example, they can charge high prices. Even worse, they may collide with other major players within the industry to drive out small businesses. It is counterproductive for the government, which seeks to develop a balanced economy that is primarily supported by small and medium-sized enterprises.

Another function of regulation is to control negative externalities (Korczynski, 2002; Kotas, 2014; Köllen, 2013; Lashley and Burgess, 2007; Le, 2017; Leary, 2001; Lee and Park, 2009). Whereas the mercantilist approach to political economy was at its height in the 15th and 16th centuries; there are still elements of that approach in international trade today. Governments may engage in "*beggar thy neighbors*" tactics such as dumping and politically motivated sanctions. Iran and other countries under sanction have complained about the effects of the international sanctions regime that never seems to target Western countries despite their misdeeds in countries like Iraq. Regulation may be a way for the affected country to ensure that foreign-backed multinational corporations do not completely take over the economy.

Figure 6.4 includes other functions of regulation such social goals (Leggett, 2007; Lengnick-Hall et al., 2009; Leuenberger, 2006; Leung et al., 2015; Li, 2009; Li et al., 2013). A case in point is where the government bans the sale of tobacco or pornography because it considers it a social ill that is going to harm the welfare of the citizenry. Other countries use regulation to control excessive profitability which might be exploitative in nature. Then there are markets which are afflicted with excessive and potentially counterproductive competitive that might be harmful to the overall efficiency of the economy. Regardless of the motivations behind the regulation, these are all examples of how the government can protect its interests in a private market.

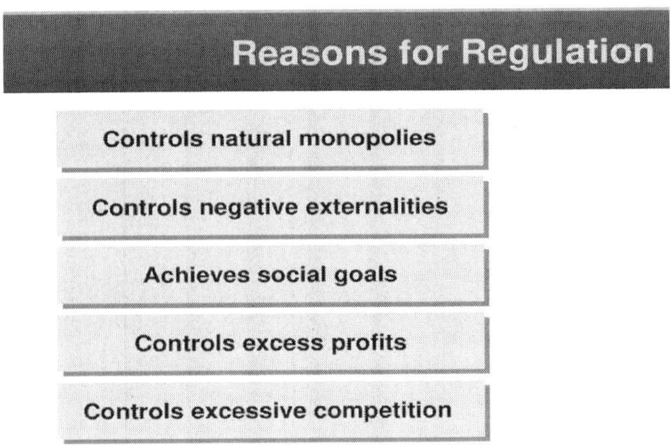

Figure 6.4. The reasons behind the regulation of business.

Source: Dana Welch via Slide Player.

The levels of regulation may vary from sector to sector depending on the perceived risk (Leggett, 2007; Lengnick-Hall et al., 2009; Leuenberger, 2006; Leung et al., 2015; Li, 2009; Li et al., 2013). Hence, there is an onus on the various establishments within a sector to ensure that they do not attract the attention of the regulator. A case in point is the increased scrutiny of companies in the financial sector that are perceived to be engaging in practices that are harmful to their customers. This is particularly relevant in situations where the customer is vulnerable. The ideal business model must be based on transparency and integrity. These are attractive features for potential customers. Moreover, they are instrumental in reducing the regulatory burden imposed on the industry or individual businesses within the sector. Some businesses will go beyond the regulatory minimum and ensure that they provide an exceptional service or products to their customers. This makes business sense because it improves their competitiveness of their establishment in the industry.

Compliance with regulation is an onus for businesses and therefore can become a burden if they are not prepared for it (Ozturk and Rumens, 2014; Papasolomou and Melanthiou, 2012; Parker et al., 2013; Parry et al., 2008; Patiar and Mia, 2009). During the problem-solving process and throughout the implementation of potential solutions, the steering committee should ensure that they are compliant with the norms and values of the society within which the organization is operating. The most realistic way of understanding the norms and values of a society from a business point of view, is to follow the rules of law. A business that is generally compliant can assume that it is acting in ways that the community expects. In most cases, such compliant businesses will gain customer bases that would otherwise shun them. Not following the rules does not save any costs. If anything, it runs the risk of increasing costs that emanate from fines and other enforcement measures.

Sometimes businesses are faced with an ethical dilemma where they are operating in an environment that is corrupt (Willmott, 1993; Wysocki, 2013; Yang and Chen, 2006; Zhang and Wen, 2008; Zheng, 2017). This is particularly prevalent within the developing world. Some businesses have responded by joining the corrupt practices. For example, they may pay bribes to avoid regulatory control. Others will hire inside officers that can help them overcome bureaucratic hurdles that are meant to protect the public. Then there are the multinational corporations that are so powerful that hardly any government will seriously challenge them. These are the corporations that will continue to engage in unethical practices without any backlash from the state. However, there are also increasing signs that the world is seeking a business community that is ethical and has integrity. We see these patterns when it comes to the sustainable use of resources. Organization that are in environmental protection legislation may find that they are picketed by campaigners and do not attract as many customers as they would otherwise get. Therefore, it makes sense for this organization to follow the regulations. Organizations also face human resource management challenges during the course of the business cycle.

6.3. HUMAN RESOURCE MANAGEMENT

Human resources play an important part in the running of an organization (Mitchell et al., 1997; Moore and Birtwistle, 2004; Moore and Doyle, 2010; Morrison and Milliken, 2003; Mosher, 2013). However, human resources can be a challenge for the organization because they involve the proclivities and complexities of dealing with a diverse workforce. The rapidly changing business landscape has also placed additional demands on the human resource management team. For example, there is increasing use of modern technology that calls for a different approach from the traditional practices that focused on work and that we are primarily operating on a manual basis. It is for this reason that the factory model has failed spectacularly when dealing with the service sector or industries that require emotional labor. Modern workers need a more sophisticated approach to their needs. Besides, the modern worker has more options than the traditional worker during the industrial revolution. Hence, the job market is competitive on both the supply and demand side. Organizations that have a poor human resource management practice are not likely to attract the best potential employees on the market. This will eventually harm their bottom line and overall efficiency. Figure 6.5 highlights some of the key challenges of human resource management.

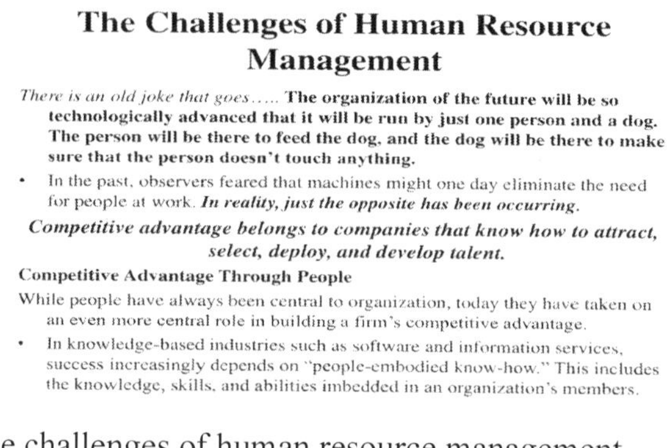

Figure 6.5. The challenges of human resource management.

Source: Dora Ana (2011) via Slide Serve.

The main challenge of human resource management is to ensure that all workers are supported and supervised to the extent that they can provide the best of their abilities to achieve the goals of the organization (Atwal and Williams, 2009; Awadh and Saad, 2013; BIS, 2015; Baker and Esherick, 2013; Bannò and Sgobbi, 2016). Clearly, this is easier said than done.

Traditional theories and formulas that have been used in human resource management have been challenged by the diversity and complexity of the needs that modern workers have. Even more challenging is the fact that it is anticipated that human resource management will continue to evolve in the next decade. For instance, there are workers that are no longer willing to come into an office and prefer to work from home. The covid-19 pandemic had shown that employers can no longer take workers for granted.

Even the public sector has not escaped the scrutiny of human resource management (WHO, 2018; Wilkinson, 1997; Williamson, 2008; Willmott, 1993; Wysocki, 2013; Yang and Chen, 2006; Zhang and Wen, 2008). The public is demanding that organizations which operate within the public sector significantly improve their efficiency. The complaints about poor quality public services and people who are sitting in jobs for life (but are not performing as expected) are increasing. At the same time there is disquiet about traditional management models that amount to bullying and harassment. Organizations can no longer afford to be perceived as being discriminatory or otherwise old-fashioned in their practices. Workers have a voice in collective bargaining. Even though trade unions are largely inactive in many industries, there are other avenues for raising complaints about employers that engage in practices that are socially unacceptable. The media to cancel does organizations that are perceived to be exploiting their workers. Even institutions such as hospitals which were traditionally well-respected have to update their human resource management systems (see Figure 6.6) to reflect the needs of human resource management.

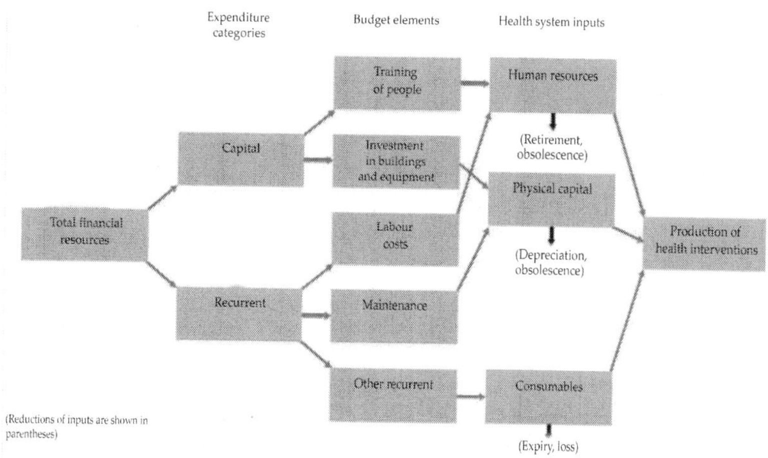

Figure 6.6. Human resource management challenges in hospitals.

Source: Sarma and Barua (2018).

Modern management practice must take on the challenge of leading the workforce that has different expectations from its counterparts that worked 100 years ago (Sendawula et al., 2018; Supply chain Management and Logistics: Zara, 2013; Sharma and Upneja, 2005). Issues such as sick pay and paternity leave are coming to the fore and organization must be active in implementing some of these innovative interventions. We have also learned that employees respond better to support than direct instruction or a dictatorial approach to leadership. It is no longer the case that uncooperative workers can be quickly silenced through the threat of instant dismissal. There are incredibly extensive and costly procedures for sacking workers that are uncooperative if they can follow certain basic rules.

The employer must cooperate with the employees to ensure that the goals of the organization are achieved (Klikauer, 2014; Kluike, 2015; de Kok et al., 2006; Korczynski, 2002; Kotas, 2014; Köllen, 2013; Lashley and Burgess, 2007). This is no longer the kind of working environment that was prevalent during the Industrial Revolution where workers were so grateful for any job that they were unable to engage in any kind of self-advocacy. The role of the human resource management is increasingly important, and organizations cannot afford to relegate this task to ordinary supervisors or leaders. Every operational team should have access to a human resource manager that is competent and updated with the latest employment law. Indeed, many organizations are developing their practices to the extent that they far exceed the minimum standards that have been set by the government.

There was once an assumption that mechanization will effectively replace the human beings that had been working in many manual labor jobs (McGill and Wooten, 1975; Memili and Welsh, 2012; Menke et al., 2007; Meyer-Sahling et al., 2018; Mia and Patiar, 2001). Empirical evidence has shown that the human touch and never be completely replaced. Even the most advanced machines require some level of inhuman input. The human beings that are operating modern machines require human resource management. No organization can afford to rely on mechanization or automation as a replacement for human resource management. The effects of neglecting the rights and responsibilities of human resource management mean that the organization cannot remain profitable. It may also be subject to legal sanctions from the state and other aggrieved parties. The media is full of stories of workers that have successfully sued their former employers for constructive dismissal, harassment, discrimination, and a host of other infringements on their rights.

In the absence of a satisfactory replacement for human beings in the working environment, the organization must identify ways of improving its human resource management practice (Berthon et al., 2009; Bilson et al., 2013; Bjerregaard, 2011; Black, 2005; Brandsen and Pestoff, 2006; Bruce and Daly, 2006). As a starting point, there should be emphasis on recruiting the right people to the right job. This includes the ways in which job adverts and person specifications are prepared. The organization must carefully plan for the workforce that it has recruited and ensure that there are sufficient resources to support staff members. This support is paid for by the motivation and productivity of the recruited workers. It is essential to streamline human resource management practices if the organization has any hope of achieving its strategic goals. The workers are an instrumentality in this endeavor. The era of exploiting workers without consequence is truly over. Modern organizations work with the employees in a symbiotic and collaborative relationship. Additionally, there have been updates to traditional Human resource management theory so that it better reflect the needs, preferences, priorities, and challenges that are face many modern organizations. One of those pressing challenges is the use of technology in an era of exploding data.

6.4. TECHNOLOGY AND EXPLODING DATA

Information and technology are key resources in modern business (Assink, 2006; Atkinson and Brander Brown, 2001; Atwal and Williams, 2009; Awadh and Saad, 2013; BIS, 2015). Nevertheless, access, and usage of technology and information can become problematic. Indeed, many businesses are facing challenges of big data and are struggling to find ways of efficiently and appropriately using the information that is available to them. Others are struggling to convert the vast amounts of data that is available to them into information that can be used in operational activities. Information and data are of limited use unless they support decision-making. That also includes the process through which information is used in solving organizational problems. Key sectors such as education (see Figure 6.7) are revisiting their technological and informational policies considering these developments.

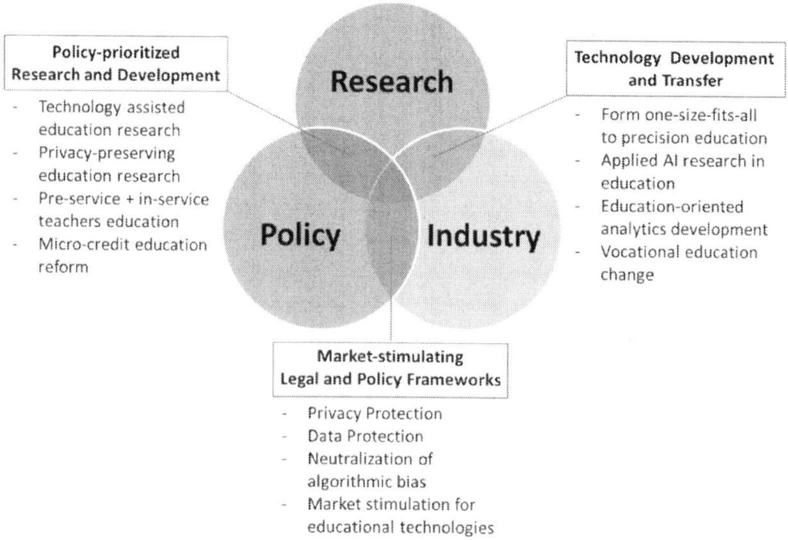

Figure 6.7. Challenges and future directions of big data and artificial intelligence in education.

Source: Luan et al. (2020).

One of the challenges that modern businesses are facing is the fact that information is gathered on a routine basis without specifying any relevant organizational needs (Morrison and Milliken, 2003; Mosher, 2013; Mujeeb and Ahmad, 2011; Nagalakhmi and Trivedi, 2015; Nagasawa and Fukunaga, 2015). The internet has become a repository of all sorts of information that can be useful depending on how it is curated and accessed. Sales information is at a premium cost and organizations that invest in data mining must be assured the resultant information that they receive is going to be used for solving organizational problems. The mere process of accessing and using information is problematic in of itself. For example, the data protection act in various jurisdictions means that it is no longer acceptable to use information for purposes that were not clear at the time it was gathered.

The sources of information or data for the organization can be internal or external (Samah et al., 2013; Schlögl, 2005; Schmid and Adams, 2008; Schuler, 1989; Sedmak and Longhurst, 2010; Sendawula et al., 2018). The organization will have more control over sources of information that come from within its departments or teams. However, the organization will have less control over information that emanates from the ecology of the business or industry within which the organization is located. Some industries or sectors are more efficient at collecting data than others. Then there are companies that rely on third parties to collect data for them. These organizations then process and utilize that data depending on the need within the organization. The quality of the data can vary significantly. Hence, if decisions are made based on faulty data there is the chance that the outcome or decision that is implemented will also is faulty. That is why businesses are encouraged to engage in quality control processes that improve the access to information that they have.

The advances in technology have been heralded as one of the breakthroughs for this century and the previous one (Carraher, 2013; Chang et al., 2006; Chen et al., 2011; Chevalier and Mazzalovo, 2008; Chung, 2015; Clegg and Palmer, 1996). However, one cannot automatically assume that technology will resolve all the problems that organizations face. Yes, there is evidence to indicate that technology has significantly improved the operations of various organizations in a range of sectors. For example, genomics has greatly benefitted from high quality information (see Figure 6.8). However, that does not mean that technology can resolve all the problems that organizations face in every circumstance. Rather, there is evidence to indicate that an abuse of technology can lead to the loss of expertise within the organization. The key issue that leaders must be aware of is that technology is not a full substitute for human beings in the workforce.

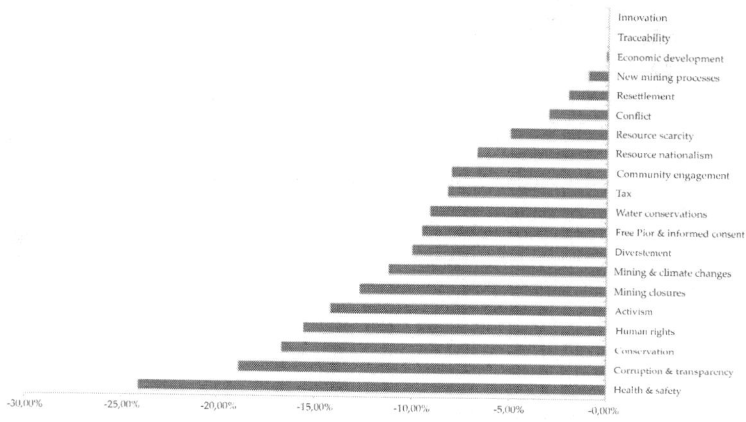

Figure 6.8. Challenges and solutions of big data in genomics.

Source: Costa (2012) via Wiley Analytical Science.

A case in point is where the organization has made employees redundant in the hope that the introduction of automation will improve productivity (Milosevic et al., 2010; Min et al., 2008; Mitchell et al., 1997; Moore and Birtwistle, 2004; Moore and Doyle, 2010; Morrison and Milliken, 2003). Clearly, this is not the right decision for all instances. There may be circumstances in which technology can improve productivity and must be incorporated into operations. However, there are certain types of labor that require the human touch. At a time when the service sector is growing in most industrialized economies, we cannot afford to underestimate the value of human beings in the organization. Hence, it is recommended that organization leverage automation and technology in ways that are complementary to existing human resources. Similarly, the use of data should be part of an overall strategy or organizational development.

The excessive accumulation of data for no other reasons other than to collect the data is harmful to organizations (Bjerregaard, 2011; Black, 2005; Brandsen and Pestoff, 2006; Bruce and Daly, 2006; Calabrese, 1997; Capko, 2003). Decision-making requires Precision in the amount of data that is produced or used. For example, data should be relevant to the problem that is being resolved. Hence, organization would prefer that it gets high-quality data in limited quantities as opposed to large quantities of data that is irrelevant to their circumstances. An organization that is facing problems with managing its data should revisit the prioritization and organization of data access and usage. That implies only collecting data that is relevant to the circumstances of the organization. More specifically, the data should be linked to specific problems that need to be resolved. From time to time, the organization should review data access procedures to ensure that they are still relevant to the mission of the organization.

Despite all the challenges and problems that are associated with big data, it is a mistake to assume that an organization can function without data (Bercu, 2012; Bernini and Cracolici, 2015; Berthon et al., 2009; Bilson et al., 2013; Bjerregaard, 2011; Black, 2005). Information is power in the corporate world where the ability to predict the future and learn from the past distinguishes the best organizations from those that are merely mediocre. An organization should map out its niche in terms of the data that is available on the market. More importantly, the organization should never invest in accessing data that is irrelevant. Then there are legal considerations to account for in terms of data protection and ethical use. The internet has become a hub of misinformation and therefore organizations must be particularly careful about what type of data they use for their decision-making.

It is for these reasons that experts recommend a cautious approach to the management and access of data (Dartey-Baah and Amoako, 2011; Day and Schoenrade, 2000; Deery and Nath, 2013; Dumay et al., 2010; Dutse, 2013). Organizations should pay attention to the industry standards and practices in relation to data access and usage. This is because the industry will lay out the rules and procedures that have been deemed to be appropriate for that niche. Because information helps diagnose and resolve organizational problems, it can become a competitive advantage. Therefore, the organization should make arrangements to ensure that access is controlled, and that the Integrity of business secrets is not compromised through laxity. For instance, some organizations have developed a comprehensive data access and usage policy that is disseminated to all the teams that work within the institution. The public sector has specific duties and responsibilities to members of the public. Therefore, the society may expect a more ethical approach to data access and usage from the public sector. That does not mean that the private sector can drop standards without consequences. The final organizational problems to be explored in this chapter are reputational risks.

6.5. REPUTATIONAL RISKS

The control and management of reputation has become an important organizational priority (Anwar and Sun, 2013; Anyim et al., 2011; Arbulú et al., 2015; Argenti, 1996; Arthur and Dworkin, 1991). Private companies and public agencies are increasingly concerned about the possibility that their reputation could be destroyed if they do not have a contingency plan. It is for this reason that many organizations are putting protocols and procedures in place for purposes of reputational risk management. Regardless of the size or scope of the organization, it is important to maintain a good reputation with the public and the sector. A good reputation is worth its weight in gold in terms of attracting new customers and retaining the ones that are existent. Figure 6.9 some of the modalities that an organization can utilize to measure and evaluate its reputational risks.

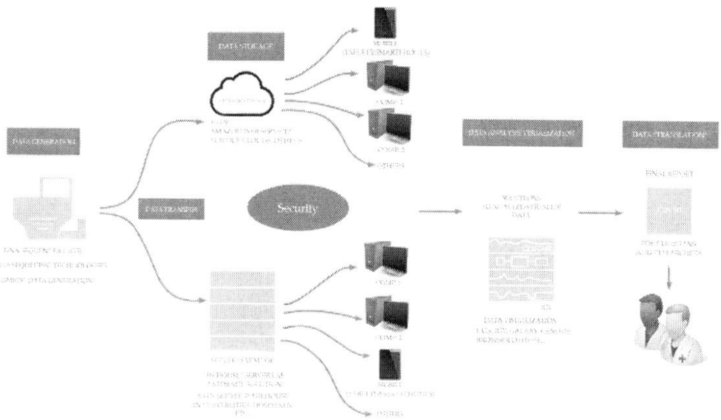

Figure 6.9. How to measure the reputational risk of your business?

Source: Alva.

The age of the internet has meant that messages can travel very far, regardless of whether they are positive or negative (Loorbach, 2010; Lorenzo-Romero et al., 2013; Loundes, 2001; Lycett et al., 2004; Maneesh et al., 2009; Manzoor, 2011). Hence, negative news about an organization or its practices can destroy its reputation across the globe in a matter of minutes. The so-called "*cancel culture*" has played an important role in creating a climate of fear online for businesses. A single disgruntled employee or customer can destroy any reputational value that the company retained online. Unfortunately, the organizations or companies that run the internet have not yet identified a suitably robust mechanism for weeding out any malicious reviews. Instead, companies are continuously afraid that someone saying the wrong thing at the wrong time in the wrong place is going to destroy their reputation and decimate their customer base.

There are certain best practices that are commonly used in the industry to manage reputations (Sedmak and Longhurst, 2010; Sendawula et al., 2018; Supply chain Management and Logistics: Zara, 2013; Sharma and Upneja, 2005). Indeed, the specialization of reputation of management has emerged from public relations circles. Certainly, no international company would ever dream of opening a business or a branch without understanding the risks to its reputation. A significant amount of investment may be required to kick-start the reputational risk management program. Additionally, the organization may need to hire experts in this field. All the operations of the organization should be subjected to a reputational risk evaluation and follow the principles that are suggested by the professionals.

The responsibility for reputation of management does not simply lie with the leadership team (Nica, 2015; Obeidat, 2012; Odrakiewicz, 2012; Okotoni and Erero, 2005; Onyx and Maclean, 1996; Ozturk and Rumens, 2014). Instead, every member of the organization should participate in protecting and building the reputation of that organization. In fact, it should be a performance management measure to evaluate the extent to which the activities of an employee are contributing to the reputation of the organization. That calls for an implementation of systems that specifically address the risky areas that have been identified. The reputation of the organization can be compared with statistical data from the past. This allows for a more holistic and realistic view of reputational management.

Through a comparative analysis, it is possible to understand the level of reputational risk across a range of departments (Huselid, 1995; Ibrahim and Zailani, 2010; Ichniowski et al., 1997; Ifinedo, 2016; Ismail et al., 2005; Jansen et al., 2008). The organization may even develop metrics that can be used as a performance management measure. Reputational risk is typically considered a quantitative issue. However, there may be instances where the reputation of an organization is a qualitative issue. Robust methods and measures should be adopted to address the specific reputational risks that the organization is facing currently. The same approach should be adopted when considering the risks that might emerge in the future. Of course, there could be a surprise event that significantly damages the reputation of the organization despite its best efforts.

With a system in place to manage enterprise risk, companies can set quantifiable performance metrics. In turn, these metrics can facilitate reputational alignment across departments or teams (Cox et al., 2021; Cox, 1999; Crane, 2013; Crawford, 2016; Cunniff and Mostert, 2012; Cunningham, 2011). A strategy can be identified to deal with individual risks and the peripatetic risks that cross departments. The organization can embed some of these measures so that they become part of the culture. There are several measures that can be used to improve the reputational risk management strategies of an organization (see Figure 6.10). These include holistic approach, valuing the brand, understanding relationships, prioritizing the problematic areas, better communication, and the development of a crisis plan.

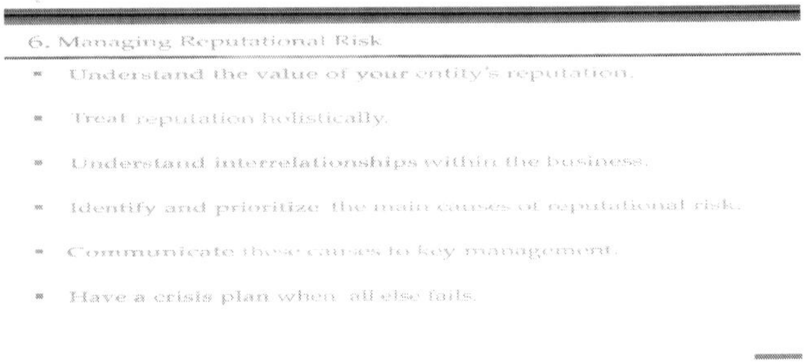

Figure 6.10. Managing reputational risk.

Source: Brett Green via Slide Player.

The necessity for reputation management emanates from an understanding of the time it takes to build a reputation after it has been destroyed (Parry et al., 2008; Patiar and Mia, 2009; Pavlatos and Paggios, 2009a, b; Peng and Huiling Chen, 2011). Organizations that are careless about their reputations will pay a very heavy price in the market where impressions matter. In certain extreme cases, the loss of reputation has meant that the customer base abandons the brand to the extent that the organization must close business. Corporate social responsibility is one of the responses to the need for reputation management. If an organization has very high ratings on corporate social responsibility, it is likely that the organization is taking care of its reputation.

There are several best practices that have been established for managing reputations in a corporate context (Ahmad and Schroeder, 2003; Alshallah, 2004; Alvesson et al., 2011; Amos et al., 2008; Anckar et al., 2002). The first option is to establish a board or oversight committee which monitors and evaluates the ways in which the reputation of the organization is maintained. Having a good reputation is not enough. You must take positive steps to ensure that the good reputation you have is maintained. The members of the oversight committee help supervise sensitive activities that take place in the organization. This is particularly important if the activities are likely to attract adverse media attention. Media is an instrumentality for building and maintaining a good reputation. For example, companies May release information strategically at times when they are and the pressure due to suppress negative rumors about the organization.

The reputation management framework should be fully integrated into the operations of the organization (Singh and Masuku, 2014; Singh et al., 2016; Slack et al., 2006; Songa et al., 2012; Sparrow and Makram, 2015). In fact, the strategic plan of the organization should detail the ways in which the reputation of the organization will be maintained. Planning is an important aid in reputation management. The planning may take the form of risk assessment and the preparation of contingency plans. Certain organizations have been able to survive some of the worst publicity nightmares through careful planning. They can do this because they have the right people who are trained and fully supported. Invest in the structures that build and maintain your reputation as an organization or brand.

Chapter 6 Summary

This chapter has explored some of the common problems that organizations face. These include uncertainty, regulation, human resources, technology, big data, and reputational risks. In doing so, the chapter has suggested some ways in which these problems can be overcome using insights into the classic problem-solving processes. The penultimate chapter of this book will consider the general problem solver paradigm as a continuation in the harnessing of competencies in this area of management practice.

CHAPTER 7

THE GENERAL PROBLEM SOLVER PARADIGM

CONTENTS

This chapter is preoccupied with the general problem-solver paradigm. We will briefly explore the work of Newell and Simon before moving on to review a means-ends analysis. The chapter will define the problem space and its implications. We will explore how subgoals can be identified and satisfied. Additionally, the chapter will explore the merits and demerits of relying on heuristics. The work of Newell and Simon on problem-solving is a good starting point for this chapter.

7.1. INTRODUCTION TO THE WORK OF NEWELL AND SIMON

Newell and Simon (1972) were critical voices in the development of the construct of a General Problem Solver. It is based on an information-processing paradigm that helps us to better understand how organizational problems are resolved. There are other associated concepts, such as the problem space and the means-ends-analysis, which have been included in the description of this model. The General Problem Solver framework involves the identification of certain subgoals, which are then satisfied using selected methods. This paradigm has been closely associated with the use of heuristics to satisfy the subgoals that have been identified. The model is summarized in Figure 7.1. Under this model, there is a mental representation of the problem situation, which includes knowledge, experience, and environment before defining the problem, identifying goals, setting criteria for solutions, search for solutions, and settle on specific solutions.

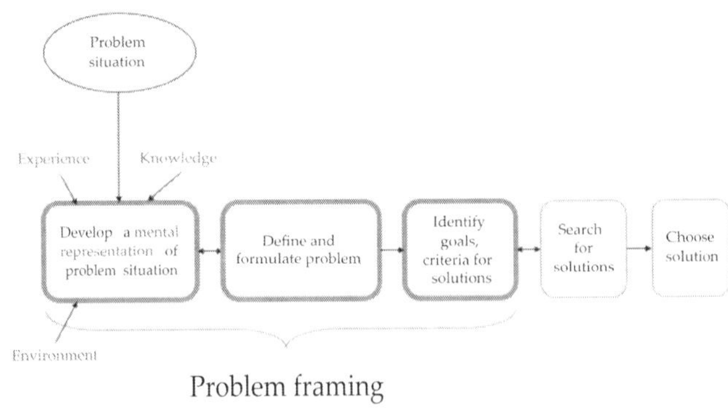

Figure 7.1. The theory of problem-framing.

Source: Pearce and Ejderyan (2020).

Psychologists have been involved in the development of modalities for understanding and resolving problems (Leung et al., 2015; Li, 2009; Li et al., 2006, 2013; Lock, 2007; Loorbach, 2010; Lorenzo-Romero et al., 2013). A case in point is Wertheimer who was part of the Gestalt school. He conducted research on the structures of a problem and the modalities for solving it. The problem has different parts that also have relationships with each other. According to DeBono, a fresh perspective is of the essence when trying to understand a problem. These theories are complemented by the work of Schoenfeld who presents a mathematical approach to problem-solving that comprises a quartet of aspects. The first are the resources. The second comprises heuristics. The third relates to control. The fourth relates to beliefs. Whereas this framework is specifically geared towards mathematical problems, it can also have relevance to other spheres of life. Indeed, Bransford seems to borrow some ideas for this model in an approach that makes use of hypermedia as anchored in instructional theory.

It is notable that problem-solving skills are closely related to other aspects of cognition (Cox, 1999; Crane, 2013; Crawford, 2016; Cunniff and Mostert, 2012; Cunningham, 2011; D'Ippolito and Timpano, 2016). Examples include the use of schema which refers to the ability to remember similar problems. Another area of relation is that of pattern recognition which allows people to recall how similar problems have occurred in the past. Furthermore, the problem-solver may go beyond recognizing similar patterns and develop new solutions to problems. In other words, the problem is linked and related to previous problems so that it provides a foundation for finding the solution to the current problem.

All these problem-solving paradigms require an ability to transfer competencies from previous problem-solving process to current problem situations (Le, 2017; Leary, 2001; Lee and Park, 2009; Leggett, 2007; Lengnick-Hall et al., 2009; Leuenberger, 2006). There will be many factors that determine the possibility of transfer. For instance, the similarity of the problem itself and circumstances can make it easier to learn the lessons of the past. If there is a marked difference between the two situations, it becomes difficult to make them relatable to each other. That means that the problem-solver must start afresh with a new perspective. Of course, there is also the problem of potentially trying to identify similarities that do not exist. If the two problems (past and present) are markedly different, it makes sense that the solution should be different also.

By intimately understanding the processes through which problems have been resolved in the past, it is possible to provide training to professional that are dealing with problems in the present and the future (Ahimbisibwe and Nkundabanyanga, 2016; Ahmad and Schroeder, 2003; Alshallah, 2004; Alvesson et al., 2011). This is the foundation of pedagogy in management science. Current managers learn from the models that were used in the past and will hopefully improve them to make them more relevant to the problems that they are facing today. Nevertheless, being able to resolve problems is a fundamental management competency. The organization should never recruit people that have difficulties resolving problems. However, that does not mean that the organization is not under any obligation to provide training and support for new managers that are learning the intricacies of their craft. You can build your team by understanding its limitations and then using training to bring them up to the level that is necessary to achieve the goals of the organization.

The problem-solving process is linked to the workings of the human brain (Lycett et al., 2004; Maneesh et al., 2009; Manzoor, 2011; Matías-Reche et al., 2009; McGill and Wooten, 1975). Hence, models such as the one presented in Figure 7.2 have been used to simulate how thinking resolves problems. At the heart of the model are elementary information processes that are surrounded by the human problem-solving behavior, the general problem solver, computer hardware, and a nervous system. Organizations are therefore called upon to solve problems using the same modalities as the one deployed by the human brain.

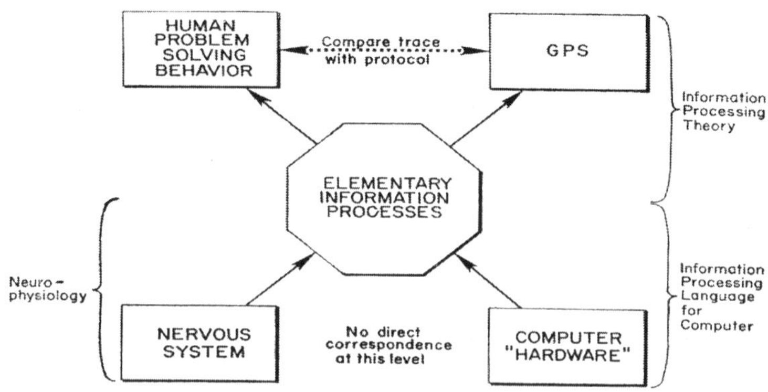

Fig. 1. Levels in an information processing theory of human thinking.

Newell, A., & Simon, H. A. (1961). Computer Simulation of Human Thinking. *Science*, *134*(3495), 2011-2017. (p. 2013)

Figure 7.2. Computer simulation of human thinking.

Source: Newell and Simon (1961) via on Writer-ing.

This is an interdisciplinary and multidisciplinary endeavor because the rain applicability across the various subject areas (BIS, 2015; Baker and Esherick, 2013; Bannò and Sgobbi, 2016; Barry et al., 2000; Bekker, 2014; Bell et al., 2011). For example, the problem-solving paradigm is related to a computer program. Yet, its principles are applied in management styles and the art of leading people. The program was created in 1959 and is different from the Logic Theorist project. The General Problem Solver has been widely adopted by organizations. It starts off by expressing a problem as a set of well-formed formulas or WFFs. These are also known as Horn Clauses.

The formulas are then constituted into a directed graph that has more than one source. These are known as axioms and sinks. Sinks are the desired conclusion. In principle, the axioms and sinks can be resolved by the General Problem Solver. The proofs are to be found in the predicate logic as well as the Euclidean geometry problem space. Hence, one can identify prime examples of the domains during the applicability of the General Problem Solver. It is notable that this was the first computer program to separate knowledge of problems from the strategy used to solve problems. The knowledge of problems is presented in the form of input data while the strategy is presented as the generic solver engine. So successful was the paradigm that it was implemented in the third-order programming language or IPL.

The general Problem Solver has been used to deal with issues such as the Towers of Hanoi. These were relatively simple problems that could be reduced to formulas. However, critics have argued that it is not capable of solving real-world problems. Organizations face problems that are more complex than a mathematical challenge (Brandsen and Pestoff, 2006; Bruce and Daly, 2006; Calabrese, 1997; Capko, 2003; Carraher, 2013; Chang et al., 2006). A combinatorial explosion meant that the search for solutions to real world problems was inevitably lost. Hence, the number of walks through the diagram was eventually untenable in computational terms. Others have argued that the prunings of the state space (such as in the Towers of Hanoi) can be improved using elementary Artificial Intelligence techniques. This requires a more detailed understanding of means-ends analysis.

7.2. MEANS-ENDS-ANALYSIS

Means-ends analysis has been mentioned as one of the more technical problem-solving strategies that can be used by organizations (Odrakiewicz, 2012; Okotoni and Erero, 2005; Onyx and Maclean, 1996; Ozturk and Rumens, 2014; Papasolomou and Melanthiou, 2012). It is part of the theories that were developed by Newell and Simon (1972). Under this paradigm, the problem is resolved by considering any obstacles that stand between the initial problem state and the desirable goal state. In other words, the problem-solver is looking for the things that prevent them from achieving the ideal solution where the problem has been eliminated or completely resolved. The elimination of these obstacles is known as sub-goals in the problem-solving process. It is arguable that the sub-goals are easier to achieve than the main goal; hence it makes sense to begin with them.

This type of analysis is not just concerned with the elimination of the obstacles but also the process through which they are eliminated (Bannò and Sgobbi, 2016; Barry et al., 2000; Bekker, 2014; Bell et al., 2011; Bercu, 2012; Bernini and Cracolici, 2015). Once all the sub-goals have been achieved, there is virtually no obstacle to resolving the problem. It is a much simpler approach than attacking the problem in its entirety at once. This analysis has been considered a search for solutions in an indirect way. Perhaps the word "solution" is not an accurate reflection of the procedure. A more accurate description would be a search for strategy. The long-term goal is kept in mind to guide to the problem solver. However, the decision-maker is expected to occupy themselves with the sub-goals in the interim. This strategy is not nearsighted and is demonstrably different from the more short-term solutions such as using the hill climbing technique. Figure 7.3 is a graphical demonstration of this process in action.

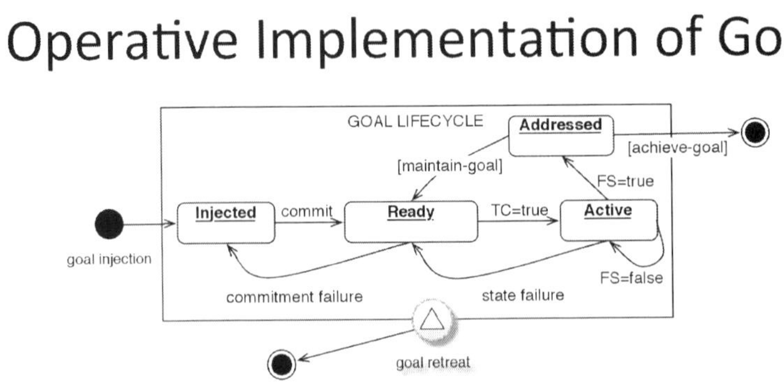

Figure 7.3. Operative implementation of goals.

Source: Sabatucci and Cossentino (2015).

Some philosophers have argued that the means-ends analysis technique is akin to the divide and conquer approach to solving problems (Harris and Brown, 1998; Harrison and Lock, 2004; Hartmann, 2014; Haworth and Hughes, 2015; Hennigs et al., 2013). Once the problem has been divided into its constituent parts or obstacles, it becomes easier to resolve it on a gradual basis. Along the way, the problem solver will learn valuable lessons that they can apply to future circumstances. We can also accurately map the ways in which decision-makers have resolved the problems by breaking it down into a series of smaller goals. This can be very useful when working with heuristics. However, there is a difference between means-ends analysis and the divide and conquer strategy. For example, the former is less obviously recursive whilst the latter is almost always visibly recursive.

In that way, means-ends analysis is the more flexible option (Anwar and Sun, 2013; Anyim et al., 2011; Arbulú et al., 2015; Argenti, 1996; Arthur and Dworkin, 1991; Ashton et al., 2010). Hence, this method has the advantage of acknowledging and embracing the nonlinearity of problems and their resolution. This can be a useful tool when dealing with a complex market that does not readily deal with formulaic resolutions. The organization can easily cope with the stop and start aspects of the problem resolving process if they rely on means-ends analysis. As for the employee that is dealing with the problem, means ends analysis is a relatively easy option because it does not put excessive pressure on them to resolve issues in a limited time frame. The employee can deal with complexity without feeling as if they are letting the organization down by taking their time.

The use of means-ends analysis has human resource management implications (Priola et al., 2014; Rasim, 2008; Rose Ragins, 2004; Rosenthal, 2013; Rosser and Eccleston, 2011; Saenz and Pérez-Bouvier, 2014). For example, it offers flexibility when handling problems that are complex. The pressure to always perform on time is markedly reduced. However, that reality also calls for a sophisticated approach to performance management. Specifically, the supervisor should not blame the problem solver for the non-linearity of the issues they are dealing with. The implication is that supervisors must be trained in the approach so that they are aware of its merits and demerits. It is an investment in the long-term future of the organization and its ability to resolve problems efficiently. As Figure 7.4 shows, heuristics, and strategy are key aspects of the means-ends analysis technique.

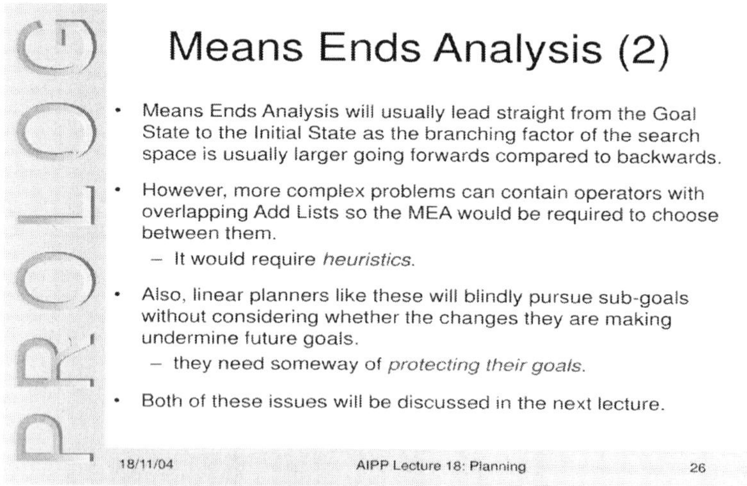

Figure 7.4. Summary of means-ends analysis.

Source: Klarika Farkas (2019) via Slide Serve.

It is important to note that means-ends analysis is a technique that is popular in artificial intelligence programs (Baker and Esherick, 2013; Bannò and Sgobbi, 2016; Barry et al., 2000; Bekker, 2014; Bell et al., 2011; Bercu, 2012). However, this does not detract from its wide applicability through association. The key take-home for managers is the process and requirements of the problem-solving process. This is a technique that has paved the way for more use of artificial intelligence in operations. Moreover, the means-ends analysis can limit some of the demerits of artificial intelligence. Hence, means-ends analysis could be useful for organizations that are dealing with a post-pandemic reality in which efficiency is of the essence. Since the 1950s, means-ends analysis 4has been used as a creativity tool. This allows for organizations to imagi4natively deal with problems rather than being effectively imprisoned by dogmatic models. Means-ends analysis is commonly associated with higher level engineering and design. However, it can also be used with other businesses and sectors. Indeed, means-ends analysis is very similar to the means-ends chain approach which is prevalent in consumer behavior analysis. Its systematic approach has relevance to public sector organizations that are looking for efficiency in their operations.

Some argue that means-ends analysis is one of the key approaches to clarifying thoughts when engaging in mathematical proofs (Songa et al., 2012; Sparrow and Makram, 2015; Speer and Potter, 2000; Steers et al., 2004; Stevens, 2002; Stewart and Walsh, 1992). Using this paradigm means that problem solving becomes a search for strategy. It is the kind of intelligent behavior that underpins the efforts by artificial intelligence to mimic the capabilities of a human. Artificial intelligence is a goal-based and goal-driven problem-solving process. Means-ends analysis develops the framework of problem-solving through which the sequences of solving the sub-goals in a problem situation can be satisfied. In doing so, there must be an understanding of the problem space and its implications.

7.3. THE PROBLEM SPACE

The problem space is complemented by the solution space in the process of resolving issues in the organization (Rosser and Eccleston, 2011; Saenz and Pérez-Bouvier, 2014; Saji and Ellingstad, 2004; Sakuramoto, 2005; Samah et al., 2013). Accordingly, the problem space comprises everything that is associated with the problem including its history and the stakeholders that are affected. It is important to remember that the stakeholders can include people who benefit from the problem and people who are negatively affected by the problem. For example, problems that are beneficial to certain groups may not be easily resolved because those interest groups ensure that the problem remains. A case in point is where a shortage of staff members results in overtime being paid. The people that are receiving overtime will be reluctant to close the recruitment gap. The person that is resolving the problem must be aware of this interest group because it can significantly impact on the processes through which the problem is resolved. Figure 7.5 is an example of the design of a problem space for a collaborative work environment.

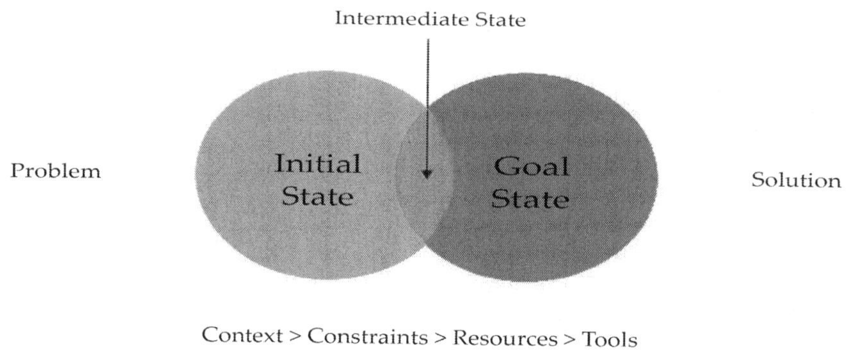

Figure 7.5. Designing a problem space for a collaborative work environment.

Source: Wikiversity.

It is also important to understand that there are people who contribute to the problem (Ashton et al., 2010; Assink, 2006; Atkinson and Brander Brown, 2001; Atwal and Williams, 2009; Awadh and Saad, 2013). The resolution must address this group of stakeholders since they are a key driver of the issues. Unless there is a transformation in their perception or behavior, the problem is going to be difficult to resolve. This goes back to the need to understand the problem fully and clearly from its Inception and the effect that it has on the organization. The history of the problem might offer clues as to the solution to that problem. For example, the lack of financing for specific projects may emanate from the acceptance of additional projects that are not fully funded. If the decision maker understands this history, they will untangle the funding process for the original project to allow the budget more room to breathe. Ignoring the history of a problem in an organization can be disadvantageous because it closes of some of the sources of potential solutions.

Another group of stakeholders within the problem space are those people that are impacted negatively to a higher degree than other members of the organization (Thursfield and Grayley, 2016; Toner, 2015; Too and Weaver, 2014; Torre Edoardo and Luca, 2013; Turyakira, 2018a). Members of the team or different teams may display a range of divergent responses to the problem. Indeed, this can be a question of the extent to which different people have resilience in their responses to the problem. All the individuals or teams will have coping mechanisms that allow them to mount a resistance or an acceptance to the problem in ways that do not disrupt operations. The decision-maker must be aware of these differential effects because they will determine the prioritization and organization of the problem-solving process. One of the criticisms of homogenous solutions is that they do not fully acknowledge the diversity in experiences of the organizational problem. This has been a criticism that has even reached developmental economics as a case in point. For example, funding during pandemics does not necessarily reflect need meaning that the more advanced economies enjoy an exponential advantage in their ability to respond.

The problem space is often closely associated with the design environment in which there are various products or ideas that must be turned into services and products for the market (Leuenberger, 2006; Leung et al., 2015; Li, 2009; Li et al., 2006, 2013; Lock, 2007; Loorbach, 2010). In that sense, the activities of the organization are meant to involve solving problems regardless of whether those problems are organizational or whether they relate to the needs of customers. The organization should get into the habit of resolving problems and learning from the process of resolving problems. In addition, there must be certain protocols for identifying challenges and potentially developing creative solutions to those challenges. This is the proverbial learning organization that has been spoken of in academic discourses. Ideally, the problem-solving process should be deliberate and part of the operations of the organization rather than merely firefighting.

Where the problem-solving process has been integrated into the operations of the organization, there is room for creativity. The organization may even market its problem-solving process. Far too often, organizations are preoccupied with problems emanating from the customer base as opposed to dealing with internal issue. A preferable option is to be proactive about problem-solving. Figure 7.6 demonstrates a proactive approach to linking the problem space to the solution space. This is the type of approach that creates organizations that are resilient and continuously developing.

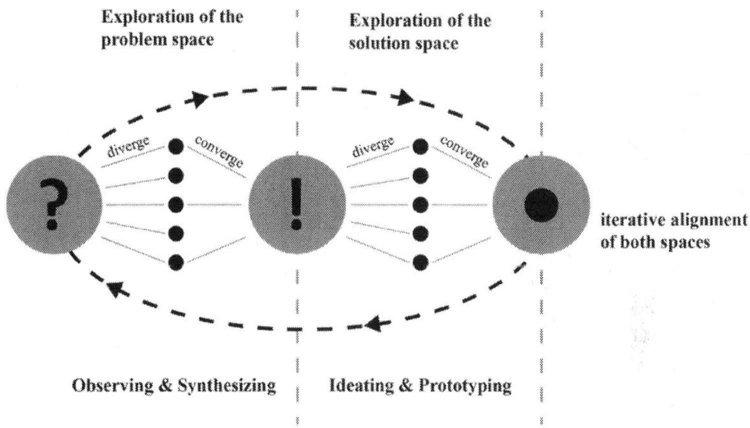

Figure 7.6. Problem and solution space in design thinking.

Source: Adikari, McDonald, and Lynch (2007).

The development of priorities is meant to reflect the needs of various segments of the organization including teams and workers (Steers et al., 2004; Stevens, 2002; Stewart and Walsh, 1992; Stone et al., 2015; Stoorvogel et al., 2017). Ideally, you should be paying a lot of attention to those people and teams that are adversely affected by the problem. Of course, the organization may have its own priorities in terms of the teams that must be allowed to operate regardless of any problems are taking place. For example, the hospital might determine that the emergency room must remain open and function regardless of any financial difficulties that are being faced. Indeed, this might be true even where the financial problems are a direct result of mismanagement in the accident and emergency department. To avoid demotivating teams and individuals, the justification for decisions must be clear and rational.

Once the problem space has been identified, the decision-makers should give consideration to identifying and responding to the solution space (Patiar and Mia, 2009; Pavlatos and Paggios, 2009a, b; Peng and Huiling Chen, 2011; Phillips and Gully, 2014). It is not enough to speak about the problems and their impact without taking into consideration the possibilities resolving those problems. Resolutions allow the organization to move forward, and the solution space provides the right opportunities for that to happen. The solution space typically constitutes the world of services, products, and policies that can be introduced to deal with the issues that are raised in the organization. These solutions are directly linked to the problem and its consequences. In that way, the decision-maker is not distracted by the general ecology within which the organization is operating.

If a problem is going to be resolved satisfactorily, the solution must be linked to the problem space (Huselid, 1995; Ibrahim and Zailani, 2010; Ichniowski et al., 1997; Ifinedo, 2016; Ismail et al., 2005; Jansen et al., 2008). This is a practical endeavor that requires an understanding of the environment within which the organization operates. When we speak of the environment in this instance, we are speaking of a combination of the internal environment and the external environment. In other words, the problem solver must identify where the problem is coming from and the potential sources of the solutions to the problem. Linking these two spaces is a management practice and competency. Where the problem is resolved effectively, there will be limited disruption in the operations of an organization. However, if the link is not handled in a professional and effective, there will be a lot of disruption, which might render the solution unacceptable. Obviously, the decision-maker should engage in cost-benefit analysis, which then becomes the justification for whatever decision that has been taken. The identification of sub-goals is a crucial facet of this process.

7.4. THE IDENTIFICATION OF SUBGOALS

The identification and labeling of subgoals in a problem-solving situation are critical because it opens possibilities of resolving the problem in a more effective manner (Jian Wang et al., 2010; John et al., 2014; Johnson and Clark, 2008; Jurevicius, 2016; Kabene et al., 2006; Kasperk et al., 2011).

First, it allows the decision-maker to break down the problem into parts that are easier to manage when compared to the whole of the problem. This will increase the chances of success when handling complex problems that require sophisticated solutions. Figure 7.7 graphically demonstrates the decompression of goals and sub-goals when solving problems.

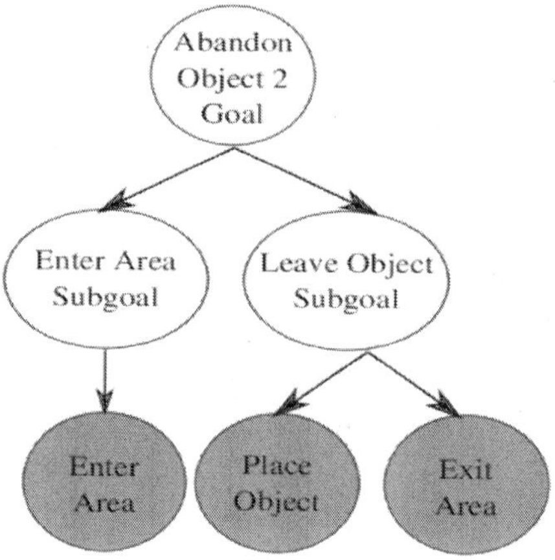

Figure 7.7. Hierarchically decomposing goal behaviors into subgoals and activities.

Source: Baxter (2012).

Once the sub-goals have been identified, the decision-maker should try to label them (Chen et al., 2011; Chevalier and Mazzalovo, 2008; Chung, 2015; Clegg and Palmer, 1996; Cold Cafe, 2018; Cole and Dawson, 2010). The label includes a series of steps that will be followed when resolving each of the sub-problems that are identified. The step-by-step description will be useful for reviewing the management of the process. There should be an explanation as to how the various steps are related to each other and how they support the achievement of the overall main goal of the organization. Such an approach forces the decision-maker to be more analytical in their engagement with the problem space and solution space. Otherwise, they would be reduced to merely apply models and theories that are not relevant to the problem.

The identification and labeling of a sub-goal has been used in psychology and other fields that support the resolution of problems (Arbulú et al., 2015; Argenti, 1996; Arthur and Dworkin, 1991; Ashton et al., 2010; Assink, 2006; Atkinson and Brander Brown, 2001). For example, it is an inherent paradigm in educational psychology as well as cognitive science. There may be a hierarchy of some goals which are identified and organized into patterns that are easier to follow when solving organizational problems. The lower levels or states will be consolidated into a narrative. This narrative comprises of grouped meanings and issues that can be resolved as a strand. Figure 7.8 is an example of the hierarchical breakdown of sub goals.

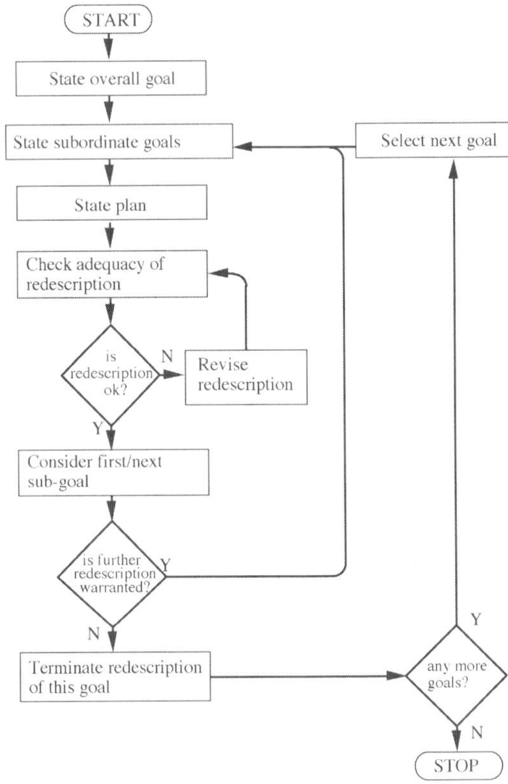

Figure 7.8. Procedure for breaking down the sub-goal hierarch.

Source: Stanton (2006).

For some organizations, dealing with problems in strands is more efficient because they can avoid the risk of duplication. However, the strands should be well-organized so that they do not miss pertinent issues. Organizations that are departmentalize will find it easier to deal with this type of problem-solving approach (Li et al., 2006, 2013; Lock, 2007; Loorbach, 2010; Lorenzo-Romero et al., 2013; Loundes, 2001; Lycett et al., 2004).

This is because of the power of division of labor which has already been recommended as a critical determinant of efficiency. The rationale is that division of labor allows for specialization, which in turn builds expertise in specific aspects of a task or problem-solving process. Each of the relevant teams or individuals will be granted leeway to perform certain tasks that contribute to the overall resolution of the problem. These groupings may be linked to the hierarchy of the organization; they could be implemented as a stopgap during the problem-solving process.

When subgoals are labeled and accurately identified, it helps the decision-maker to identify the structure information that is necessary to accomplish the task of resolving the problem (Hunter and Katz, 2012; Huselid, 1995; Ibrahim and Zailani, 2010; Ichniowski et al., 1997; Ifinedo, 2016; Ismail et al., 2005). That structure information is differentiated from the incidental information that may not be relevant to the management of the problem. In other words, the creation of sub-goals helps in reducing the cognitive load for the individuals and teams that are finding ways of creatively resolving problems. Additionally, this type of activity can provide a decision-maker with a momentum of the framework that they can rely on when dealing with the issues that emanate from the problem. In fact, this approach has been used in pedagogy even at the lowest levels of learning. The implication is that simple and effective.

The procedural approach to problem-solving, which is the default for many organizations, may not offer this kind of detailed breakdown of the issues surrounding the problem (Saenz and Pérez-Bouvier, 2014; Saji and Ellingstad, 2004; Sakuramoto, 2005; Samah et al., 2013; Schlögl, 2005). However, the labeling of subgoals can also be incorporated into the procedures that are used when solving problems. Indeed, it may not necessarily affect the chronology within which the problem is being addressed. However, the decision-maker should prioritize the areas of the structures within the organization that are most likely to provide the most significant impact on the problem. The overarching goal remains the operational effectiveness of the organization without being hindered by obstacles and other organizational problems. The final section of this chapter will consider the use of heuristics in decision-making.

7.5. USE OF METHODS INCLUDING HEURISTICS TO SATISFY SUBGOALS

Heuristics have been referenced throughout the course of this book because they are relevant to different problem-solving strategies that are adopted by organizations in a range of circumstances (Farndale et al., 2008; Fetscherin and Heinrich, 2014; Finkelstein et al., 2007; Gil-Pareja et al., 2007; Gruman and Saks, 2011). We all like to learn from the past and apply the lessons of the past to our present, as well as towards predicting the future. However, relying excessively on the past and misinterpreting the information from the past can be problematic when solving problems that are markedly different from the ones that we experienced before. The trick is being able to differentiate between problems and learn the right lessons that must be acquired; whilst ensuring that one is creative as they resolve problems that are in their present and in their future. The heuristic method is summarized in Figure 7.9.

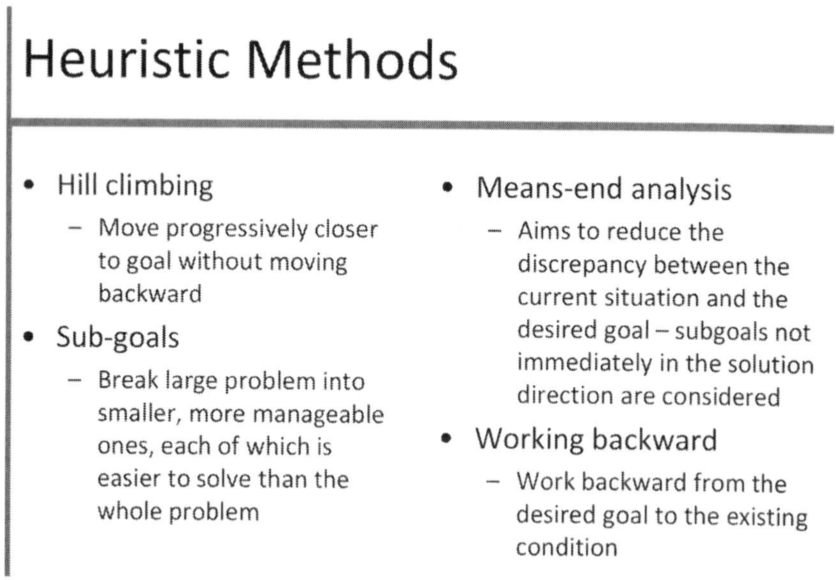

Figure 7.9. Summary of heuristic methods.

Source: Phillip Nicholson via Slide Player.

The notion of heuristics is quite ancient (Atkinson and Brander Brown, 2001; Atwal and Williams, 2009; Awadh and Saad, 2013; BIS, 2015). For example, the term has been associated with Greek traditions and classic philosophy. The heuristic technique relies on solving problems through self-discovery and exploration. It is essentially a practical method that might not be optimal in its outcome. However, many turn to it in times of need when they do not have access to many alternatives. Heuristics generally do not pretend to be perfect or even rational. Nevertheless, they are useful for reaching an immediate or short-term goal when resolving problems. This approach relies on approximation, whilst some organizations prefer accuracy. There might be some disagreement about the appropriateness of heuristics when solving organizational problems if accuracy is of the essence.

At other times, the heuristic is used as the second-best option when there is no practical possibility of resolving the problem in the short term (McGill and Wooten, 1975; Memili and Welsh, 2012; Menke et al., 2007; Meyer-Sahling et al., 2018; Mia and Patiar, 2001). The heuristic is therefore used to speed up the process and reach an emergency conclusion that can prevent the problem from becoming a crisis. Some critics have argued that heuristics are nothing more than mental shortcuts and will necessarily not provide the kind of problem-solving prowess that would occur in alternative methodologies. One of the benefits of using heuristics nevertheless is that they reduce the cognitive load associated with resolving problems. That means that the organization or individual can remain largely functional despite the problem. They can also be useful for newly appointed or inexperienced managers. Figure 7.10 is an example of how independent sub-goals can be organized so that they can be resolved using heuristics.

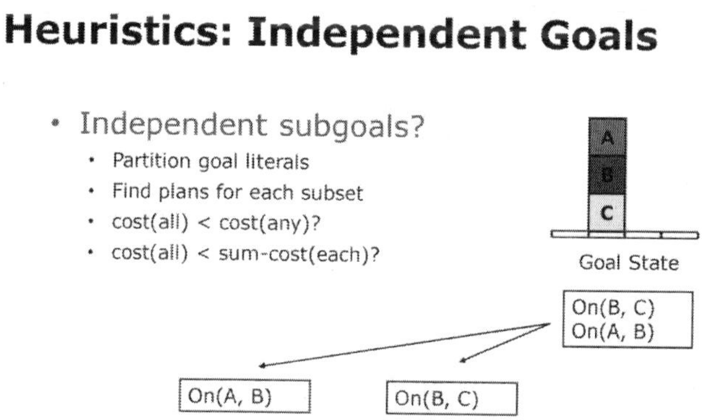

Figure 7.10. Using heuristics to satisfy independent subgoals.

Source: Felicia Houston via Slide Player.

Although not many people would admit to using heuristics in their day-to-day lines; the reality is that heuristics are an integral part of social life (Li, 2009; Li et al., 2006, 2013; Lock, 2007; Loorbach, 2010; Lorenzo-Romero et al., 2013; Loundes, 2001). For example, heuristics are used when adopting a trial-and-error approach to the problem. Here, there is no definite conclusion or answer. Instead, the decision-maker is looking to experiment with variables in the environment before they can settle on one that seems to work best. Of course, the availability of resources such as time will be a significant consideration before one can use heuristics in a professional context. Besides, the owners of the organization or a designated supervisor may not have a lot of confidence in an approach that is based on trial and error. However, it must be acknowledged that many of the scientific discoveries that we enjoy today are a result of experimentation. Therefore, it would be a mistake to completely ignore the role of experimentation in solving organizational problems.

Additionally, the decision-maker must be wary of the imprecise notion of heuristics and the reliance on anecdotal evidence (Kerzner, 2003; Khan et al., 2011; King et al., 2000; Klikauer, 2014; Kluike, 2015; de Kok et al., 2006; Korczynski, 2002). A case in is the reliance on evidence that is acquired through the usage of a rule of thumb. It sounds comforting to think of a rule of thumb that provides solutions that are basic. However, the problems that organizations must deal with on a regular basis are not always simplistic. There is an implicit requirement for sophistication when dealing with issues that pertain to the management of an organization. Heuristics are oversimplifications of situations that can be quite complex indeed.

Another modality that is used in heuristics is the educated guess (Ifinedo, 2016; Ismail et al., 2005; Jansen et al., 2008; Jian Wang et al., 2010; John et al., 2014; Johnson and Clark, 2008). Once again, the experienced decision-maker can refer to their knowledge and experiences to make a decision about the current situation. There is an expectation that the decision-maker who is relying on heuristics will have a good working memory. Additionally, there is an assumption that this decision-maker will be able to relate information from past events to the current circumstances in ways that are not entirely biased. This calls for a sense of judgment and a significant amount of experience in dealing with problems so that the heuristics do not become a reflection of bad practices in the past.

Chapter 7 Summary

This chapter has briefly explored the notion of a general problem solver, which is gleaned from mathematics and information science. We have specifically highlighted some of the key aspects of the work that was done by Newell and Simon. Some of the emerging concepts included means-ends analysis, the problem space, the solution space, the identification of sub-goals, and the use of heuristics in the problem-solving process. Chapter 8 will close this book by considering the elements of the Schoefield model of problem-solving.

CHAPTER 8

THE SCHOENFELD MODEL OF PROBLEM-SOLVING

CONTENTS

The Schoenfeld model of problem-solving offers an opportunity to revisit many of the issues that have been discussed in Chapter 7. It considers the role of resources, heuristics, control, beliefs, cognition, schema, pattern recognition, and creativity. Many of the issues that will be discussed in this chapter are reiterations of concepts that were introduced earlier. This chapter, therefore, aims to demonstrate the applicability of the problem-solving process in a range of situations. Let us open the chapter by exploring the role of resources when solving problems.

8.1. RESOURCES IN PROBLEM-SOLVING

Organizational resources play an important role in the problem-solving process (Cold Cafe, 2018; Cole and Dawson, 2010; Collinson and Hearn, 1994; Connell et al., 2009; Cooke, 2003; Cox et al., 2021). Indeed, some managers are so convinced about the importance of quick results that they fail to recognize the full extent of the problems that the organization is facing. These are the managers that inject resources into a problem in the hope that they can resolve it. The primary role of resources in the problem-solving process is that they are an instrumentality in achieving a goal that has been set by the organization. Because the organizational problem is one which hinders the achievement of this goal, resources are the ideal pathway towards addressing these problems. The organization will utilize different resources to accomplish its goal depending on the context and the demands of the task at hand. The proper allocation of resources is a performance management issue and should be taken seriously by managers and leaders.

The typical organization will have several resources that are available to resolve problems or achieve the strategic goals (Argenti, 1996; Arthur and Dworkin, 1991; Ashton et al., 2010; Assink, 2006; Atkinson and Brander Brown, 2001). The first and perhaps most important resource is the human resource. People make an organization, and an organization contributes to the formation of the personalities, perspectives, and behavior of people. Organizations are routinely advised to invest heavily in human resources. That investment is guided by human resource management as a specialization. Another major resource that is available to the organization is financial resources. The finances of an organization can determine whether it survives or is it closed. In fact, one of the criteria for deciding that an organization is no longer functional is where its financial resources can no longer cover its liabilities. This is when the organization can be declared bankrupt and a process of winding it down commences. Understandably, organizations invest a lot of time and expertise in ensuring that their finances are in proper order. The accountancy team will play an important role in reminding the organization of its financial responsibilities and highlighting potential problems. An organization may have physical resources like buildings and materials which are used for the production process (Haworth and Hughes, 2015; Hennigs et al., 2013; Hermansson, 2020; Hopkin et al., 1979; Hunter and Katz, 2012). This can be a variable input and will require significant investment for the organization to start operating. The physical resources can undergo a process of depreciation in value with time. In fact, the accountancy team will account for depreciation as part of its management of the deterioration in the value of these physical assets. Besides, the organization must take steps to ensure that the physical assets are kept in good working order. Research has shown that organizations which do not look after their physical assets or protect them may find that they can no longer operate because the physical resources become so depreciated that they can no longer significantly contribute to the productive process. Of course, this could also be a purchasing issue where the organization should aim to acquire physical assets that are of the highest quality possible. Planning and problem-solving in an organization (see Figure 8.1) must incorporate the acquisition and use of all the resources available to it, including physical assets. These are typically placed in the tools that are used for dealing with a problem.

Figure 8.1. Role of robust planning in problem-solving.

Source: Jakubik and Kagan (2015) via Planet Lean.

The organization may also be endowed with information resources (DyReyes, 2008; Egan, 2009; Egloff and Bhalla, 2014; Evans, 2005; Farndale et al., 2008; Fetscherin and Heinrich, 2014). We live in an age where information is power. The internet has allowed organizations to gather significant amount of data. However, data is not as important as information because it is not yet processed. The organization must prepare systems and procedures to ensure that it can require the most relevant information for any situation. This is particularly important if the situation becomes problematic. That information is then applied in the problem-solving process. The quality of the information that the organization uses to make decisions has a profound impact on its success in the market. This is particularly important if there are competitors that have the same information or even a better quality of information. Hence, the organizations that has high-quality information have a greater chance of success than those that rely on poor-quality information.

The leadership and management team within the organization will be responsible for identifying, collecting, protecting, and deploying various resources towards the achievement of the strategic goals within the organization (Mujeeb and Ahmad, 2011; Nagalakhmi and Trivedi, 2015; Nagasawa and Fukunaga, 2015; Najam, 2000; Nath, 2011). This is the very essence of management practice. The term management can be understood and utilized in different ways. Some researchers suggest that management is the art of getting things done through people. This definition is an acknowledgment of the centrality of human resources in the accomplishment of strategic goals. Management operates within a context that is complex and perhaps nonlinear. That means that management must be both an art and a science. There are qualitative and quantitative aspects of management. Neither can be ignored if a manager is going to be successful. Managers are responsible for giving direction to the organization and providing leadership to the various operational units that are under their control so that the achievement of organizational goals is as effective as possible. Management is defined by its procedures, values, and outcomes. The organization can only tell whether a manager is effective depending on the ability of their teams to achieve certain organizational objectives and hence contribute to the sustainability of the organization.

There is a hierarchy of responsibilities in management practices which emanates from the various professionals that have contributed to this field of study (Chen et al., 2011; Chevalier and Mazzalovo, 2008; Chung, 2015; Clegg and Palmer, 1996; Cold Cafe, 2018). For example, there is leadership at the top which provides directive or consultative support to the organization in terms of developing a vision. Leaders do not necessarily become engaged in the day-to-day running of the organization. In fact, there are situations where frontline members of staff may never meet the leader at all. However, the modern and flatter organizational structures that are currently popular tend to encourage leaders to engage with all parts of the organization. There is less emphasis on different hierarchical protocols or silos and more emphasis on achievement through collaboration. This is the modality of co-production which has become very important for contemporary organizations.

In effect, the modern manager has been given the responsibility of directing resources to specific activities that achieve strategic goals, yet they must do this in a way that is supportive of the entire staff team (Haworth and Hughes, 2015; Hennigs et al., 2013; Hermansson, 2020; Hopkin et al., 1979; Hunter and Katz, 2012). The traditional organizations do not allow managers to create a vision. Instead, managers are required to implement the vision. However, the flatter management structures have allowed certain managers to contribute towards the development of the organizational vision or mission settlement. This is designed to allow for an exchange of information and to prevent the leadership from being completely isolated from what is happening on the ground. It seems that the more modern an organization is, the less likely it is to be imprisoned by the strict rigidity of traditional hierarchical structures. These changes reflect the modern preference for an egalitarian approach that treats all people with dignity. Whereas the traditional manager was judged depending on their ability to command obedience, if not respect; the modern manager is judged on their ability to bring people together towards the achievement of organizational goals. Both types of management style may reach the same destination, but they have different styles. In any case, regardless of the style that is eventually adopted by the organization; issues of protecting and strategically deploying resources remain of paramount importance.

Below the manager there is a supervisor, a role which is critical for achieving the targets and objectives of a specific team (Najam, 2000; Nath, 2011; Newell and Simon, 1972; Nica, 2015; Obeidat, 2012; Odrakiewicz, 2012; Okotoni and Erero, 2005). The supervisor is expected to oversee the teams on a day-to-day basis. They are at the front line of management practice and will often be unpopular with members of the team because they are the people that tell them off when they are not accomplishing certain tasks. Unfortunately, some organizations do not provide sufficient support to be supervisor such that they end up firefighting or becoming scapegoats for the mistakes that have been made by the leadership or management team.

This is often the beginning of the insidious blame culture that has destroyed public sector organizations. The supervisor is not a scapegoat or workhorse. They are an integral part of the leadership team and will link the leadership team to the rest of the workforce.

To be effective, the organization must provide supervisors with support and information that allows them to undertake their duties in a responsible and professional manner (Toner, 2015; Too and Weaver, 2014; Torre Edoardo and Luca, 2013; Turyakira, 2018a, b). The role of the supervisor can be challenging when you are dealing with higher-level professionals such as doctors, lawyers, and healthcare workers. These are highly trained professionals who are required to engage in self-management as part of their competencies. They may require management support, but they are less likely to accept supervision from anyone that is not qualified in their field of study. Yes, management has been developed as a profession that is separate from the other professions. We are seeing these challenges in health services when doctors are being asked to become managers, and managers are finding it difficult to supervise doctors. The line between a professional and a manager can become blurred during these contexts. Unfortunately, the failure to clarify the roles may mean that organizational resources and opportunities are consequently wasted.

Managers can be perceived to be the link that drives the agenda that has been set by the leadership team (Awadh and Saad, 2013; BIS, 2015; Baker and Esherick, 2013; Bannò and Sgobbi, 2016; Barry et al., 2000; Bekker, 2014). Hence, managers may contribute to the development of the mission and vision for the organization. Yet, managers are also involved in communicating this mission or vision to the rest of the team. Whereas managers may not supervise their teams on a day-to-day basis, there are ultimately responsible for the outcomes of those teams. Indeed, it can be a disciplinary issue if the manager is unable to produce results. Managers cannot claim that a supervisor has not done their job or that a frontline member of staff is failing to do theirs. It is the job of the manager to inspire and motivate the team to achieve the organization's goals through the effective use of resources. That is why some researchers argue that management involves the attainment organizational goals in an efficient and effective manner through organizing, planning, leading, and controlling the resources that belong to the organization. One of the practice modalities for these roles is where managers utilize resources to solve organizational problems as demonstrated in Figure 8.2.

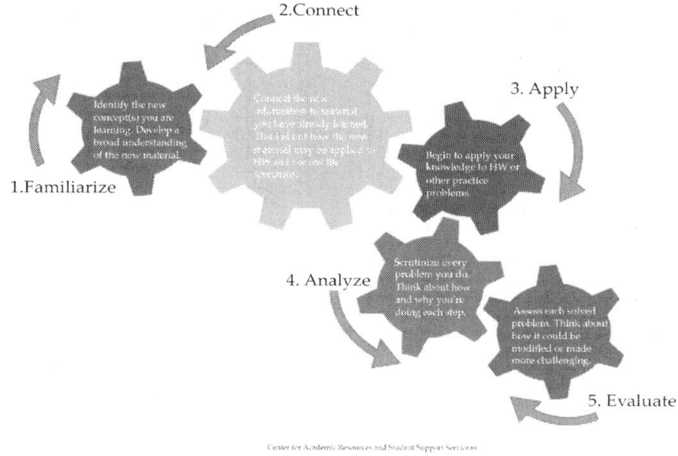

Figure 8.2. Example of a problem-solving strategy.

Source: University of New Hampshire.

Contemporary definitions of management underpin two important ideas about the relationship between management and resources (Leary, 2001; Lee and Park, 2009; Leggett, 2007; Lengnick-Hall et al., 2009; Leuenberger, 2006; Leung et al., 2015). The first idea relates to the four major functions of management which include controlling, leading, organizing, and planning. The second aspect relates to the attainment of goals that have been set within the strategic plan. Perhaps there is also a side element which requires that managers achieve these tasks in ways that are efficient and effective. Modern organizations cannot afford managers that are either wasteful or do not understand the importance of protecting resources. Even the notoriously bloated public sector now requires that managers have a clear understanding of efficiency measures. Indeed, the more senior level manager may be disciplined (including the option of sacking them) for failing to make savings that are identified in the budget. The public can no longer tolerate a wasteful public sector that is not producing results. Hence, the managers within those public sector structures are being asked to behave in much the same way as those in the private sector. Certainly, the protection of resources remains a key priority from a management practice perspective.

Part of the training for a manager is to ensure that they clearly understand the possibilities and limitations of the resources that are available to the organization (Bilson et al., 2013; Bjerregaard, 2011; Black, 2005; Brandsen and Pestoff, 2006; Bruce and Daly, 2006; Calabrese, 1997). The second part of the training will involve attuning the manager to the most efficient ways of utilizing the available resources to achieve the goals that are in the vision and mission statement of the organization that has employed them. This can turn out to be an orientation exercise that embeds the culture of the organization among new recruits. Indeed, there are organizations that prefer to promote their own members of staff as opposed to recruiting external managers. This is because internal recruitment allows them to build expertise through cultural socialization. The business model is supported by resources and the managers should be aware of how the resources can be deployed to specific aspects of the business model. Some aspects require more resources than others. These are the nuanced decisions that managers will have to make from time to time.

One way to look at the success of the organization is the extent to which it can achieve its goals within the constraints of the limited resources that are available to it (Rosenthal, 2013; Rosser and Eccleston, 2011; Saenz and Pérez-Bouvier, 2014; Saji and Ellingstad, 2004). This is the comparative modality that is used in the public sector to ensure that various institutions can compete for funding. There may be budget priorities and there could be some discretionary spending that is dependent upon the efficiency of organizations. Those organizations that is unable to implement effective efficiency measures may lose funding and could be closed. Indeed, the press and the public have been very vocal about the need to eliminate those public sector institutions that are not delivering a high-quality service. The clamor for more efficient management has become so heated that previously sacrosanct institutions like the police are now being openly questioned. During the Black Lives Matter protests in the United States of America for example, there were certain politicians and campaigners that were openly calling for the police to be abolished. Such a campaign would have been unthinkable 100 years ago or even 50 years ago.

Managing results as can be challenging and managers should be encouraged to share good practice (Too and Weaver, 2014; Torre Edoardo and Luca, 2013; Turyakira, 2018a, b; Visser, 2012; WHO, 2018). If there are challenges with managing resources, the managers should be able to communicate with the leadership team and other stakeholders (such as the owners) to ensure that an appropriate level of resources is made available. Ideally, competent managers can develop strategies for acquiring more resources for their teams and reducing the wastage of resources that are pre-existent. Some of these strategies emerge from existing theory while others are developed through practice knowledge. The organization should develop, record, and evaluate specific systems that allow new managers to review the work that was done by previous managers. This allows for continuity in the management of resources and ensures that the problems that the organization has faced are used as an opportunity to learn.

Managers should pay extra attention to economic resources because there are open subjected to microeconomics structures that determine how there are accessed and how they are eventually utilized (Moore and Doyle, 2010; Morrison and Milliken, 2003; Mosher, 2013; Mujeeb and Ahmad, 2011; Nagalakhmi and Trivedi, 2015). In other words, the diligent manager should be aware of how the economy is run and the impact of economic policy on the organization. Nowhere is this more prevalent and pertinent than in the taxation a private enterprise. There are legal loopholes that allow organizations to reduce the tax burden. In fact, countries like the USA have celebrated those entrepreneurs that have been able to play the tax system within the legal boundaries. However, that is a different proposition from organizations engaging in illegal activities to avoid paying tax. The consequences for managers and leaders that allowed this illegality can be fatal to the organization. Indeed, in the case of Enron, it became clear that senior managers can be imprisoned for significant periods of time for failing to follow the law. Of course, the case of Enron was also a case of large-scale fraud that was driven by a corporate culture that lack of accountability. The lessons of Enron are still being taught and learned in management schools. However, learning from the past through heuristics is not always understood as a problem-solving modality.

8.2. HEURISTICS IN PROBLEM-SOLVING

Heuristics have been used as a problem-solving instrumentality (Ahmad and Schroeder, 2003; Alshallah, 2004; Alvesson et al., 2011; Amos et al., 2008; Anckar et al., 2002). Typically, the use of heuristics is closely associated with algorithms. Organizations tend to use heuristics for solving problems that are linked to mathematical issues. However, heuristics can be used for structured and unstructured problems. Researchers have distinguished algorithms from heuristics because each of these concepts resolves problems in slightly different ways. There are also different issues in the terms abuse as well as the possibilities of success. Hence, the choice of heuristics or algorithms is also a choice about the potential for dealing with an organizational problem. It is a management decision and shows a sense of judgment or otherwise.

Several scholars states that ann organization main commission problem-solving algorithm which constitutes a procedure that is guaranteed to produce a certain solution if the rules are followed in a strict manner (Mosher, 2013; Mujeeb and Ahmad, 2011; Nagalakhmi and Trivedi, 2015; Nagasawa and Fukunaga, 2015; Najam, 2000). The algorithm is about predictability through adherence to procedures. Therefore, it can be argued that the algorithm works best if you have predictable variables and situations that are not likely to change in the short run. Certain problems could arise if the situation is unpredictable, and the variables are unstable. In such situations, organizations may opt to use heuristics. The problem with algorithms is that they can take a lot of time because they go through a lot of processes and iterations before they arrive as a solution. Hence, the decision to use an algorithm can imply a waste of time. Some problems are so urgent that there is no room to wait for an algorithm to go through all its iterations. Overall, the criticism of algorithm is that they are almost certain to succeed but they take a long time. The business world may not be prepared for such a length of time.

The language and conceptualization of heuristics and an algorithm are important considerations during the problem-solving process (Nagasawa and Fukunaga, 2015; Najam, 2000; Nath, 2011; Newell and Simon, 1972; Nica, 2015; Obeidat, 2012). This is based on the notion that the ability to communicate is linked to the ability to conceptualize. Indeed, child psychologists argue that children learn to conceptualize and communicate at the same time. The combination of these competencies will determine where the child is linguistically competent or otherwise. In the same way, an organization that can conceptualize and communicate the nature of its problems is more likely to succeed in resolving them. There is a difference between the technical resolutions of a program question in computing, as opposed to the resolution of an organizational problem that may not involve any computers at all. Heuristics and algorithms necessarily reduce the conceptualization and measurement of problems to computer programs. There is some debate as to whether this is an appropriate approach. However, organizations have much to learn from the ways in which algorithms or heuristics can resolve computer-related problems.

The nature of the problem-solving heuristic will determine how effective it is at resolving organizational problems (Dartey-Baah and Amoako, 2011; Day and Schoenrade, 2000; Deery and Nath, 2013; Dumay et al., 2010; Dutse, 2013). For example, such a heuristic is typically informal and intuitive. That can be a problem when solving problems in an organization that is highly structured and requires resolution that a streamlined to fit into a specific narrative. Moreover, the problem-solving heuristic is speculative in nature and yet some organizations require certainty throughout the problem-solving process. That is not to say that the speculation that can be garnered through the problem-solving heuristic is necessarily inaccurate. Indeed, there have been instances where the problem-solving heuristic has effectively resolved an issue through speculation.

The critical point is how the speculation is conceived and executed when using heuristics (Connell et al., 2009; Cooke, 2003; Cox et al., 2021; Cox, 1999; Crane, 2013; Crawford, 2016; Cunniff and Mostert, 2012). Although the problem-solving heuristic can be faster than an algorithm, the certainty of resolution is not clear. The heuristic is possibly accurate on some occasions. This contrasts with the algorithm, which is always accurate, albeit taking a lot of time in the process. The time spent resolving the problem can be reduced significantly by searching for it heuristically as opposed to algorithmically. The problem with the heuristic is that if it is wrong, the search must be completed several times until the right answer is found. That is a different proposition from the algorithm that is bound to get to the right answer eventually. In any case, this is a balancing question that must be answered through a sense of judgment that is exercised by the manager or the system that has been developed to resolve problems in the organization.

There are several problem-solving heuristics on the market today (Connell et al., 2009; Cooke, 2003; Cox et al., 2021; Cox, 1999; Crane, 2013; Crawford, 2016; Cunniff and Mostert, 2012). However, issues of accuracy mean there is only a few that are used repeatedly. From the perspective of a business, it makes sense to focus on those heuristics that work. In terms of the algorithm, the situation is different because the algorithm is bound to reach the right answer at some point. If the organization is not hampered by timescales, it may be able to use algorithms instead of heuristics. The alternative is to select a set of heuristics that have a good record and then use them repeatedly. The heuristics that are used frequently include means-ends analysis, working backward, working forward, and the generate-and-test approach. These approaches maybe change depending on the situation and the needs of the organization. A management decision will have to be made about the heuristics that are most suitable for that situation or even the ones that must be purchased to be used routinely in the organization. Extensive consultation with analysts and other experts is of the essence. Other organizations have the flexibility to use both algorithms and heuristics depending on the problem that they are resolving. Figure 8.3 is an example of a problem-solving heuristic in action.

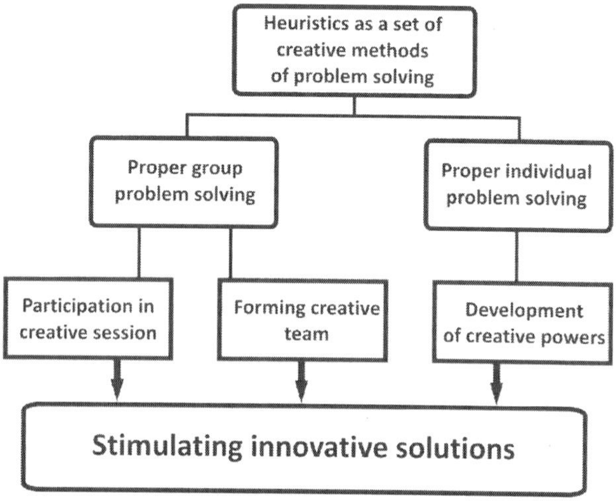

Figure 8.3. Example of the application of the heuristic method.

Source: Wasilewska and Ryszard (2014).

We have already explored some of the basic tenants of the means-ends analysis in previous chapters. The basic tenet of this approach is to begin by envisioning the end of the problem or the solution (Harney and Dundon, 2006; Harris and Brown, 1998; Harrison and Lock, 2004; Hartmann, 2014; Haworth and Hughes, 2015). The goal is then idealized in terms of trying to move from a bad situation and towards one which is desirable. The decision-maker will determine the most efficient and effective strategy for achieving the end status, which is the goal. There will be several obstacles that prevent the decision-maker from reaching that goal. Hence those obstacles will be turned into sub-goals which must be overcome before achieving the overall goal of the problem-solving exercise.

Working forward is another heuristic that is commonly used (Guest et al., 2003; Hansen and Wernerfelt, 1989; Hansen and Olsson, 2011; Harney and Dundon, 2006; Harris and Brown, 1998). It starts with an ambition to achieve a goal and then systematically working one's way towards that goal. The problem is resolved from beginning to end. Hence the notion that working forward is a modality that requires chronology. Some organizations may have problems that lack chronology because the nature of the problem may be nonlinear. For example, achievements that are made in resolving the problems may be lost afterwards and then the problem solver must go back one to try and resolve the remaining problems before they move forward. Moreover, working forward requires a certain level of predictability which is not always available when resolving complex problems in organizations. To move forward, the decision-maker must have a clear plan of the journey.

The working-backward approach is that exact opposite where the solver of the problem first seeks the endpoint (Arthur and Dworkin, 1991; Ashton et al., 2010; Assink, 2006; Atkinson and Brander Brown, 2001; Atwal and Williams, 2009). By working backwards to resolve the problems or issues that has prevented them from getting there. It seems like a counter-intuitive approach to problem-solving. However, some organizations have successfully resolved many problems using the working-backwards approach. In some instances, the organization will not risk arriving at the endpoint and not being able to map its journey to that point. Instead, the designated decision-makers will operate on an experimental basis by using the working-backwards approach as a test before rolling it out to the entire organization. Indeed, this approach has been used to improve the learning within the organization because the detail that is required to map the journey necessarily calls for a high level of analysis.

The three forms of heuristics that have been discussed previously are systematic in their conceptualization and execution (Rasim, 2008; Rose Ragins, 2004; Rosenthal, 2013; Rosser and Eccleston, 2011; Saenz and Pérez-Bouvier, 2014; Saji and Ellingstad, 2004). That is a different proposition from the problem-solving heuristic that works based on a generate-and-test method. Under this paradigm, the organization will generate a series of alternative courses of action. Typically, these courses of action are random in nature. The next stage is to determine for each course of action the extent to which it can achieve the goal of solving the problem. In other words, this is a particularly tiresome and time-consuming exercise. The benefits of the generate-and-test method might arise from the diversity of options. The advantage of this approach is that there are many alternatives that might be used in the future if a similar (but slightly different) problem is encountered.

The processes of experimenting with various options can also be instructive to managers who are trying to understand how the organization operates (Schuler, 1989; Sedmak and Longhurst, 2010; Sendawula et al., 2018; Supply chain Management and Logistics: Zara, 2013). A distinction is made between an optimizing strategy and a satisficing strategy. That satisficing strategy is one that gives the first acceptable solution to a problem. By way of contrast, the optimizing strategy is one that offers the best path to a solution. If the organization is under pressure to resolve a problem quickly, it may opt for the satisficing strategy. However, if the organization has a bit more time, it could invest in identifying the optimizing strategy did. The main advantage of optimizing is better to use the best possible strategy for the organization. Meanwhile, the satisficing strategy is one that can save time and energy that would otherwise be expended in meticulous planning. That approach might be considered when dealing with technological challenges, as demonstrated in Figure 8.4.

Set of Heuristics	Nature of heuristics	Methodological framework	References
Inventive Principles	Induction from empirical analysis	Supposed to be primarily used after identification of Technical/Pair Contradictions (TRIZ)	e.g. Altshuller, 2004
Separation Principles	Induction from empirical analysis	Supposed to be primarily used after identification of Physical/Point Contradictions (TRIZ)	e.g. Savranksy, 2000
Standard Solutions	Induction from empirical analysis	Supposed to be primarily used after establishment of Su-Field Models (TRIZ)	e.g. Altshuller and Seljuzki, 1983
Solution Operators	Induction form empirical analysis	Supposed to be primarily used after establishment of problem structure (SIT) or Closed World Model (USIT)	Horowitz, 1999; Sickafus, 1997
Design Heuristics	Aggregation from laboratory experiment	-	Daly et al., 2012
AD Corollaries	Deduction from design axioms	Derived from axioms of Axiomatic Design theory	Suh, 1998

Figure 8.4. Examples of heuristics for technological and design problem-solving.

Source: Schoenfeld (2016).

One of the lessons of problem-solving is related to understanding the nature of the obstacles that prevent managers and decision-makers from engaging in effective thinking (Maneesh et al., 2009; Manzoor, 2011; Matías-Reche et al., 2009; McGill and Wooten, 1975; Memili and Welsh, 2012). In other ones, part of the problem-solving process is designed to correct cognitive biases and cognitive deficits that prevent optimal decision making. The starting point is always a better understanding of the human mind and how it works. Several factors may prevent optimal thinking when resolving problems. For example, a person may be socialized into a certain mental state that does not allow him to open their mind to alternative solutions. In that sense, the person or the decision-maker may lose out in terms of identifying solutions that are not immediately obvious but are otherwise effective. On other occasions, the decision-makers may suffer from a mental block that does not allow them to think clearly about the problem that they are resolving. Then there is the problem of functional fixedness in which the decision-maker is unwilling to change their strategy because they have lurched onto a certain way of operating that they are unwilling to change.

Some decision-makers tend to oversimplify the problems that they are faced with (Chevalier and Mazzalovo, 2008; Chung, 2015; Clegg and Palmer, 1996; Cold Cafe, 2018; Cole and Dawson, 2010). Heuristics may be unhelpful because they rely on the past. Yet, recollections of the past may not be necessarily accurate. Other decision-makers are hampered by the reality that they are prejudiced and are willing to follow stereotypes instead of investigating the true nature of the problem. There is a very good reason why organizations are moving towards a more inclusive approach to recruitment and development. Stereotypes appear to be a shortcut, but they are an inefficient one. If the problem-solving strategy is based on stereotypes, there is a high likelihood that the decisions that are made will not be appropriate. Prejudice costs money and lost opportunities. Then there is the problem of negative transfer in which interventions that are meant to elicit positive output do not follow that trajectory. Instead, the inputs reduce the effectiveness of the solution or make the problem worse.

The mental state of the decision-maker has a critical role to play in the decisions that they make (Nath, 2011; Newell and Simon, 1972; Nica, 2015; Obeidat, 2012; Odrakiewicz, 2012; Okotoni and Erero, 2005). That is why some researchers refer to the mental sent as an entrenchment. The entrenchment is a frame of mind that involves a model that represents a problem or context within which a problem occurs. It can also represent a procedure for resolving the problem. Where the problem solver has a fixated mental state, they will focus on a solution or description of the problem, which may not be accurate. Therefore, fixation on certain strategies might mean that the problem is poorly understood and poorly resolved. Some strategies work well on certain occasions, but there is no guarantee that they work well all the time. The issue is that someone that is firmly set in their way of thinking may find it challenging to adjust. For example, they may opt for strategies that are inappropriate or irrelevant to the current situation. Where the decision-maker is used to operating in a certain way, it is difficult for them to switch easily when the problem demands so. This is where the problem-solving process fails.

The inappropriate fixation on certain mental schemas may relate to functional fixedness (Ashton et al., 2010; Assink, 2006; Atkinson and Brander Brown, 2001; Atwal and Williams, 2009; Awadh and Saad, 2013). This relates to the inability to realize that something that is known to be used in a particular way can also have alternative uses. Hence, the decision-maker believes that a certain tool can only be used for certain tasks, whereas there are opportunities to use that tool for different tasks. When the decision-maker is faced with a new problem, they may be hampered by functional fixedness, which blocks the ability to use pre-existing tools to solve problem. The creative manager should be able to use old tools in new ways to solve problems creatively. Overcoming functional fixedness can be a sign of high levels of analysis and creativity. These are the types of managers that are resourceful. Such managers can scan the environment and look at old tools in a new way.

It is only recently that society and its institutions have started understanding the full impact of stereotypes on decision-making (Dumay et al., 2010; Dutse, 2013; DyReyes, 2008; Egan, 2009; Egloff and Bhalla, 2014; Evans, 2005; Farndale et al., 2008). Previously, stereotypes were deemed legitimate decision-making paradigm. For example, it was perfectly acceptable to stereotype African Americans, ethnic minorities, sexual minorities, women, old people, and foreigners. The insidious impact of stereotyping could also be perceived in areas such as law and medicine. Stereotypes are a block on mental functionality. Typically, a stereotype comprises irrationally supported generalizations about the putative practices of most or all members of a social group. For example, there is a stereotype that women cannot be leaders whilst men are natural leaders. This type of stereotyping means that the organization misses out on a highly competent people. It is a loss in every sense of the word. Most stereotypes are garnered through our childhood experience. However, most of us soon grow out of those stereotypes or learn to hide them very well. Social pressure means that we can no longer make critical decisions based on stereotypes. Of course, such decisions can be made in secret. It is no secret that juries are prejudiced, for example. Hence, certain trials have been overturned because evidence has emerged that juries made decisions outside their scope and based on stereotypes.

Negative transfer is an interesting mental block that may occur without the decision-maker even realizing it (Milosevic et al., 2010; Min et al., 2008; Mitchell et al., 1997; Moore and Birtwistle, 2004; Moore and Doyle, 2010). Here, the process of solving an earlier problem makes it more challenging to resolve a later problem. It is the opposite of positive transfer in which solving an earlier problem makes it easier to solve a later problem. The problems of negative transfer may stem from activities that are ostensibly similar when they are markedly different. At other times, the decision-maker is not paying enough attention. The previous success may have been due to luck or other externalities which have not been fully considered in the later decision. In some rare cases, there are activities whose positive performance can have a negative effect on the performance of other activities. For example, a savings fanatic is not going to make a good investor. Dealing with all these obstacles involves a certain level of control over the situation.

8.3. CONTROL WHEN SOLVING PROBLEMS

Exercising control when solving organizational problems can become a critical issue (Storey et al., 2006; Subhas Chandra et al., 2010; Tarafdar et al., 2014; Thursfield and Grayley, 2016; Toner, 2015; Too and Weaver, 2014). Typically, the problem occurs in a context that is full of uncertainties. The manager is trying to bring control and predictability to the circumstances. This is the same approach that is used in research. However, the term control means something different depending on whether one is engaged in an experiment or not. In an experiment, control is the variable that is introduced or a circumstances that introduced to ensure that the veracity of the findings of the experiment can be supported in all circumstances. Without controls, the experiment will only produce evidence that supports preconceived assumptions as opposed to the reality of the situation. As demonstrated in Figure 8.5, the exercise of control can be a proactive way of either preventing problems from occurring or alternatively reducing the negative impact that they have on organizations.

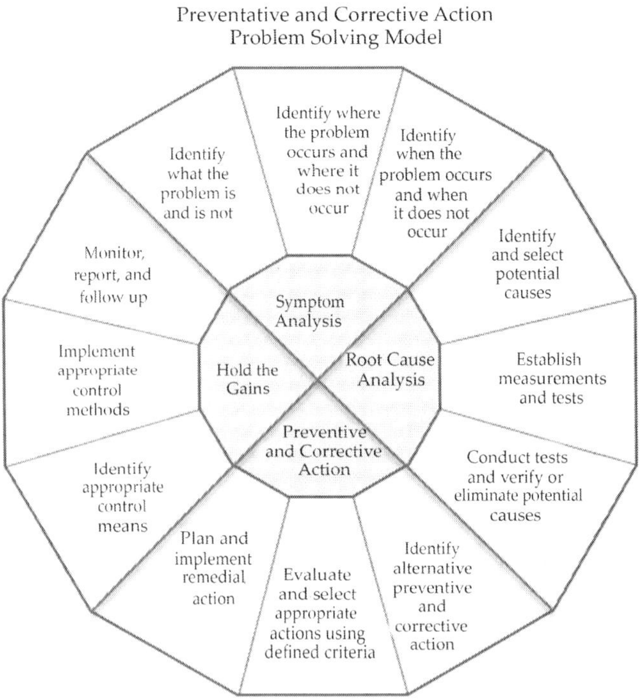

Figure 8.5. Preventative and correct problem-solving model.

Source: Quality Help Community.

In an organizational context, control means looking at the variables that contribute to a problem and then bringing some order to then (Stoorvogel et al., 2017; Storey et al., 2006; Subhas Chandra et al., 2010; Tarafdar et al., 2014; Thursfield and Grayley, 2016; Toner, 2015). The manager may be empowered to exercise this control. However, there are managers that took control using known techniques that are established in theory. For example, some managers use a "management by objectives" technique which motivates workers to achieve certain tasks that contribute to the overall strategic goals of the organization. In any case, managers are expected to be in full control of their teams. Indeed, it has been argued that effective management starts with self-management. A manager that is not able to control their own activities is unlikely to be able to control the activities of subordinates. Hence, psychometric testing during the recruitment process will identify creative people that are able to work independently whilst retaining certain social skills that are necessary to operate in the modern organization. These social skills can help to connect the manager to a feedback loop as demonstrated in Figure 8.6 which in turn facilitates problem-solving.

Figure 8.6. Example of managing feedback.

Source: Adapted from FAVPNG.

One of the performance indicators for good management is the ability to control the team and circumstances (Stewart and Walsh, 1992; Stone et al., 2015; Stoorvogel et al., 2017; Storey et al., 2006; Subhas Chandra et al., 2010). However, the environment within which problems arise may not be controllable. For example, the problems may emanate from external sources which are not easily controlled. Alternatively, the problem may emanate from someone or an entity with a significant power advantage when compared to the organization or the person that is supposed to resolve the problem. This has been the case for organizations that operate in the developing world where systems are neither predictable nor fair. There have been cases where a government has unilaterally decided to nationalize private property and deprive the owners of their business. These are the dynamic externalities that the organization must deal with even as it resolves problems.

That is not to say that managers and decision-makers are entirely powerless (Jian Wang et al., 2010; John et al., 2014; Johnson and Clark, 2008; Jurevicius, 2016; Kabene et al., 2006). As already noted in this book, a manager is expected to have some control over the resources that are available to them. Therefore, the manager can allocate resources and deploy them strategically to deal with problems that arise in the organization. This is the business of management. If the resources are not sufficient or in the right configuration, the manager can speak to the leadership team to change the configuration or even increase the level of resources. The managers should not feel as if they are out of control. There are always ways of finding control within the remit that the management position elicits. That does not mean that the managers should overstep the parameters that have been set in terms of their responsibilities. If the manager is breaking boundaries, there is a risk that they will create chaos in the teams that they manage. The art and science of management is knowing when and how to deploy resources to deal with organizational problems.

There is a pertinent question as whether control can become excessive (Parker et al., 2013; Parry et al., 2008; Patiar and Mia, 2009; Pavlatos and Paggios, 2009a, b). Indeed, some managers have faced criticism from their teams for being controlling. The control that is exercised by a manager should be undertaken with responsibility. The manager can do a lot of good in an organization, but they cannot resolve every problem. Some of the challenges are simply beyond their remit. At the same time, excessive control can stifle creativity among the team members. A manager should give people the room to grow and explore problems. This is a critical determinant of learning in an organization. Indeed, some professions call for autonomy in the workplace to allow creative people to engage their capabilities. The decision-making manager or entity must take the time to understand the nature of the team that they are leading and ensure that their management style is appropriate. Of course, the manager may have to make tough decisions that involve annoying creative people or even changing systems that have become entrenched in a negative way. These are the challenges of leadership and management which must be embraced throughout the problem-solving process. It is pertinent to consider the levers of control in the problem-solving process.

8.4. LEVERS OF CONTROL IN THE PROBLEM-SOLVING PROCESS

There are four levers of control that can be exercised in the problem-solving process (Bernini and Cracolici, 2015; Berthon et al., 2009; Bilson et al., 2013; Bjerregaard, 2011; Black, 2005; Brandsen and Pestoff, 2006). This model was developed by Robert Simons in the 1990s. This research was based on the study of the management practice of leaders in organizations. However, the levers of control also developed from other disciplines and practice knowledge that is gained through leading and managing people. The decision-maker may deploy some or all these livers when solving problems in the organization. However, it is important to understand their merits and limitations so that these levers are not used inappropriately. The quartet of levers comprises diagnostic control, interactive control, boundary systems, and belief systems. These levels can be very powerful. For example, in Figure 8.7, we see that teachers can be influenced by their beliefs in teaching and assessing students.

Aspect	Category		
	Good	*Very Good*	*Excellent*
teacher's beliefs about problem solving learning	The teacher considers that learning about mathematical problem solving is emphasized on *performance* (emphasizing to know rules and procedures without understanding) of the mathematical problem-solving process	The teacher considers that learning about mathematical problem solving is emphasized in understanding the process of solving mathematical problems	The teacher considers that learning about mathematical problem solving is emphasized on how students construct a mathematical problem-solving process.
teacher's beliefs about problem solving teaching	The teacher considers that if given a mathematical problem then the student completes by receiving knowledge from the teacher	The teacher sees that if given a mathematical problem then the student finishes by constructing his knowledge with the teacher's direction	The teacher considers that if given a mathematical problem the student completes by exploring the problem-solving strategy based on their own interests
teacher's beliefs about what is the positions of mathematical knowledge to learning about mathematical problem solving	Teacher considers that in the process of mathematical problems, solving we must remember the definitions/ rules needed to solve the problem	Teacher considers that in the process of solving mathematical problems, we must understand the definitions/rules needed to solve the problem	Teacher considers that in the process of solving mathematical problems, we must be able to adjust and differentiate the definitions used to solve the problem

Figure 8.7. Ranking of teacher's beliefs when solving mathematical problems.

Source: Harisman et al. (2019).

In diagnostic control, the decision-maker will make use of standard performance measures (Hansen and Olsson, 2011; Harney and Dundon, 2006; Harris and Brown, 1998; Harrison and Lock, 2004; Hartmann, 2014). In this case, the decision-maker is using feedback control to achieve certain objectives. Hence, performance is measured against a target which operates as a goal for the employee. The manager will then monitor and evaluate any variance between the target and performance. If there is performance beyond the target, then the employee is credited and rewarded. However, if the performance falls below the target, then the employee is supported or put through performance management measures. The performance can be reviewed on a regular basis using formal avenues such as team meetings, departmental meetings, a board meeting, or personal development plans.

Managers may also use interactive control which is a completely different approach to diagnostic control (Fetscherin and Heinrich, 2014; Finkelstein et al., 2007; Gil-Pareja et al., 2007; Gruman and Saks, 2011; Guest et al., 2003). In these instances, the senior management team will create meaningful and purposeful conversations with many members of the overall team at all levels. This interaction builds relationships and allows the senior managers to understand what is going on at the grass-root level of the organization. There are cases where an organization will select an issue or problem area that will be subjected to interactive control. Once a measure of success is agreed, it is deployed across the organization to ensure that every member of the team understands their responsibilities within this goal. Of course, it is expected that managers with superior social skills will excel at interactive control. For members of staff, interactive control means that at any moment, a senior manager can walk in and ask them to explain what they are doing. This can have a dramatic effect on motivation. However, interactive control should not be exercised in ways that are humiliating or discriminatory. In fact, some organizations could use this modality to embed work beliefs, as demonstrated in Figure 8.8. This shows that the levers of control are never mutually exclusive. They can be used as a combination.

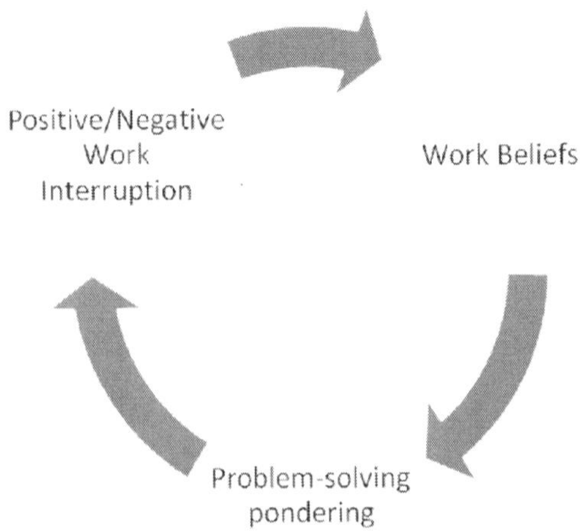

Figure 8.8. Role of work beliefs and work interruptions in problem-solving.

Source: Zoupanou, Cropley, and Rydstedt (2013).

One of the benefits of interactive control is that it can create attention to a single issue and ensure that it is given priority across the organization (Schmid and Adams, 2008; Schuler, 1989; Sedmak and Longhurst, 2010; Sendawula et al., 2018; Supply chain Management and Logistics: Zara, 2013). However, the decision-makers must be wary of giving too much attention to an issue and neglecting the critical aspects of the organization which allows operations to continue. In fact, it is possible to use interactive control with diagnostic control if the manager understands which aspects are being allocated to each modality. Another advantage of interactive control is that it can ensure that senior managers speak with one voice. It can be very confusing for the rest of the team if mixed messages are being sent from the senior management team. Some organizations allow senior managers to have pet issues that are put through the interactive control framework from time to time in an orderly manner. In that sense, there is no feeling of unfairness. The interruption allows for feedback and learning across the board. This can create a cohesive organization that can withstand pressure from the external forces in the ecology within which the organization is operating.

Boundary systems are another form of control (Songa et al., 2012; Sparrow and Makram, 2015; Speer and Potter, 2000; Steers et al., 2004; Stevens, 2002). It can simply comprise a statement of what the company is not going to do. On the face, it may appear counterintuitive and even counterproductive to tell people that you are not going to do certain things. However, organizations need to set boundaries and boundary systems are an effective way of ensuring that everyone knows where they stand. The statement that explains what the organization is not going to do can set limits on the activities of other workers so that they do not engage in any relevant issues. It is a means of ensuring that there is a focused on the priorities of the organization. Moreover, boundary systems help to ensure that senior members of staff do not waste time and opportunities in exploring prospects that are never going to come to fruition. The organization must be very clear about its priorities and its capabilities. Being too many things at the same time is a recipe for disaster.

The fourth and perhaps most controversial lever of control is the belief system (Papasolomou and Melanthiou, 2012; Parker et al., 2013; Parry et al., 2008; Patiar and Mia, 2009; Pavlatos and Paggios, 2009a). Organizations are reluctance to be presented or perceived as being overly religious. This is because religiosity in its extreme forms has been associated with prejudice and discrimination. Additionally, we have seen many cases of organizations that are perceived to be bigoted when they claim to be merely following the religious beliefs of the owners or members of staff. Nevertheless, belief systems are a powerful lever of control. The organization can make belief systems neutral in the sense that they are not attached to any form of organized religion. The classic example of this is the vision statement and a mission statement. The organization can also communicate values of inclusivity and hard work which are not controversial. Through this communication, the organization can influence its employees to follow his priorities. Indeed, coherent belief systems can markedly change the behavior of organizations and the people that operate in them. A belief system can also give workers as a sense of purpose. In that sense, beliefs can motivate workers to achieve certain goals that are in line with the beliefs that they have taken on. Beliefs will guide the trajectory of problem-solving so that it is in line with the expectations and priorities of the organization.

Chapter 8 Summary

This chapter has explored the Schoenfeld model of problem-solving as an example of key aspects of theory and practice emerge. The chapter has shown the importance of using resources in an imaginative way. It has also highlighted the merits and demerits of relying on heuristics as a problem-solving strategy. The chapter has explored the importance of control throughout the problem-solving process and the potential risks of exercising too much control. The enduring take-home from the chapter is that management requires flexibility, creativity, and nuance when solving organizational problems.

CHAPTER 9

CONCLUDING REMARKS

This book has explored the problem-solving process as an important dimension of performance in an organization. The book has provided an overview of problem-solving as a technical exercise whilst simultaneously offering practical insights into how this model can be applied to everyday challenges in management. Managers face many challenges when conceptualization and dealing with organizational problems. They must necessarily follow certain rules which can be restrictive and counterproductive. Besides, there is a lot of theory about problem-solving that is not informed by management practice. In that sense, problem-solving can become something of a guessing game. The insights provided in this book should offer some guidelines and support to new and aspiring managers that are trying to make sense of it all. I hope you have enjoyed the book and will explore the other books in the series.

BIBLIOGRAPHY

1. Aboulian, L., Charnley, P., & Watkins, H., (2008). Case review: Adidas AG, adidas Benelux BV v Marca mode CV, CA Nederland CV, HM Hennes Mauritz Netherlands BV, Vendex KBB Nederland BV. *The Journal of Brand Management, 16*(3), 213–215.
2. Abramovsky, L., Griffith, R., & Sako, M., (2004). *Offshoring of Business Services and its Impact on the UK Economy.* London: Advanced Institute of Management Research.
3. Abu-Saifan, S., (2012). Social entrepreneurship: Definition and boundaries. *Technology Innovation Management Review,* 22–27.
4. Ahimbisibwe, G. M., & Nkundabanyanga, S. K., (2016). Knowledge absorptive capacity: Do all its dimensions matter for export performance of SMEs?. *World Journal of Entrepreneurship, Management, and Sustainable Development, 12*(2), 139–160.
5. Ahmad, S., & Schroeder, R. G., (2003). The impact of human resource management practices on operational performance: Recognizing country and industry differences. *Journal of Operations Management, 21*(1), 19–43.
6. Alshallah, S., (2004). Job satisfaction and motivation: How do we inspire employees?. *Radiology Management, 26*(2), 47.
7. Alvesson, M., Bridgman, T., & Willmott, H., (2011). *The Oxford Handbook of Critical Management Studies.* Reprint ed. Oxford: OUP.

8. Amos, T., Ristow, A., Pearse, N. J., & Ristow, L., (2008). *Human Resource Management* (3rd edn.). Cape Town (SA): Junta and Company.
9. Anckar, B., Walden, P., & Jelassi, T., (2002). Creating customer value in online grocery shopping. *International Journal of Retail & Distribution Management, 30*(4), 211–220.
10. Anwar, S., & Sun, S., (2013). Foreign entry and firm R&D: Evidence from Chinese manufacturing industries. *R&D Management, 43*(4), 303–317.
11. Anyim, F. C., Ikemefuna, C. O., & Mbah, S. E., (2011). Human resource management challenges in Nigeria under a globalized economy. *International Journal of Economics and Management Sciences, 2011*(4).
12. Arbulú, I., Lozano, J., & Rey-Maquieira, J., (2015). Tourism and solid waste generation in Europe: A panel data assessment of the environmental Kuznets curve. *Waste Management, 46*(1), 628–636.
13. Argenti, P. A., (1996). Corporate communication as a discipline. *Management Communication Quarterly, 10*(1), 73–97.
14. Arthur, J. B., & Dworkin, J. B., (1991). Current topics in industrial and labor relations research and practice. *Journal of Management, 17*(3), 515–551.
15. Ashton, D., Brown, P., & Lauder, H., (2010). Skill webs and international human resource management: Lessons from a study of the global skill strategies of transnational companies. *International Journal of Human Resource Management, 21*(6), 836–850.
16. Assink, M., (2006). Inhibitors of disruptive innovation capability: A conceptual model. *European Journal of Innovation Management, 9*(2), 215–233.
17. Atkinson, H., & Brander, B. J., (2001). Rethinking performance measures: Assessing progress in UK hotels. *International Journal of Contemporary Hospitality Management, 13*(3), 128–136.
18. Atwal, G., & Williams, A., (2009). Luxury brand marketing-the experience is everything. *Brand Management, 16*(1), 338–346.
19. Awadh, A. M., & Saad, M., (2013). Impact of organizational culture on employee performance. *International Review of Management and Business Research, 2*(1), 168.

20. Baker, R. E., & Esherick, C. D., (2013). *Fundamentals of Sport Management (Human Kinetics' Fundamentals of Sport and Exercise Science)*. Champaign (IL): Human Kinetics.

21. Bannò, M., & Sgobbi, F., (2016). Family business characteristics and the approach to HRM in overseas ventures. *Journal of Small Business Management, 54*(2), 640–658.

22. Barry, P. J., Ellinger, P. N., Hopkin, J. A., & Baker, C. B., (2000). *Financial Management in Agriculture*. S.L.:S. N.

23. Bekker, M. C., (2014). Project governance: "schools of thought." *South African Journal of Economic and Management Sciences, 17*(1).

24. Bell, M. P., Özbilgin, M. F., Beauregard, T. A., &Sürgevil, O., (2011). Voice, silence, and diversity in 21st century organizations: Strategies for inclusion of gay, lesbian, bisexual, and transgender employees. *Human Resource Management, 50*(1), 131–146.

25. Bercu, A. M., (2012). The impact of human resource management practices on SMEs performance in Romania. *Annals. Economic Science Series, 8*(1), 377–385.

26. Bernini, C., & Cracolici, M. F., (2015). Demographic change, tourism expenditure and life cycle behavior. *Tourism Management, 47*(1), 191–205.

27. Berthon, P., Pitt, L., Parent, M., & Berthon, J. P., (2009). Aesthetics and ephemerality: Observing and preserving the luxury brand. *California Management Review, 52*(1), 45–66.

28. Bilson, A., Nyeko, J., Baskott, J., & Rayment, C., (2013). *Developing Social Care and Support Services in Uganda: A Literature Review of International Experience in Implementing Social Care and Support Services: Considerations for the Ugandan Context*. Oxford Policy Management.

29. BIS, (2015). *Leadership and Management Skills in SMEs: Measuring Associations with Management Practices and Performance (BIS Paper No. 211)*. London: Department for Business Innovation & Skills.

30. Bjerregaard, T., (2011). Studying institutional work in organizations: Uses and implications of ethnographic methodologies. *Journal of Organizational Change Management, 24*(1), 51–64.

31. Black, B., (2005). Comparative industrial relations theory: The role of national culture. *International Journal of Human Resource Management, 16*(7), 1137–1158.

32. Brandsen, T., & Pestoff, V., (2006). Co-production, the third sector and the delivery of public services: An introduction. *Public Management Review, 8*(4), 493–501.
33. Bruce, M., & Daly, L., (2006). Buyer behavior for fast fashion. *Journal of Fashion Marketing and Management: An International Journal, 10*(3), 329–344.
34. Calabrese, G., (1997). Communication and co-operation in product development: A case study of a European car producer. *R&D Management, 27*(3), 239–252.
35. Capko, J., (2003). Five steps to a performance evaluation system. *Family Practice Management, 10*(3), 43.
36. Carraher, S. M., (2013). ISI, social entrepreneurship, and research. *Journal of Management History, 19*(1), 1–4.
37. Carraher, S. M., Welsh, D. H. B., &Svilokos, A., (2016). Validation of a measure of social entrepreneurship. *European Journal of International Management, 10*(4), 386.
38. Chang, H., Huang, K., & Wu, C., (2006). Determination of sample size in using central limit theorem for Weibull distribution. *International Journal of Information and Management Sciences, 17*(3), 31.
39. Chen, F. H., Hsu, T. S., & Tzeng, G. H., (2011). A balanced scorecard approach to establish a performance evaluation and relationship model for hot spring hotels based on a hybrid MCDM model combining DEMATEL and ANP. *International Journal of Hospitality Management, 30*(4), 908–932.
40. Chevalier, M., & Mazzalovo, G., (2008). *Luxury Brand Management: A World of Privilege.* London: John Wiley & Sons.
41. Chung, D. J., (2015). How much is a win worth? An application to intercollegiate athletics. *Management Science, 63*(2), 548–565.
42. Clegg, S. R., & Palmer, G., (1996). *The Politics of Management Knowledge.* New York: Sage.
43. Cold Cafe, (2018). *History of Human Resource Management.* [Online] Available at: https://www.youtube.com/watch?v=22uS6YJnHCE (accessed on 29 March 2022).
44. Cole, T., & Dawson, P. M., (2010). *Footy Mates and Football Professionals: A Case Study of Change at an Australian Rules Football Club* (pp. 1–18). Adelaide, ANZAM.

45. Collinson, D., & Hearn, J., (1994). Naming men as men: Implications for work, organization, and management. *Gender, Work & Organization, 1*(1), 2–22.

46. Connell, J., Page, S., & Bentley, T., (2009). Towards sustainable tourism planning in New Zealand: Monitoring local government planning under the resource management act. *Tourism Management, 30*(6), 867–877.

47. Cooke, B., (2003). The denial of slavery in management studies. *Journal of Management Studies, 40*(8), 0022–2380.

48. Cox, A. E., Beasley, L., & Hardin, R., (2021). Application of social work theory in sport management curriculum: Ecological systems theory. *Sport Management Education Journal, 1*(aop), 1–5.

49. Cox, A., (1999). Power, value, and supply chain management. *Supply Chain Management: An International Journal, 4*(4), 167–175.

50. Crane, A., (2013). Modern slavery as a management practice: Exploring the conditions and capabilities of human exploitation. *Academy of Management Review, 38*(1), 49–69.

51. Crawford, G. C., (2016). Realism, empiricism, and fetishism in the study of entrepreneurship. *Journal of Management Inquiry, 25*(2), 168–170.

52. Cunniff, L., & Mostert, K., (2012). Prevalence of workplace bullying of South African employees. *Sa Journal of Human Resource Management, 10*(1), 15.

53. Cunningham, G. B., (2011). The LGBT advantage: Examining the relationship among sexual orientation diversity strategy, and performance. *Sport Management Review, 14*(4), 453–461.

54. D'Ippolito, B., & Timpano, F., (2016). The role of non-technological innovations in services: The case of food retailing. *Creativity and Innovation Management, 25*(1), 73–89.

55. Dartey-Baah, K., & Amoako, G. K., (2011). Application of Frederick Herzberg's two-factor theory in assessing and understanding employee motivation at work: A Ghanaian perspective. *European Journal of Business and Management, 3*(9), 1–8.

56. Day, N. E., & Schoenrade, P., (2000). The relationship among reported disclosure of sexual orientation, anti-discrimination policies, top management support and work attitudes of gay and lesbian employees. *Personnel Review, 29*(3), 346–363.

57. De Kok, J. M. P., Uhlaner, L. M., & Roy, T. A., (2006). Professional HRM practices in family owned-managed enterprises. *Journal of Small Business Management, 44*(3), 441–460.

58. Deery, S., & Nath, V., (2013). Customer service work, employee well-being and performance. In: Bach, S., & Edwards, M., (eds.), *Managing Human Resources: Human Resource Management in Transition* (pp. 100–121). Chichester: John Wiley & Sons.

59. Dumay, J., Guthrie, J., & Farneti, F., (2010). GRI sustainability reporting guidelines for public and third sector organizations: A critical review. *Public Management Review, 12*(4), 531–548.

60. Dutse, A. Y., (2013). Linking absorptive capacity with innovative capabilities: A survey of manufacturing firms in Nigeria. *International Journal of Technology Management & Sustainable Development, 12*(2), 167–183.

61. DyReyes, J., (2008). *Strategic Project Management: Aligning Strategic Business Objectives with Project Management Strategy.* [Online] Available at: https://scholarsbank.uoregon.edu/xmlui/bitstream/handle/1794/7678/2008-dyreyes.pdf?sequence=1 (accessed on 29 March 2022).

62. Egan, G., (2009). *The Skilled Helper: A Problem Management and Opportunity Development Approach to Helping* (9th edn.). London: Brooks.

63. Egloff, C., & Bhalla, V., (2014). *Governance for Family Businesses: Sustaining the "Magic" for Generations to Come.* [Online] Available at: https://www.bcgperspectives.com/content/articles/corporate_strategy_portfolio_management_leadership_talent_governance_family_business/ (accessed on 29 March 2022).

64. Evans, N., (2005). Assessing the balanced scorecard as a management tool for hotels. *International Journal of Contemporary Hospitality Management, 17*(5), 376–390.

65. Farndale, E., Brewster, C., &Poutsma, E., (2008). Coordinated vs. liberal market HRM: The impact of institutionalization on multinational firms. *International Journal of Human Resource Management, 19*(11), 2004–2023.

66. Fetscherin, M., & Heinrich, D., (2014). Consumer brand relationships: A research landscape. *Journal of Brand Management, 21*(1), 366–371.

67. Finkelstein, L. M., Demuth, F. R. L., & Sweeney, D. L., (2007). Bias against overweight job applicants: Further explorations of when and why. *Human Resource Management, 46*(2), 203–222.
68. Gil-Pareja, S., Llorca-Vivero, R., & Martínez-Serrano, J., (2007). The impact of embassies and consulates on tourism. *Tourism Management, 28*(2), 355–360.
69. Gruman, J. A., & Saks, A. M., (2011). Performance management and employee engagement. *Human Resource Management Review, 21*(2), 123–136.
70. Guest, D., Michie, J., Conway, N., & Sheehan, M., (2003). Human resource management and corporate performance in the UK. *British Journal of Industrial Relations, 41*(2), 291–314.
71. Hansen, G. K., & Olsson, N. O. E., (2011). Layered project–layered process: Lean thinking and flexible solutions. *Architectural Engineering and Design Management, 7*(2), 70–84.
72. Hansen, G. S., & Wernerfelt, B., (1989). Determinants of firm performance: The relative importance of economic and organizational factors. *Strategic Management Journal, 10*(5), 399–411.
73. Harney, B., & Dundon, T., (2006). Capturing complexity: Developing an integrated approach to analyzing HRM in SMEs. *Human Resource Management Journal, 16*(1), 48–73.
74. Harris, P. J., & Brown, J. B., (1998). Research and development in hospitality accounting and financial management. *International Journal of Hospitality Management, 17*(2), 161–182.
75. Harrison, F. L., & Lock, D., (2004). *Advanced Project Management: A Structured Approach.* Aldershot: Gower Publishing.
76. Hartmann, R., (2014). Dark tourism, thanatourism, and dissonance in heritage tourism management: New directions in contemporary tourism research. *Journal of Heritage Tourism, 9*(2), 166–182.
77. Haworth, N., & Hughes, S., (2015). International production, global governance and IHRM. In: *The Routledge Companion to International Human Resource Management* (pp. 86–98). New York: Routledge.
78. Hennigs, N., et al., (2013). Brand extensions: A successful strategy in luxury fashion branding? Assessing consumers' implicit associations. *Journal of Fashion Marketing and Management: An International Journal, 17*(4), 390–402.

79. Hermansson, T., (2020). *Sacked in the Morning? The Effect of Within-Season Coach Replacement in Swedish Football.* Dissertation, KTH, School of Industrial Engineering and Management.
80. Hopkin, J. A., Barry, P. J., & Baker, C. B., (1979). *Financial Management in Agriculture* (2nd edn.) Danville, IL: Interstate.
81. Hunter, L. W., & Katz, H. C., (2012). The impact of globalization on human resource management and employment relations in the US automobile and banking industries. *International Journal of Human Resource Management, 23*(10), 1983–1998.
82. Huselid, M. A., (1995). The impact of human resource management practices on turnover, productivity, and corporate financial performance. *Academy of Management Journal, 38*(3), 635–672.
83. Ibrahim, H. W., & Zailani, S., (2010). A review on the competitiveness of global supply chain in a coffee industry in Indonesia. *International Business Management, 4*(3), 105–115.
84. Ichniowski, C., Shaw, K. L., &Prennushi, G., (1997). The effects of human resource management practices on productivity: A study of steel finishing lines. *The American Economic Review, 87*(3), 291–313.
85. Ifinedo, P., (2016). Applying uses and gratifications theory and social influence processes to understand students' pervasive adoption of social networking sites: Perspectives from the Americas. *International Journal of Information Management, 36*(2), 192–194.
86. Ismail, M., Mohd, R. R., &Wahiza, A. W. N., (2005). High-flyer women academicians: Factors contributing to success. *Women in Management Review, 20*(2), 117–132.
87. Jansen, B. J., Booth, D., & Spink, A., (2008). Determining the informational, navigational, and transactional intent of web queries. *Information Processing & Management, 44*(3), 1251–1266.
88. Jian, W. Y., Doss, S. K., Guo, C., & Li, W., (2010). An investigation of Chinese consumers' outshopping motives from a culture perspective: Implications for retail and distribution. *International Journal of Retail & Distribution Management, 38*(6), 423–442.
89. John, R., Smith, A., Chotipanich, S., & Pitt, M., (2014). Awareness and effectiveness of quality function deployment (QFD) in design and build projects in Nigeria. *Journal of Facilities Management, 12*(1), 72–88.

90. Johnson, R., & Clark, G., (2008). *Service Operations Management: Improving Service Delivery* (3rdedn.). London: FT Prentice Hall.

91. Jurevicius, O., (2016). *Starbucks SWOT Analysis.* [Online] Available at: https://www.strategicmanagementinsight.com/swot-analyses/starbucks-swot-analysis.html (accessed on 29 March 2022).

92. Kabene, S. M., et al., (2006). The importance of human resources management in health care: A global context. *Human Resources for Health, 4*(20), https://doi.org/10.1186/1478-4491-4-20.

93. Kasperk, G., Drauz, R., Wilhelm, J., &Laeuppi, U., (2011). *Internationalization of Chinese Automobile Companies.* Aachen: Center for International Automobile Management.

94. Kay, R. D., Edwards, W. M., & Duffy, P. A., (1994). *Farm Management.* New York: McGraw-Hill.

95. Kerzner, H., (2003). *Project Management: A Systems Approach to Planning, Scheduling, and Controlling* (8thedn.) London: John Wiley and Son.

96. Khan, R. A. G., Khan, F. A., & Khan, M. A., (2011). Impact of training and development on organizational performance. *Global Journal of Management and Business Research, 11*(7), 62–68.

97. King, M., et al., (2000). Randomized controlled trial of non-directive counselling, cognitive-behavior therapy and usual general practitioner care in the management of depression as well as mixed anxiety and depression in primary care. *Health Technology Assessment, 4*(19), 1–83.

98. Klikauer, T., (2014). *Seven Moralities of Human Resource Management.* New York: Palgrave McMillan.

99. Kluike, M., (2015). Host-country effects in coordinated, liberal, and hybrid market economies: US subsidiaries in Switzerland, Germany, and the UK. *International Journal of Human Resource Management, 26*(17), 2211–2226.

100. Köllen, T., (2013). Bisexuality and diversity management—Addressing the B in LGBT as a relevant 'sexual orientation' in the workplace. *Journal of Bisexuality, 13*(1), 122–137.

101. Korczynski, M., (2002). Chapter 8: Managing emotions. In: Korczynski, M., (ed). *Human Resource Management in Service Work* (pp. 139–157). Basingstoke: Palgrave.

102. Kotas, R., (2014). *Management Accounting for Hotels and Restaurants.* London: Routledge.

103. Lashley, C., & Burgess, C., (2007). Do hotel managers have sufficient financial skills to help them manage their areas?. *International Journal of Contemporary Hospitality Management.*

104. Le, T., (2017). *Revenue Management: Development of a Case Study for Higher Education*. California State Polytechnic University Masters Dissertations.

105. Leary, M. R., (2001). *Impression Management, Psychology of.* [Online] Available at: https://sciencedirect.com/science/article/pii/b0080430767017277 (accessed on 29 March 2022).

106. Lee, S., & Park, S. Y., (2009). Do socially responsible activities help hotels and casinos achieve their financial goals?. *International Journal of Hospitality Management, 28*(1), 105–112.

107. Leggett, C., (2007). From industrial relations to manpower planning: The transformations of Singapore's industrial relations. *International Journal of Human Resource Management, 18*(4), 642–664.

108. Lengnick-Hall, M. L., Lengnick-Hall, C. A., Andrade, L. S., & Drake, B., (2009). Strategic human resource management: The evolution of the field. *Human Resource Management Review, 19*(2), 64–85.

109. Leuenberger, D., (2006). Sustainable development in public administration a match with practice?. *Public Works Management & Policy, 10*(3), 195–201.

110. Leung, Y. F., Spenceley, A., Hvenegaard, G., & Buckley, R., (2015). *Tourism and Visitor Management in Protected Areas: Guidelines Towards Sustainability.* Gland, Switzerland, IUCN, Best Practice Protected Area Guidelines Series No XX.

111. Li, D. W. P., (2009). Is China's bond market really inefficient?. *Journal of Risk Management in Financial Institutions, 2*(2), 141–154.

112. Li, N., Robson, A., & Coates, N., (2013). Chinese consumers' purchasing: Impact of value and affect. *Journal of Fashion Marketing and Management, 17*(4), 486–508.

113. Li, S., Ragu-Nathan, B. S., Ragu-Nathan, T. S., & Rao, S. S., (2006). The impact of supply chain management practices on competitive advantage and organizational performance. *Omega-international Journal of Management Science, 34*(2), 107–124.

114. Lock, D., (2007). *Project Management* (9thedn.) Aldershot: Gower Publishing.

115. Loorbach, D., (2010). Transition management for sustainable development: A prescriptive, complexity-based governance framework. *Governance, 23*(1), 161–183.

116. Lorenzo-Romero, C., Constantinides, E., & Alarcón-Del, A. M., (2013). Social media as marketing strategy: An explorative study on adoption and use by retailers. *Advanced Series in Management, Social Media in Strategic Management, 11*(1), 197–215.

117. Loundes, J., (2001). Management and industrial relations practices and outcomes in Australian workplaces. *Australian Journal of Labor Economics, 4*(1), 19–39.

118. Lycett, M., Rassau, A., & Danson, J., (2004). Program management: A critical review. *International Journal of Project Management, 22*(1), 289–299.

119. Maneesh, K., Jijum, A., & Byung, R. C., (2009). Project selection and its impact on the successful deployment of six sigma. *Business Process Management Journal, 15*(5), 669–686.

120. Manzoor, Q. A., (2011). Impact of employees motivation on organizational effectiveness. *European Journal of Business and Management, 3*(3), 36–44.

121. Matías-Reche, F., Rubio-López, E. A., & Rueda-Manzanares, A., (2009). Human resource management in relation to CEOs in nonprofit organizations. *Employee Relations, 31*(5), 489–502.

122. McGill, M. E., & Wooten, L. M., (1975). Management in the third sector. *Public Administration Review, 35*(5), 444–455.

123. Memili, E., & Welsh, D. H., (2012). Towards a theory of nonfamily employees' organizational identification and attachment in family firms. *Journal of Technology Management in China, 7*(3), 255–269.

124. Menke, M., Xu, Q., & Gu, L., (2007). An analysis of the universality, flexibility, and agility of total innovation management: A case study of Hewlett–Packard. *Journal of Technology Transfer, 32*(1), 49–62.

125. Meyer-Sahling, J. H., Mikkelsen, K. S., & Schuster, C., (2018). *Civil Service Management and Corruption: What We Know and What We Don't* (Vol. 96, No. 2, pp. 276–285). Public Administration.

126. Mia, L., & Patiar, A., (2001). The use of management accounting systems in hotels: An exploratory study. *International Journal of Hospitality Management, 20*(2), 111–128.

127. Milosevic, D. Z., Patanakul, P., &Srivannaboon, S., (2010). *Case Studies in Project, Program, and Organizational Management.* London: John Wiley & Sons.

128. Min, H., Min, H., Joo, S. J., & Kim, J., (2008). Data envelopment analysis for establishing the financial benchmark of Korean hotels. *International Journal of Services and Operations Management, 4*(2), 201.

129. Mitchell, R. K., Agle, B. R., & Wood, D. J., (1997). Toward a theory of stakeholder identification and salience: Defining the principle of who and what really counts. *The Academy of Management Review, 22*(4), 853–886.

130. Moore, C. M., & Birtwistle, G., (2004). The Burberry business model: Creating an international luxury fashion brand. *International Journal of Retail & Distribution Management, 32*(8), 412–422.

131. Moore, C. M., & Doyle, S. A., (2010). The evolution of a luxury brand: The case of Prada. *International Journal of Retail & Distribution Management, 38*(11, 12), 915–927.

132. Morrison, E. W., & Milliken, F. J., (2003). Speaking up, remaining silent: The dynamics of voice and silence in organizations. *Journal of Management Studies, 40*(6), 1353–1358.

133. Mosher, G. A., (2013). Trust, safety, and employee decision-making: A review of research and discussion of future directions. *The Journal of Technology, Management, and Applied Engineering, 29*(1).

134. Mujeeb, E. U., & Ahmad, M. S., (2011). Impact of organizational culture on performance management practices in Pakistan. *International Management Review, 7*(2), 52.

135. Nagalakhmi, L. R. A., & Trivedi, M. J., (2015). Utilization of online survey tools for academic research: A practical approach to survey monkey. *Research Journal of Science & IT Management, 4*(3), 21–27.

136. Nagasawa, S., & Fukunaga, T., (2015). Strategic brand management of the luxury brand GUCCI. *Waseda Business & Economic Studies, 50*(1), 37–54.

137. Najam, A., (2000). The four C's of government third sector-government relations. *Nonprofit Management and Leadership, 10*(4), 375–396.

138. Nath, V., (2011). Aesthetic and emotional labor through stigma; national identity management and racial abuse in offshored Indian call centers. *Work, Employment, and Society, 25*(4), 709–725.

139. Newell, A., & Simon, H. A., (1972). *Human Problem Solving.* Englewood Cliffs, NJ: Prentice-Hall.

140. Nica, E., (2015). Public administration as a tool of sustainable development. *Journal of Self-Governance and Management Economics, 3*(4), 30–36.

141. Obeidat, B. Y., (2012). The relationship between human resource information system (HRIS) functions and human resource management (HRM) functionalities. *Journal of Management and Research, 4*(4), 192–211.

142. Odrakiewicz, D., (2012). The connection between health and economic growth: Policy implications re-examined. *Global Management Journal, 4*(1).

143. Okotoni, O., & Erero, J., (2005). Manpower training and development in the Nigerian public service. *African Journal of Public Administration and Management, 16*(1), 1–13.

144. Onyx, J., & Maclean, M., (1996). Careers in the third sector. *Nonprofit Management and Leadership, 6*(4), 331–345.

145. Ozturk, M. B., & Rumens, N., (2014). Gay male academics in UK business and management schools: Negotiating heteronormativities in everyday work life. *British Journal of Management, 25*(3), 503–517.

146. Papasolomou, I., & Melanthiou, Y., (2012). Social media: Marketing public relations' new best friend. *Journal Of Promotion Management, 3*(1), 319–328.

147. Parker, D., Charlton, J., Ribeiro, A., & Raghuvar, P. D., (2013). Integration of project-based management and change management: Intervention methodology. *International Journal of Productivity and Performance Management, 62*(5), 534–544.

148. Parry, E., Dickmann, M., & Morley, M., (2008). North American MNCs and their HR policies in liberal and coordinated market economies. *International Journal of Human Resource Management, 19*(11), 2024–2040.

149. Patiar, A., & Mia, L., (2009). Transformational leadership style, market competition and departmental performance: Evidence from luxury

hotels in Australia. *International Journal of Hospitality Management, 28*(2), 254–262.

150. Pavlatos, O., & Paggios, I., (2009a). A survey of factors influencing the cost system design in hotels. *International Journal of Hospitality Management, 28*(2), 263–271.
151. Pavlatos, O., & Paggios, I., (2009b). Management accounting practices in the Greek hospitality industry. *Managerial Auditing Journal,24*, 81–98.
152. Peng, N., & Huiling, C. A., (2011). Consumer perspectives of cultural branding: The case of Burberry in Taiwan. *The Journal of Brand Management, 19*(4), 318–330.
153. Phillips, J. M., & Gully, S. M., (2014). *Human Resource Management.* Mason (OH): Cengage.
154. Pitts, D., (2009). Diversity management, job satisfaction, and performance: Evidence from US federal agencies. *Public Administration Review, 69*(2), 328–338.
155. Podoshen, J. S., Andrzejewski, S. A., Venkatesh, V., & Wallin, J., (2015). New approaches to dark tourism inquiry: A response to Isaac. *Tourism Management, 51*(1), 331–334.
156. Priola, V., Lasio, D., De Simone, S., &Serri, F., (2014). The sound of silence. Lesbian, gay, bisexual, and transgender discrimination in 'inclusive organizations.' *British Journal of Management, 25*(3),488–502.
157. Rasim, T. S., (2008). The role of psychology in human resources management. *Europe's Journal of Psychology, 4*(4).
158. Rose, R. B., (2004). Sexual orientation in the workplace: The unique work and career experiences of gay, lesbian, and bisexual workers sexual orientation in the workplace: The unique work and career experiences of gay, lesbian, and bisexual workers. In: Rose, R. B., (ed.), *Research in Personnel and Human Resources Management* (pp. 35–120). London: Emerald Group Publishing Limited.
159. Rosenthal, C., (2013). Plantations practiced modern management. *Harvard Business Review, 91*(9), 30–33.
160. Rosser, B. A., & Eccleston, C., (2011). Smartphone applications for pain management. *Journal of Telemedicine and Telecare, 17*(6), 308–312.

161. Saenz, J., & Pérez-Bouvier, A., (2014). Interaction with external agents, innovation networks, and innovation capability: The case of Uruguayan software firms. *Journal of Knowledge Management, 18*(2), 447–468.

162. Saji, B. S., & Ellingstad, P., (2004). Social innovation model for business performance and innovation. *International Journal of Productivity and Performance Management, 65*(2), 256–274.

163. Sakuramoto, N., (2005). Development of bookkeeping and management analysis system for small-scale farmers (pocket bookkeeping system). *Agricultural Information Research (Japan), 14*(4), 273–286.

164. Samah, A., et al., (2013). Influence of coaches 'behavior on athletes' motivation: Malaysian sport archery experience. *International Journal of Research in Management, 5*(3), 136–142.

165. Schlögl, C., (2005). Information and knowledge management: Dimensions and approaches. *Information Research: An International Electronic Journal, 10*(4), 235.

166. Schmid, B., & Adams, J., (2008). Motivation in project management: The project manager's perspective. *Project Management Journal, 39*(2), 60–71.

167. Schuler, R. S., (1989). Strategic human resource management and industrial relations. *Human Relations, 42*(2), 157–184.

168. Sedmak, M., & Longhurst, P., (2010). Methodological choices in enterprise systems research. *Business Process Management Journal, 16*(1), 76–92.

169. Sendawula, K., Turyakira, P., &Alioni, C., (2018). Sustainable entrepreneurship intention among university students in Uganda: A conceptual paper. *African Journal of Business Management, 12*(6), 131–139.

170. Shandilya., A,(2013). *Supply Chain Management & Logistics: Zara.* [Film] UK: YouTube.

171. Sharma, A., & Upneja, A., (2005). Factors influencing financial performance of small hotels in Tanzania. *International Journal of Contemporary Hospitality Management, 17*(6), 504–515.

172. Shatte, A., Holdsworth, J., & Lee, I., (2014). Mobile augmented reality based context-aware library management system. *Expert Systems with Applications, 41*(5), 2174–2185.

173. Sinclaire, J., & Vogus, C., (2011). Adoption of social networking sites: An exploratory adaptive structuration perspective for global organizations. *Information Technology & Management, 12*(4), 293–314.

174. Singh, A. S., & Masuku, M. B., (2014). Sampling techniques & determination of sample size in applied statistics research: An overview. *International Journal of Economics, Commerce, and Management, 2*(11), 1–22.

175. Singh, H., Kryscynski, D., Li, X., & Gopal, R., (2016). Pipes, pools, and filters: How collaboration networks affect innovative performance. *Strategic Management Journal, 37*(8), 1649–1666.

176. Slack, N., Chambers, S., Johnston, R., & Betts, A., (2006). *Operations and Process Management.* London: FT Prentice Hall.

177. Songa, H., Gartnerb, W., &Tascic, A., (2012). Visa restrictions and their adverse economic and marketing implications–evidence from China. *Tourism Management, 33*(2), 397–412.

178. Sparrow, P. R., & Makram, H., (2015). What is the value of talent management? Building value-driven processes within a talent management architecture. *Human Resource Management Review, 25*(3), 249–263.

179. Speer, S. A., & Potter, J., (2000). The management of heterosexist talk: Conversational resources and prejudiced claims. *Discourse & Society, 11*(4), 543–572.

180. Steers, R. M., Mowday, R. T., & Shapiro, D. L., (2004). Introduction to special topic forum: The future of work motivation theory. *Academy of Management Review, 29*(3), 379.

181. Stevens, M., (2002). *Project Management Pathways.* London: APM Publishing Limited.

182. Stewart, J., & Walsh, K., (1992). *Change in the Management of Public Services* (Vol. 70, No. 4, pp. 499–518). Public Administration.

183. Stone, D. L., Deadrick, D. L., Lukaszewskic, K. M., & Johnson, R., (2015). The influence of technology on the future of human resource management. *Human Resource Management: Past, Present, and Future, 25*(2), 216–231.

184. Stoorvogel, J., Segura, R., &Erima, R., (2017). *The Relationship Between Soil Management and the Sustainable Development Goals: The Case of Global Banana Production* (p. 18973). S.L., EGU.

185. Storey, J., Emberson, C., Godsell, J., & Harrison, A., (2006). Supply chain management: Theory, practice, and future challenges. *International Journal of Operations & Product Management, 26*(7), 754–774.

186. Subhas, C. M., Vinod, K., & Uma, K., (2010). Identifying some critical changes required in adopting agile practices in traditional software development projects. *International Journal of Quality & Reliability Management, 27*(4), 451–474.

187. Tarafdar, M., D'Arcy, J., Turel, O., & Gupta, A., (2014). The dark side of information technology. *MIT Sloan Management Review.* Research Feature (Winter).

188. Thursfield, D., & Grayley, K., (2016). Exploring performance management in four UK trade unions. *Employee Relations, 38*(5), 789–804.

189. Toner, J., (2015). *Slaves or Wage Slaves: Incentives, Rewards, Bonuses, and Bonding Experiences – Roman Slaveowners Were the First Management Theorists.* [Online] Available at: https://aeon.co/essays/were-roman-slave-owners-the-first-management-theorists (accessed on 29 March 2022).

190. Too, E. G., & Weaver, P., (2014). The management of project management: A conceptual framework for project governance. *International Journal of Project Management, 32*(8), 1382–1394.

191. Torre, E. D., & Luca, S., (2013). High-performance work systems and the change management process in medium-sized firms. *International Journal of Human Resource Management, 24*(13), 2583–2607.

192. Turyakira, P. K., (2018a). Corporate social responsibility activities that influence customer loyalty of SMEs. *International Journal of Business and Management, 13*(6), 255–266.

193. Turyakira, P. K., (2018b). Ethical practices of small and medium-sized enterprises in developing countries: Literature analysis. *South African Journal of Economic and Management Sciences, 21*(1), 1–7.

194. Visser, W., (2012). *CSR 2.0: Reinventing Corporate Social Responsibility for the 21st Century.* [Online] Available at: http://www.managementexchange.com/hack/csr-20-reinventing-corporate-social-responsibility-21st-century (accessed on 29 March 2022).

195. WHO, (2018). *Management of Substance Abuse: Facts and Figures.* [Online] Available at: http://www.who.int/substance_abuse/facts/en/ (accessed on 29 March 2022).

196. Wilkinson, D., (1997). Whole system development-rethinking public service management. *International Journal of Public Sector Management, 10*(7), 505–533.

197. Williamson, O., (2008). Outsourcing: Transaction cost economics and supply chain management. *Journal of Supply Chain Management, 44*(2), 5–16.

198. Willmott, H., (1993). Strength is ignorance; slavery is freedom: Managing culture in modern organizations. *Journal of Management Studies, 30*(4), 0022–2380.

199. Wysocki, R. K., (2013). *Effective Project Management: Traditional, Adaptive, Extreme* (7thedn.). London: John Wiley & Sons.

200. Yang, D. J., & Chen, Y., (2006). A study of the effect of social influence on the college student's attitude and behavior for playing online games. *The Journal of Global Business Management, 2*(2), 33.

201. Zhang, K. M., & Wen, Z. G., (2008). Review and challenges of policies of environmental protection and sustainable development in China. *Journal of Environmental Management, 88*(4), 1249–1261.

202. Zheng, H., (2017). *IT Project Management Case Study- NiteRest Hotels Management System.* [Online] Available at: https://medium.com/@kiaorahao/project-management-case-study-niterest-hotels-management-system-df8e29a60e52 (accessed on 29 March 2022).

INDEX